REVOLUTIONS OF THE HEART

This fascinating account of heterosexual love presents a radical challenge to the contemporary view that the pursuit of 'intimacy' is leading us to greater humanity and equality between the sexes. The author argues that, on the contrary, the current emphasis on personal fulfilment in relationships based on attraction is more likely to intensify destructive power dynamics which are fuelled by desire itself.

This conclusion is reached via a detailed analysis of accounts from women who describe their attempts to realise 'the new romantic ideal' – a relationship which is intimate, equal and emotionally satisfying. Through an innovative application of psychoanalytic theories to empirical data, the book reveals how the highs and lows of love follow a systematic, even predictable course – a course which involves the reproduction of gender identities and the playing out of gendered power dynamics.

Through identifying the processes of love's transmutation, *Revolutions of the Heart* shows how and why love is blind. Falling in love is experienced as liberating and deeply gratifying because it allows the individual to 'break out' of the confines of a limited masculine or feminine identity, plunges them into the pleasures of intimacy and mutuality and 'heals' the suffering caused by previous loves. Tragically, however, unaware of how this 'romantic transformation' is based upon illusion, and impelled by the very desire to 'make it last', lovers unwittingly resort to well-worn habits of control and manipulation. As each attempts to make the relationship fit with their own particular fantasy of ideal love, partners alienate themselves from each other and destroy the possibility of happiness.

So how can we move beyond the suffering which we inflict and endure in the name of love? The author's conclusion is uncompromising: we must face up to the fact that our faith in this kind of love is a faith tragically misplaced. To the extent we remain attached to the myth that happiness is to be attained through the pursuit of romantic attraction, relationships will continue to be determined by destructive craving and the play of power. The possibility of real personal and social transformation begins when we see the limitations of love's transient pleasures, and recognize the very real dangers which inhere in our own 'revolutions of the heart'.

Wendy Langford is a Research Associate at the University of Lancaster.

REVOLUTIONS
OF THE HEART

Gender, power and the delusions of love

Wendy Langford

London and New York

First published 1999
by Routledge
11 New Fetter Lane, London EC4P 4EE

Simultaneously published in the USA and Canada
by Routledge
29 West 35th Street, New York, NY 10001

Routledge is an imprint of the Taylor & Francis Group

Typeset in Garamond by
J&L Composition Ltd, Filey, North Yorkshire
Printed and bound in Great Britain by
TJ International Ltd, Padstow, Cornwall

British Library Cataloguing in Publication Data
A catalogue record for this book is available from the British Library

Library of Congress Cataloguing in Publication Data
Langford, Wendy:
Revolutions of the heart:
gender, power, and the delusions of love / Wendy Langford.
p.   cm.
Includes bibliographical references and index.
1. Love. 2. Man–woman relationships. I. Title.
BF575.L8L266 1999
306.7—dc21   98–50255

ISBN 0–415–16297–1 (hbk)
ISBN 0–415–16298–x (pbk)

Hoping to escape suffering, it is to suffering that they run.
In the desire for happiness, out of delusion, they destroy
their own happiness, like an enemy.

Śāntideva, seventh century

CONTENTS

CONTENTS

ACKNOWLEDGEMENTS

I would like to thank everyone who has helped and supported me in the work that has resulted in this book. A special mention goes to Jackie Stacey, Stevi Jackson and Thomas Jones for reading and commenting on earlier versions. Thank you too to all the friends who have offered inspiration, encouragement and practical support.

The original research on which this book is based was funded by the Economic and Social Research Council.

Revolutions of the Heart would not have been possible without the women who so generously shared their insights and experiences with me. I dedicate this book to them.

INTRODUCTION

It is probable that in one form or another the 'couple' has always been viewed as a fundamental human relationship. Certainly the formation of a new couple is regarded almost everywhere as a central organising principle of domestic, economic and social life. Perhaps less obvious is that the significance given to the couple relationship is not universal and that in modern Western societies it is endowed with a very particular set of meanings. Increasingly, we have come to look to 'coupledom' for the satisfaction of a range of 'emotional' and existential needs and desires; we want it to be 'meaningful' and to provide us with 'intimacy' and companionship as well as a feeling of security, and a sense of 'who we really are' as individuals. Our faith that couple relationships can, and ideally should, meet these needs and desires is rooted in turn in a faith in the process through which they come into being, the process of 'falling in love'. We romanticise attraction between individuals, telling ourselves that it is the natural and humane foundation of relationships. Whatever difficulties might come afterwards, we assume that falling in love itself is essentially liberating and beneficial. Indeed we construct and experience love as a means of salvation, a means by which we may 'transcend' the meaninglessness of an unsatisfactory and alienating world. Through 'falling' we aim to create the world anew, so that it becomes a place where we are wanted, where we are loved 'for ourselves' and where we can be 'somebody' who matters. Since our 'deliverance' arises upon the formation of a deep emotional attachment, and since lasting happiness is held to depend upon the quality and durability of this attachment, we must somehow find a way to make it last, to 'make the relationship work'. Otherwise we risk being turned out of our haven and cast into the abyss. Where then would we belong?

Despite, or perhaps because of, its fundamental place in personal and social life, this form of love has rarely been subject to radical criticism. One particular exception is the feminist critique which gave rise to this powerful indictment: not only are couple relationships often characterised by cruelty, violence and the economic and sexual exploitation of women, but it is through the attempt to realise the romantic ideal that women make themselves 'subject to love'. Falling in love causes a woman to enter into a particularly deluded state of being in which, as Simone de Beauvoir (1988: 653) put it, 'she chooses to desire her enslavement so ardently that it will seem to her the very expression of her liberty'. Love does not create a private domain in which humanity thrives apart from a competitive and alienating public world; on the contrary, life 'within the refuge' is itself determined by the exercise of power, and love in itself helps to underpin an inhumane and unequal society.

Attempts to close the gulf between the romantic ideal and the picture painted by critics have most recently taken the form of a 'democratisation thesis'. This does not deny that love relationships have often been sites of tyranny. However, oppression is seen to have been caused largely by religious, legal and social regulation which represented the interests of an outdated patriarchal, Christian, industrial society. Nowadays, the story goes, constraints have been swept aside and the existence, content and duration of love relationships is increasingly determined by democratic negotiation between the partners. So great is this supposed change that one writer even declares 'romantic' love to be a thing of the past and heralds the arrival of a new kind of love – 'confluent love', pioneered by women who have demanded equality and reciprocity in personal relationships. The impetus for this change has not come only from feminist resistance but from the greater emphasis on the pursuit of individual satisfaction in couple relationships. The quest for 'intimacy' implies equality, it is argued, because if individuals fail to get the 'satisfaction' they seek, they will simply pursue their heart's desire elsewhere. Separation, divorce and social instability should not be understood as evidence that love is oppressive. On the contrary, this is evidence that love is fast becoming a 'transactional negotiation of personal ties between equals' who are no longer forced to remain in cruel or unsatisfying unions (Giddens 1992: 3).

In a culture where we want to 'believe in love', the democratisation thesis is seductive. It provides us with a reassuring narrative of social progress while leaving untouched the basic tenets of romanticism: love in itself remains unanalysed and love for its own sake remains as a path to salvation. Meanwhile, empirical social science has found little to contradict the theory. Even studies which have specifically set out to identify power in couple relationships have largely failed to find it. This could be interpreted as evidence that we are indeed entering a new era of humane and equal love. It could also represent, however, the failure of the social sciences to do more than create sophisticated justifications for what we want to believe about the world. Certainly, love itself as a compelling emotional experience has been left largely unexplored and untheorised. Writers tend to either lapse into romanticism and assume love to be essentially mysterious and inexplicable, or quite contrarily portray it as measurable, negotiable, and readily amenable to the principles of social justice.

It seems dangerous indeed to maintain that we can know little about love while assuming that we are progressive in basing our social world upon it. *Revolutions of the Heart* develops the ground between 'surface sociology' and romanticism. It aims to realise the conviction that it *is* possible to understand what love is, and thus determine how far love, in and of itself, is a route to freedom or a road to servitude. The project is inspired by the radical questioning of feminist critiques, pursued through engagement in empirical enquiry, developed using the explanatory power of psychoanalytic theories, and driven by a personal quest to find the 'truth' about love. On one level the resulting account is a very particular one; it is a story of heterosexual love constructed through a detailed analysis of the attempts of a group of 'ordinary' women to realise the romantic ideal. It follows them through hope and despair, through success and defeat, and reveals exactly how the dynamics of couple relationships are determined by the play of power. While this love story *is* a particular one, however, its implications are far-reaching – for as we journey to the heart of the romantic ideal, we begin to discover the truth about love itself. If we are prepared to look this truth in the face, love will never seem the same again.

1

GOVERNMENT BY LOVE

The main objective of this book is to tell a story of contemporary love, grounded in the first-hand accounts of fifteen women. Before I tell the story, however, I need to set the scene. It is a scene about which there is some general agreement: we live in a society where romantic or passionate love has become the predominant basis of domestic and social life and where couple relationships are invested with an unprecedented range of meanings in respect of our desires for personal identity, emotional fulfilment, sexual satisfaction and existential security. The fundamental desirability of this situation is commonly assumed. It has not, however, been entirely uncontested. In particular, the eruption of feminist resistance in the West during the 1970s brought assertions that romantic love is an ideology which obscures the violent and conflictual nature of sexual relations and which therefore, particularly in its heterosexual forms, serves to reproduce the oppression of women. For a while, some researchers attempted to address questions of power in their work on marriage, although the nature of love itself remained largely unexamined and little understood. By the 1990s, however, prominent social theorists were again constructing the sexual couple as progressive and humane – claiming, moreover, that partly in response to feminism, love relationships are becoming more equal and more negotiable than ever before. This chapter examines these different arguments, and establishes the political position occupied by the 'subject of love' at the close of the twentieth century.

The rise of the passionate couple

In modern Western societies, couple relationships almost always come into being through a more or less powerful experience of emotional 'bonding', infused with erotic attraction. Being part of such a couple is held to be fundamental to our happiness, well-being and sense of place in the world. Reproduction, the family, and to a great extent social life itself, are seen as ideally based upon and around the loving (heterosexual) couple. Thus, while 'falling in love' remains something of a mystery, it is generally understood and experienced as a beneficial and foundational life event; everything, it seems,

1

begins when we fall in love, and everything, it seems, depends upon the quality and durability of the resulting emotional attachment. Therefore if the relationship should end so, it can seem, does everything else, leaving us to pick up the pieces of our lives and 'start all over again'. With divorce, serial monogamy and the 'reconstitution' of families now commonplace phenomena, the fact that couple relationships are at the centre of rapid social change is part of our everyday awareness. However, it is not just the increasing speed with which we repeat the 'love cycle' that is specific to our particular historical and cultural location. Perhaps less obvious is that love as we know it today has come into being over time and needs to be understood in its specificity. It is true that sexual attraction and emotional attachment between partners are omnipresent human experiences. It is also true that at a very general level of analysis, all such love is 'romantic' love in the sense that it is always necessarily mediated through cultural conditioning – through the stories that societies tell their members about the nature and meaning of desire and attachment. However, the very recognition that emotional life is always already 'cultured' along with the observation that human cultures are extremely variable means that any consideration of love must address it as a phenomenon which takes qualitatively different forms across different societies, and within the same society during different phases of its history (Averill 1985; Dion and Dion 1996). Love is therefore here addressed as a universal kind of human experience, but one which is manifest in a particular form and invested with particular meanings.

It has been claimed that love as we know it, 'love as passion', gained ascendancy in Europe during the upheavals of industrialisation, when dramatic social change produced the need for a new means of communication which would facilitate the establishment of couple relationships. Through an analysis of love literature from the period, Niklas Luhmann charts the development of 'a symbolic code which shows how to communicate effectively in situations where this would otherwise appear improbable', a code which 'encourages one to have the appropriate feelings' (Luhmann 1986: 8–9). Crucially, this new code was closely tied to the legitimation of individualism; for the first time, a passionate involvement with one other person began to be constructed as a primary ground for identity formation, rather than wider kinship networks or social position.

Any particular 'language of love' must be spoken at the emotional level, raising the question of how the articulation of new romantic codes came to involve such an intense and significant focusing of emotional and sexual energies. Persuasive in this respect is Max Weber's argument that 'erotic love' in its modern form came into being largely as a result of religious change, precipitated in particular by the influence of puritan salvationism (Weber 1948; Bologh 1987). The puritan salvation ethic centred on 'brotherly love' which was universalistic, self-abnegating and valued neighbourliness rather than individual ties. It also, however, involved an overly formal, regulatory, instrumental and sexually repressive approach to everyday life which ultimately undermined spirituality, leaving individuals with a lack of a sense of mystery or meaning in their lives. Weber argued that this over-rationalisation led to a reactive eruption of eroticism, which took an oppositional form to brotherly love. The desire to please others and serve God gave way to individualism and self-indulgence, and the quest for spiritual salvation became a search for self-realisation through an irrational, fatalistic, exclusive and erotically charged 'fusion of souls'.

Changes in love should not be viewed as sudden, smooth or uncontested processes. For example, while a spiritualised ideal of the couple figured prominently in Victorian society, and a discourse of companionate marriage emerged from the mid-1850s onwards, prevailing fears that the foundations of marriage were threatened by lust ensured that the languages of love and sex remained largely separate (Shorter 1976; Seidman 1991). As Steven Seidman (1991) has pointed out, the explicit 'sexualization of love' did not occur to any extent until the twentieth century, which has seen the emergence of a new 'intimate culture'. As this became established, sexual attraction increasingly came to be interpreted as a sign of love, and sustained sexual longing and satisfaction as a way of enhancing 'intimate solidarity in a social context where other unifying forces (e.g. kinship, patriarchy, economic dependency) were losing their power to do so' (ibid.: 2). Couple relationships have, of course, continued to be structured by legal, economic, religious and social ties. The crucial point is, however, that it is the emotional attachment between sexual partners, formed through 'falling in love', that has increasingly come to be understood as the *basis* of the relationship. This is reflected, for example, in changing divorce laws: where once evidence of cruelty, adultery or other wrongdoing on the part of a spouse was required, the advent of the 'no fault' divorce allows lack of love alone to be a sufficient reason for the dissolution of a marriage (Kayser 1993: 4). Marriage may remain popular, but its meaning has shifted; once a binding contract which fixed one's position within the social structure, it has become an optional and soluble sign of commitment to someone with whom one has fallen in love.

As the love bond has become the priority in relation to coupledom, so the couple has become the focus of an ever greater range of needs and desires, not only for sexual fulfilment and 'spiritual' meaning, but for identity, self-expression, companionship and emotional security – a trend documented in the work of many social scientists (Burgess and Locke 1945; Blood and Wolfe 1960; Berger and Kellner 1974). Peter Berger and Hansfried Kellner, for example, argue that ideologies of self-discovery and self-realisation through romantic love and sexual expression have come into being to encourage individuals to enter into marriage, 'a crucial nomic instrumentality in our society' (Berger and Kellner 1974: 160). Through an ongoing 'marital conversation', 'the partners "discover" themselves and the world, "who they really are," "what they really believe," "how they really feel", and always have felt, about so-and-

3

so' (ibid.: 168). This process of identity construction gives the partners a sense of stability and helps to 'assuage the existential anxiety' that accompanies the isolation of life in the modern world (ibid.).

We can see, then, that love does not exist in a fixed or unchanging form; our contemporary experience of love is something which has come into being. Love has become an exclusively focused, 'spiritualised', erotic passion which is articulated through romantic codes, and which forms the basis of our social identity. It has been suggested, moreover, that the importance and meaning attached to romantic love is undergoing further, rapid, intensification. Ulrich Beck and Elizabeth Beck-Gernsheim (1995) argue that as the structure of industrial society breaks down, as the labour market grows more competitive and ruthless, and as people become more mobile in their search for work, traditional sources of stability and identity are fast disappearing. Secularisation has further contributed to a society in which life is experienced as empty and soulless. Even for the lucky ones, new 'freedoms' offer little compensation for a lonely and hollow life. It is in such a society that romantic love is gaining ever greater significance as a 'secular religion', 'a faith quickly finding followers in a society of uprooted loners' (Beck and Beck-Gernsheim 1995: 173). Yet, paradoxically, the more that love appears as the escape from social instability and meaninglessness, the more impermanent and chaotic love becomes. The more we look for happiness through love, the more miserable love relationships seem to become. The more we marry, the more we divorce. The more desperately we grasp at the hope of 'intimacy', the more surely we are cast down into loneliness and alienation. While a burgeoning 'agony industry' ministers to the broken-hearted, and popular songs articulate the anguish of love gone wrong, the new religion seems only to thrive on its failure to deliver.

Historical social processes have thus brought us to a time when our tendency to attach ourselves to the object of our desire has become an exalted tendency, and the resulting 'bond' is endowed with the power to satisfy an extensive range of human needs and personal wishes. Never, it seems, have we wanted so much from another human being. Never, it seems, have we been so disappointed. Yet despite its crucial place in our world, our attempts to realise the new romantic ideal, and their failures, remain little studied and less understood. 'Love' remains ill-defined, assumed rather than explained, seeming to reflect rather than elucidate a lived experience of something mysterious and impenetrable. What can account for this neglect and hesitancy? What prevents us from subjecting love to more incisive and systematic enquiry? It can hardly be the belief that the subject is unimportant. Perhaps, on the contrary, it is precisely our own deep investments in love which hold us back. Certainly, those relatively few critiques which have emerged have come from those with a particularly strong motivation to question the wisdom of 'investing in love'. Such motivation has perhaps been most manifest in the form of feminist resistance. Rooted in the articulation and politicisation of women's personal experiences of love, feminist analyses have rejected the view that romantic love is a vehicle of freedom and satisfaction, and portrayed it instead as a road to servitude.

A diminishing life in chains

Within feminist thought there is a long tradition which identifies a direct relationship between the practice of love and the reproduction of patriarchal power. Feminists in the nineteenth century, for example, argued that the blind, passionate, seductive and conflictual nature of romantic love undermined women's interests. They envisioned a more equal model of 'rational love', based on knowledge rather than fantasy or passion (Leach 1981). Here, however, I am going to concentrate on more recent feminist analyses of love, particularly those rooted in the explosion of feminist discourse which emerged in Europe and the United States from the late 1960s. A radical politicisation of heterosexual love relationships was a central theme at this time, drawing its intellectual inspiration largely from the work of the French philosopher Simone de Beauvoir.

In *The Second Sex*, first published in 1949, de Beauvoir developed a Hegelian analysis of patriarchy. The key dynamic is a fundamental tendency of human consciousness, when it becomes aware of itself as a subject, and in turn becomes aware of the existence of other subjects, to see them as objects, as 'other', and as inferior, as a defence against its own fear of their subjectivity. If no effort is made to construct reciprocity (the recognition of each other as free and equal beings), this tendency, combined with the varying life conditions of different groups, leads inevitably to relations of domination and subordination. Members of dominant groups become the 'Ones', who reduce the existential threat of the 'Others' by objectifying them. This is the basic dynamic that, historically, has shaped relations between men and women, producing gendered forms of consciousness which are in turn reinforced through the actual life situations of the sexes. Women, defined as 'Others', are directed towards a life of dependence, vulnerability and self-sacrifice in a sphere of 'immanence'. Men are defined as the 'Ones' who are capable of 'transcendence', and are directed towards a life of independence, strength and self-determination.

According to de Beauvoir, the ideology of romantic love plays a significant part in maintaining this pattern of social arrangements. Denied a vision of her own transcendence, a woman learns that devoting herself completely to a man is the way that her own life can have a meaning beyond the realm of immanence. In an account which adds a gendered dimension to the claim that modern love has a religious or spiritual significance, de Beauvoir argues that feminine consciousness in particular is structured to seek freedom through self-sacrifice in love:

> She chooses to desire her enslavement so ardently that it will seem
> to her the expression of her liberty; she will try to rise above her
> situation as inessential object by fully accepting it; through her flesh,

her feelings, her behaviour, she will enthrone him as supreme value and reality: she will humble herself to nothingness before him. Love becomes for her a religion.

(de Beauvoir 1988: 653)

In order to pursue this apparent route to salvation, a woman must believe in the impossible: liberation through servitude. She may employ 'bad faith' in an attempt to resolve this paradox, but this involves entering into a series of manipulations and self-deceptions which trap her even further. Only ending the liaison can free her, but this is terrifying because it means facing up to that which caused her to enter it in the first place: her failure to achieve her own transcendence. Romantic love is thus an 'existential fraud' (Morgan 1986). De Beauvoir has been criticised by some feminists for overdrawing women's responsibility for their oppression within love relationships, while failing to highlight the ways in which men benefit from a corresponding use of 'bad faith' (Douglas 1990: 111). For others, however, it is the way de Beauvoir stresses women's complicity which makes her theory compelling.

De Beauvoir's analysis was taken up, for example, by the US group The Feminists, who integrated it into a Marxist framework in order to argue that love is an ideological device, a form of 'false consciousness' which serves the interests of the 'ruling class', men, through preventing women from bonding with their own 'sex class'. Being 'in love' acts as a self-defence against the painful truth of subordination by offering women the delusion that they are both givers and receivers. Since this secures women's identification with men, The Feminists argued that '[w]e must destroy love (an institution by definition)' (1973: 375). A founder member of the group, Ti-Grace Atkinson, later developed this argument:

I propose that the phenomenon of love is the psychological pivot in the persecution of women. Because the internalization of coercion must play such a key functional part in the oppression of women due to their numbers alone, and because of the striking grotesqueness of the one-to-one political units 'pairing' the Oppressor and the Oppressed, the hostile and the powerless, and thereby severing the Oppressed from any kind of political aid, it is not difficult to conclude that women by definition must exist in a special psycho-pathological state of fantasy both in reference to themselves and to their manner of relating to the counterclass. This pathological condition, considered the most desirable state for any woman to find herself in, is what we know as the phenomenon of love.

(Atkinson 1974: 43–44)

Other writers focused less on the 'deluded' state of the woman in love, and more on the dynamics of power in heterosexual relationships. Also inspired by de Beauvoir's Hegelian analysis, the 'New York Radical Feminists', for example, saw male power as operating at the psychological level through the ability of the male ego to have power over the female ego. These 'politics of the ego' are ensured through the construction and maintenance of particular institutions: marriage, motherhood and sexual intercourse, at the centre of which is the definition of what counts as 'love':

> Love, in the context of an oppressive male–female relationship, becomes an emotional cement to justify the dominant–submissive relationship. The man 'loves' the woman who fulfills her submissive ego-boosting role. The woman 'loves' the man she is submitting to – that is, after all, why she 'lives for him.' LOVE, magical and systematically unanalyzed, becomes the emotional rationale for the submission of one ego to the other. And it is deemed every woman's natural function to love. Radical feminism believes that the popularized version of love has thus been used politically to cloud and justify an oppressive relationship between men and women, and that in reality there can be no genuine love until the need to *control* the growth of another is replaced by the love *for* the growth of another.
>
> (New York Radical Feminists 1971: 442)

Love was also a central theme in the work of many other feminist thinkers in the 1970s. In *Sexual Politics*, for example, Kate Millett argued that a subordinate female sexuality is largely defined and experienced in relation to ideologies of heterosexual romance (Millett 1971). Shulamith Firestone, in *The Dialectic of Sex*, argued that the gendered dynamics of romantic love underpin a patriarchal culture which is 'parasitical, feeding on the emotional strength of women without reciprocity' (Firestone 1979: 122). Ideologies of romantic love were deemed to obscure women's economic exploitation within marriage (Greer 1970; Comer 1974), and male violence and the abuse of women were seen to be facilitated by a kind of love which is experienced as a 'frenzied passion which compels a woman to submit to a diminishing life in chains' (Dworkin 1976: 105).

During the 1980s and 1990s, romance as a cultural form continued to be subject to critical analysis (see e.g. Modleski 1984; Radway 1984; Christian-Smith 1990; Pearce and Stacey 1995). However, the same period saw feminists lapse into silence on the experience of love. There were probably several reasons for this. The development of divisive 'identity politics' within the women's movement impeded the honest exploration of love as lived experience (Mainardi 1975; Allen 1982; Campbell 1987). This was reflected in some strands of theory which posited a set of polarized oppositions between patriarchy, heterosexuality and victimhood on the one hand, and feminism, lesbianism and resistance on the other (Leeds Revolutionary Feminist Group 1981; Wilson 1981; Jeffreys 1990; Wilkinson and Kitzinger 1993). Within this model, the destructive nature of heterosexual relationships was reduced to their heterosexuality, which gained popularity over romantic love as the crucial form of 'false consciousness'. With one or two exceptions, critiques of love were never extended at all to gay and lesbian relationships, which therefore remained a conceptual haven for the romantic ideal. Despite its limited development, however, the radical feminist critique of the 1970s stands as a cogent challenge to an ideal which promises comfort, security and identity within a cosy world of coupledom. It certainly paints a very different picture to the one that prevailed in 'malestream' sociology at this time, which departed little from the romantic ideal in its portrayal of the couple as an increasingly 'symmetrical' and humane relationship between intimate equals (Young and Willmott 1973; Berger and Kellner 1974).

If it is true that romantic love underpins and facilitates the exploitation of women within Western societies, *and* it is true that romantic love has become a popular mass movement pursued with religious fervour, an obvious question presents itself: Are love relationships becoming ever more important as sites of the exercise of power? Perhaps surprisingly, a surge of interest in love among sociologists has tended towards the contrary view. The arguments concerned hinge on the claim that love is undergoing a process of 'democratisation'.

The democratisation of love

For Niklas Luhmann (1986), 'democratisation' refers to the historical process through which cultural codes offering individual fulfilment through 'love as passion' have become increasingly available to the population as a whole. Beck and Beck-Gernsheim (1995: 184) similarly argue that the modern history of love can be understood in terms of the democratisation of romanticism: 'Love as an encounter of egos, as a re-creation of reality in terms of you–me . . . is becoming a mass phenomenon: a secular religion of love.' The nature of love, however, has not gone unchanged. Because couple relationships are no longer determined by external meanings or constraints, the quest of the traditional romantic hero or heroine who sought their true destiny in defiance of social norms has been reduced to 'a trivialised Romanticism without any prohibitions attached' (ibid.). Lovers, it seems, have won the right to determine their love: '[t]he actual content of the love package is a subjective mutual invention' (ibid.: 193). Post-traditional love has thus become 'a radical form of democracy for two, personal responsibility in its purest form' (ibid.: 192).

Democratised love is not necessarily happy love, however, since wider processes of social change mean that 'contradictions are piling up behind the facade of the ideal relationship' (ibid.: 15). In particular, while traditional love depended on women being the 'backstage person', this is no longer fashionable. Women's demands for equality in the labour market, combined with labour market demands for mobile and flexible workers, mean that couples must constantly negotiate two separate, and often competing, biographies. So

8

while lovers have won the freedom to determine their own relationships, this itself is increasingly difficult and demanding work, with relationships often breaking down under the strain. Thus the disintegration of traditional patriarchal industrial society is being partly played out within intimate relationships; conflict and instability in love are the 'private signs of the crumbling of a whole social framework' (ibid.: 23). Beck and Beck-Gernsheim predict 'a long and bitter battle; in the coming years there will be a war between men and women' (ibid.: 14). Such predictions suggest that while romantic love may have become 'democratised', caution should be exercised in respect of any claim that the relationships which result are necessarily becoming more humane or more equitable.

Some writers, however, apply the concept of 'democratisation' to the actual content and dynamics of love relationships in a direct, and particularly optimistic, way. Anthony Giddens, for example, claims that the sexual couple is fast becoming a site of emancipation. An increased emphasis on 'intimacy', together with the separation of sexuality from reproduction, has led to the emergence of the 'pure relationship': 'a social situation entered into for its own sake . . . and which is continued only in so far as it is thought by both parties to deliver enough satisfactions for each individual to stay within it' (Giddens 1992: 58). This new freedom for individuals to pursue their pleasure and gratification wherever they will 'implies the wholesale democratising of the interpersonal domain in a manner fully compatible with democracy in the public sphere' (ibid.: 3). Moreover, according to Giddens, this 'transformation of intimacy' is emerging largely as a result of the fact that 'ordinary women, going about their day-to-day lives, as well as self-consciously feminist groups – have pioneered changes of great, and generalisable, importance' (ibid.: 1–2). It is women's expression of their dissatisfaction with heterosexual arrangements, in particular men's unwillingness to be 'intimate', which has brought into being 'a relationship of sexual and emotional equality, which is explosive in its connotations for pre-existing forms of gender power' (ibid.: 2). Thus while Beck and Beck-Gernsheim portray a romantic ideal in crisis as the 'private sphere' is hit by the contradictory pressures of a deindustrialising society, for Giddens, romantic love has already fragmented 'under the pressure of female sexual emancipation and autonomy', giving way to a new form of love: 'confluent love' (ibid.: 61). This new, equal kind of love is not merely the hoped-for outcome of an escalating conflict between men and women, but evidence of a sex war already fought and, at least in part, won. The current 'chaos of love' represents the success of feminism and the triumph of intimacy: 'The "separating and divorcing society" of today here appears as an effect of the emergence of confluent love rather than its cause' (ibid.: 61).

Jeffrey Weeks similarly argues that a process of democratisation is being driven by the fact that emotional satisfaction has become the *raison d'être* of the couple. While desired levels of intimacy are hard to maintain, 'the emphasis on personal commitment as the key to emotional satisfaction . . . has radical implications. For commitment implies the involvement of consenting, more or less equal individuals' (Weeks 1995: 37). Since individuals will simply leave relationships that are not emotionally 'satisfying' this does lead to a high degree of instability, but this is the price of democracy: 'the emphasis on individual autonomy and choice provides a radicalizing dynamic that is making possible the transformation of personal life' (ibid.). Weeks does observe, if only briefly, that love is 'mediated through a host of socio-economic and gender factors' (ibid.). While thus conceding that the democratisation of love is not yet as advanced as it might be, Weeks is nevertheless optimistic that attempts to realise the new ideal provide the basis of a 'radical humanism' 'which respects diversity and the maximisation of individual choice while affirming at the same time the importance of the human bond' (ibid.: 42).

None of the democratisation theorists claim that the world is no longer characterised by hierarchical social relations. However, all represent love as ever more loosened from its everyday practice in such a world. Feminist critiques of love itself are not directly addressed, and even appear to be heading for obsolescence in a society where any failure to maintain intimacy and mutuality by fair negotiation leads increasingly, and swiftly, to separation or divorce. Even where love relationships are depicted as sites of continuing conflict, love itself is not seen as productive of power relations; the private sphere is 'only the setting, not the cause of events' (Beck and Beck-Gernsheim 1995: 24). So, only two decades after feminists declared romantic love to be the political ideology of an oppressive patriarchal society, even the least optimistic of writers on 'democratic love' consider that the union between partners 'no longer serves any political ends' (ibid.: 172).

It is all too easy to slip between articulating a new ideal and assuming it to be realised in the world. Given this, perhaps the question of the 'politics of love' is one which is best settled empirically. There have been several studies by sociologists who, in response to feminist critiques, have set out specifically to identify and study power in couple relationships. It is to these that I now turn.

The political economy of love

The study of domination in couple relationships has proved to be something of a challenge to researchers. Not least of the problems has been the failure to find it, leading to expressions of frustration and bewilderment that the structures of power seem so elusive (see Komarovsky 1988). This failure might readily be taken as supporting evidence by those keen to herald the advent of egalitarian coupledom. However, closer analysis suggests that the appearance of equality may be due more to the limitations of popular methodologies than to social progress. In particular, lessons are to be learned from the widespread employment of 'decision-making' and 'exchange' theories, which have important implications for any study on love.

The decision-making model of power, pioneered by Blood and Wolfe (1960), involves the attempt to measure in/equality between partners by looking at how important decisions are made, and at who gets their own way. Studies using this type of approach have generally found couple relationships to be relatively equal (for an exception, see Edgell 1980). However, the model is deeply flawed and methodologies based upon it have been subject to widespread criticism (see Safilios-Rothschild 1976; Eichler 1981; Komarovsky 1988; Komter 1991). Problems identified include the assumption that power can be understood as a conflict between competing wills, abstracted from relations of class and gender; the folly of attempting to analyse power on the basis of isolated decisions, without taking account of their embeddedness in ongoing relational processes; and the assumption of an overly 'rational' model of power which fails to address how dynamics of power may function at the emotional level.

Partly in response to these kinds of criticisms a second model, based on 'exchange theory', was developed. This aimed to measure power in terms of an exchange of desirable goods, or 'resources', between spouses, and the dependency of each partner on what the other controls (see e.g. Scanzoni 1972; Safilios-Rothschild 1976; Eichler 1981; O'Connor 1991). According to this model, 'a love relationship is a particular case of social exchange' in which the objective is 'to try and strike the "best bargain" possible' (Scanzoni 1972: 51, 53). Examination of the exchange model, however, reveals it to have very similar limitations to the decision-making approach. Safilios-Rothschild, for example, uses exchange theory to explain the existence of marital stability in conditions of gendered socio-economic inequality. Using subjective measures of which spouse was 'more in love' or 'less in love', she concludes that 'the spouse more in love with the other is more anxious to maintain the relationship even at high cost, that is, by offering many resources and by receiving few in return' (Safilios-Rothschild 1976: 358). Thus, although a woman has less control over socio-economic resources, indeed even if she has no access to such resources, she may nevertheless 'gain advantage' in a relationship to the extent that her partner is more in love with her, through exchanging the affection and sex her partner wants for power (ibid.: 360–361). Safilios-Rothschild does not discuss, however, the probable *dis*empowering effect on a woman of giving affection which she does not feel, or having sex which she may not want, in order to 'pay for her keep'. Neither does she discuss the fundamental question of what 'love' is anyway, when a husband who would expect this of his wife is considered to be 'more in love' with her.

Similar problems can be identified in a more recent study by Pat O'Connor who also uses an exchange model. O'Connor argues that women in her study felt themselves to be powerful in direct relation to the balance of emotional dependency between them and their partners: 'Those who felt powerful were most likely to be in marriages either characterized by a high pattern of mutual dependence and/or to be less dependent on their spouse than he was on them'

11

(O'Connor 1991: 840). Furthermore, even though the women in O'Connor's study were financially dependent, '[a] sizeable minority of them experienced power within this relationship – partly through manipulating the balance of emotional dependence within it' (ibid.: 841). Again, these claims rest on an assumption that terms such as 'powerfulness', 'powerlessness' and 'emotional dependency' are in themselves transparent and ungendered. In reality things may be much more complex. For example, as Sandra Bartky (1990) has argued in respect of the gratification and sense of competence that women can experience when 'feeding egos and tending wounds', a woman's *feelings* of powerfulness may be a particularly unreliable measure of her real power or ability to act in the world in her own interests.

These problems with exchange theories stem from the fact that in order to conceive of love relationships in terms of the logic of the marketplace, the subjective experiences of the 'traders' such as being 'in love', or feeling powerful, powerless or dependent, are assumed to have an equivalence that renders them quantifiable and comparable. 'Love' and 'power' are abstracted from the relational processes through which they manifest and, once made into essences, become a kind of currency. This is then exchanged in transactions between individuals who, apparently untrammelled by the baser human emotions, conduct their affairs 'rationally', and in accordance with the principles of rights, justice and fairness. Rather than revealing power, exchange theories serve to *obscure* it: power is assumed to operate along market lines, relationships are converted into the language and concepts of the market, relationships are then found to be exchanges which operate along market lines, and, because the market is assumed to be fair, relationships appear to be equal.

It is precisely this tautology, moreover, which structures the analyses of 'democratic love' theorists. Love itself is seen to have become a market relationship, 'a transactional negotiation of personal ties by equals', a 'rolling contract' held together by 'the acceptance on the part of each partner, "until further notice", that each partner gains sufficient benefit from the relation to make its continuance worthwhile' (Giddens 1992: 3, 63). Couples are held to operate increasingly on the basis of reason, engaging in democratic practices such as 'tenacious negotiations' and 'mini summit conferences' (Beck and Beck-Gernsheim 1995: 99). Thus love relationships are (by definition) contracts, contracts are (by definition) negotiated, negotiations imply the desire to reach a mutual agreement, love relationships are thus mutually agreed, and mutual agreement implies equality.

But does mutual agreement imply equality? It may certainly appear so, but as Carole Pateman (1988) has similarly argued, such appearances may result simply from the fact that the notion of equality between contractors is built into the very concept of the 'contract'. Given this, the advent of 'contractual love' may not so much imply the end of domination as an effective means by which consent of the subordinate is at once secured and made hidden. This appearance is further advanced by the ever greater intangibility of what is exchanged between partners. Once, when exchanges were viewed in more material terms, exchange theories could be readily criticised for presupposing the equivalence of different goods on offer while overlooking the constitution of these values within gendered social relations. As Colin Bell and Howard Newby put it in 1976: 'The crucial question is . . . what is the "going rate of exchange" and how is it arrived at? How many hours of household drudgery are a bunch of flowers on the wedding anniversary worth? And who decides?' (Bell and Newby 1976: 156). Within the new economy of love, however, partners are no longer seen to exchange the different goods and services which might reveal their embodied existence in a gendered social structure. The only commodity now traded is 'emotional satisfaction', something which remains as ill-defined as the traders themselves. But how far does this picture resemble what occurs in actual relationships? How far do individuals experience love as a negotiable contract? How do they understand and experience 'emotional satisfaction'? Do partners receive it in equal measure? If not, what are they able to do about this?

Concrete love

While the relationship between love and power has been neglected empirically, there have been some studies which have addressed the emotional aspects of heterosexual couple relationships (Brannen and Collard 1982; Hite 1988; Mansfield and Collard 1988; Duncombe and Marsden 1993). These studies allow us to invest concepts such as 'love' and 'emotional satisfaction' with at least some meaning in respect of concrete social relations, and in so doing they reveal the existence of important contradictions.

In a study of sixty-five newly-wed couples, for example, Penny Mansfield and Jean Collard (1988) found that while both partners were eager to present their relationships to the researchers as conforming to the egalitarian ideal of 'sharing and caring', much of what they actually said revealed a very different picture. The women had generally entered marriage seeing it as a relationship and seeking a 'common life' involving everyday companionship and an exchange of intimacy which would make them feel valued as individuals. Men, on the other hand, saw marriage as a 'life in common', home-based rather than relationship-based: 'somewhere and someone to set out from and return to' (Mansfield and Collard 1988: 179). They did not generally feel a need for self-disclosure. After only three months of marriage, the authors found women to be seriously disappointed and feeling ignored. Talking about the problem, moreover, proved extremely difficult, since men were simply baffled and saw their wives as 'rabbitting on' and being 'a pain in the neck' (ibid.: 173–174). The study highlights a sharp distinction between the promise of emotional fulfilment that is the *ideal* of modern love, and a wide gender gap of expectation in its practice: '[t]here is, it seems, "his" marriage and "her" marriage existing apart from "their" marriage' (ibid.: 179). The authors conclude that '[i]t is a life founded upon notions of coupleness, togetherness and equality. Yet at each point in the story it becomes clear that the worlds of husband and wife are separate and asymmetrical' (ibid.: 194).

Very similar patterns have been found in a more recent study of the relationship between the economic and emotional lives of sixty mature married or cohabiting couples. Jean Duncombe and Dennis Marsden (1993) did not set out to investigate asymmetry of emotional response, but this emerged during the research process as the dominant pattern described by their female interviewees. The women sought validation from, and wanted to feel emotionally 'special' to, their male partners. They were disappointed however by the men's lack of spontaneity and 'emotional participation' in the relationship. Thus Duncombe and Marsden suggest that an increase in conflict and unhappiness within relationships may be occurring; gender differences in emotionality may be highlighted and intensified by the shift from marriage as an 'institution' to the ideal of fulfilment within personal relationships.

These empirical studies find, then, that there is a major, and possibly increasing, tension between the contemporary ideal of love and its practice. While the ideal of an intimate relationship offers salvation and solace to the notional 'individual', actual men and women appear to have quite different relationships to that ideal. For example, while Beck and Beck-Gernsheim's abstract partners undertake endless 'relationship work', Duncombe and Marsden found that only real women and not real men were doing what they call 'emotion work'. While abstract lovers negotiate the content of the 'love package', real women, it seems, have considerable difficulty in persuading real men even to sit at the negotiating table. And while abstract relationships last only as long as they are emotionally satisfying for both parties, real relationships seem to continue anyway, despite the fact that women, in particular, say that they find them most unsatisfying. This gendered concretisation of 'emotional satisfaction' thus suggests three things: first, women and men do not appear to agree either about how important it is, or indeed what it is. Second, whatever it is, women seem to think they are getting less of it than men. And third, there is little evidence of couples utilising democratic practices to sort these differences out. What, then, might this tell us about the relationship between love and power?

Different but equal?

Researchers themselves have generally been reluctant to stray too far from the democratisation narrative. Mansfield and Collard argue that while 'traditional' marriage was oppressive to women, '[i]n the current emphasis on the relationship, *both partners are oppressed* by an ideology which fails to understand and appreciate the vitality and complexity of their differences' (Mansfield and Collard 1988: 231, my emphasis). Duncombe and Marsden suggest that the differences may be related to power, citing women in their study who experienced their partner's emotional 'remoteness' as a form of power (ibid.: 236). They also stress, however, that women have at least the possibility of exercising emotional power over men by deliberately withholding emotional 'services' which men want. Only Shere Hite (1988), whose large-scale popular survey revealed similar gendered patterns of difference, claims that it is the existence of an unequal 'emotional contract' which leaves women feeling frustrated and dissatisfied.

Some writers have addressed the question of gender differences in love at a theoretical level, but have concluded that these are evidence of 'complimentarity' rather than power differentials. Francesca Cancian, for example, echoes earlier functionalist models of coupledom which contrast the 'instrumental' role of the male breadwinner with the 'expressive' role of his wife (see Parsons and Bales 1956). She claims that 'women and men prefer different styles of love that are consistent with their gender role. Women prefer emotional closeness and verbal expression; men prefer giving instrumental help and sex' (Cancian 1985: 253). Current difficulties result, according to Cancian, from a failure to understand and respect this difference. A 'feminization of love' over the last century means that 'only women's style of love is recognized, and women are assumed to be more skilled at love' (ibid.). This has led to misguided pressure being put on men to show their feelings and a denial of the 'legitimacy' of men's claims that sex is their expression of love. Cancian considers that the existence of male domination in love relationships has been exaggerated. Indeed, she concludes that 'men's power over women in intimate relationships is *severely limited* by the social organization of love' (ibid.: 259, my emphasis).

The different but equal thesis draws popular support from Deborah Tannen's sociolinguistic theory (1986, 1992). Also basing her argument on 'separate spheres' logic, Tannen argues that men and women belong to different 'language cultures' which have evolved to equip them for their different 'public' and 'private' social roles. Miscommunication is rife as 'women speak and hear the language of connection and intimacy, while men speak and hear the language of status and independence' (Tannen 1992: 42). Tannen gives numerous examples of women feeling ignored, put down, emotionally distanced, interrupted and lectured to by male partners, but argues that these feelings result from women 'misunderstanding' men's intentions. Men and women, Tannen asserts, have 'different *but equally valid* styles' (ibid.: 15). The contradictions in Tannen's thesis are revealed by her own example of how little girls demonstrate their ability to issue orders and operate in a hierarchical structure when playing at parent–child relationships, but do not consider it 'appropriate' to behave like this with their peers (ibid.: 46–47). This suggests either that grown men, unlike small children, lack the ability to make such judgements, or that they do in fact see it as quite appropriate to relate to their female partners using the language of independence and domination. Moreover, Tannen fails to explain why, even though men and women spend a good deal of time together in public as well as in private, this has not resulted in the development of a more 'appropriate' 'language culture'. Could it be that this absence is in fact due to the presence of another particular language culture, one within which men and women are differently, and hierarchically, situated?

The contradictions within 'different but equal' arguments are evidence of a power–love dichotomy which, as Joan Meyer (1991) argues, inheres in Western thought and maps directly on to a public–private dichotomy. This in turn is linked to abstract ideas about 'masculine' and 'feminine' behaviour. These conceptual dualisms serve to obscure the operation of gendered power by making it difficult to conceive of intimate relations as vehicles for both love *and* power. What happens is that even where men's behaviour is identified as domineering, this is not viewed as having any relation to love itself, but rather as something determined by conditions outside the bounds of the 'private sphere'. Victor Seidler (1989, 1991, 1994), for example, argues that men are both controlling and 'emotionally undeveloped' in their personal lives. However, he portrays men's problematic behaviour as a side effect of an assumed greater involvement in an alienating 'public realm'. Like Cancian and Tannen, Seidler thus makes the mistake of equating actuality with abstract thought systems. The dynamics of heterosexual love then appear merely as a reflection of men's and women's supposedly discreet 'private' and 'public' roles, rather than as means by which gender identities and the social order are constructed and reproduced. So, although empirical evidence of dissatisfied women and distant men contradicts abstract constructions of the 'contractual couple', the relation of this contradiction to power can be easily obscured by this paradoxical presupposition: love exists in a social zone which is *by definition* free of power, even when obviously domineering behaviour is exhibited within it.

However, even if we reject this 'separate spheres' logic, adding this to a rejection of the 'market' model of love, there is yet another obscuration to be faced. That is, whatever goes on in love relationships cannot really be understood anyway, because it is determined by the language of the heart itself.

The language of the heart

Passionate love, it is often argued, is fundamentally rebellious in nature and emerges in *resistance* to power and control. In traditional societies, the maintenance of the social order is seen to depend in part upon the *regulation* of love: 'love must be controlled *before* it appears. Love relationships must either be kept to a small number or they must be so directed that they do not run counter to the approved kinship linkages' (Goode 1974: 150). In modern Western societies, however, marriage and family life have increasingly come to be *based upon* the experience of falling in love. Ernest Van den Haag points to the contradictory nature of this practice; commenting on the famous claim that 'love and marriage go together like a horse and carriage', he suggests instead that 'love is a very unruly horse, far more apt to run away with the carriage than to draw it' (Van den Haag 1974: 135). In contemporary society the horse, it seems, has indeed run off with the carriage; love, it appears, has finally broken free from the shackles of social constraint. The truth of this victory is rarely disputed, for in theory, as in experience, love appears to come from outside of the social. Love, that is, 'grows from below, from the power and persistence of sexual drives and from deep personal wishes' (Beck and Beck-Gernsheim 1995: 176–177). Love now recognises 'only one authority – the language of the heart' (ibid.: 81). For many, falling in love is thus synonymous with freedom itself. Ethel Person (1990: 353–354), for example, argues that romantic love has become 'perhaps the most important of our cultivated freedoms . . . perhaps in our time the primary vehicle for self-realization, transformation, and transcendence'. If we really want to be free, we must surrender to 'the power of romantic passion' a power which 'rewrites the narrative of our lives through its own compelling force' (ibid.: 350). The prevailing view appears to be that while the 'language of the heart' may be irrational, mysterious and incomprehensible, whosoever speaks in a different tongue speaks against freedom itself. At last, it seems, the individual is free to fall in love and live happily ever after.

From the feminist perspectives outlined above, however, the contradictions which inhere in love are only intensified by this 'victory of the heart'; if falling in love is becoming ever more important as a means of 'transcendence', then there is every reason to suppose that it is at once growing more important as a means of reproducing the mundane and the oppressive. This supposition draws support from Max Weber's analysis of modern love. Weber is in no doubt that love's rebellion *appears* as the most profound expression of freedom:

> [T]he erotic relation seems to offer the unsurpassable peak of fulfilment of the request for love in the direct fusion of the souls of one to the other. This boundless giving of oneself is as radical as possible in its opposition to all functionality, rationality and generality. It is displayed here as the unique meaning which one creature in his irrationality has for another, and only for this specific other . . . this meaning, and with it the value-content of the relation itself, rests upon the possibility of a communion which is felt as a complete unification, as a fading of the 'thou'. . . . The lover realizes himself to be rooted in a kernel of the truly living, which is eternally inaccessible to any rational endeavour. He knows himself to be freed from the cold skeleton hands of rational orders, just as completely as from the banality of everyday routine.
>
> (Weber 1948: 347)

However, this resistance is no remedy to the destructive forces which give rise to it. On the contrary, the substitution of an overly rational, repressive and generalistic ethic with an irrational, spiritualised, erotic passion rooted in a 'fading of the thou' results not in a more humane morality, but rather in a destructive amorality. For Weber, it is precisely because erotic desire is experienced as emanating from the depths of the soul itself, and therefore appears to be beyond social regulation, that it facilitates the exercise of power:

> Unavoidably, [the erotic relation] is considered to be a relation of conflict. This conflict is not only, or even predominantly, jealousy and the will to possession, excluding third ones. It is the most intimate coercion of the soul of the less brutal partner. This coercion exists because it is never noticed by the partners themselves. Pretending to be the most humane devotion, it is a sophisticated enjoyment of oneself in the other. No consummated erotic communion will know itself to be founded in any other way than through a mysterious *destination* for one another: *fate*, in this highest sense of the word. Thereby, it will know itself to be 'legitimized' (in an entirely amoral sense).
>
> (ibid.: 348)

Thus, while falling in love appears to transport the individual into a realm of 'the most humane devotion', it in fact creates a new domain for the most effective and insidious exercise of power. Power is hidden because it is at once the language of the heart, precisely the radical feminist view of how romantic love facilitates the reproduction of patriarchal social relations.

The path of freedom?

The 'democratisation thesis', which I outlined above, has two aspects: the spread of passionate love to the masses and the growing application of principles of justice and fairness to love relationships. If the former trend results, as Weber's argument implies, in a social system founded upon coercive love relationships fuelled by conflict and irrationality, then it may seem that the latter is just what is required – it would at least mitigate the worst effects of the 'dangerous passions' which rule us. Claims that lovers already conduct their relationships on a contractual basis do seem to be premature. However, perhaps we should nevertheless welcome the spirit of such claims, seeing them both as an expression of a desire for social progress and as a means by which it can be brought about. Egalitarian love may not yet be realised, but all the more reason, it might be argued, for us to aspire to the ideal of the 'pure relationship' and take seriously the suggestion that love should be built around the 'consitutional device' of 'an implicit "rolling contract" to which appeal may be made by either partner when situations arise felt to be unfair or oppressive' (Giddens 1992: 192). Giddens is optimistic that such an approach can succeed, and proposes that women should adopt the suggestions of popular advice books and open a 'rule book' to share with their male partners in order to help them develop more satisfying relationships.

However, even leaving aside empirical and practical questions, such as the non-compliance of the powerful, there are deep contradictions within the very ideal of democratic love. How can a powerful force which has broken free from all social regulation be made subject to the principles of social democracy? How can a freedom sought through surrender to unconscious forces become a freedom built through conscious negotiation? How can a mysterious power which determines our lives be made a power which we determine? And how can a clash of wills which threatens to crush the very soul be transformed into an 'equal emotional contract'? How can emotion beyond reason, that is, be tamed by reason beyond emotion? Such a task, if possible at all, appears to require rather more than good intentions and a few popular advice books. Nevertheless, some argue that this process is already well underway, leading us to a future where 'the chaos of love is tidied up and properly organized along market lines: equality, carefully worded contracts . . . a social hybrid of market forces and personal impulses . . . which is safe, calculable and medically optimized' (Beck and Beck-Gernsheim 1995: 141). However, the result of this is not the maintenance of deeply intimate and emotionally satisfying love but its end: 'the secular religion known as love is suffering the fate of other religions; it is losing its mythology and turning into a rational system' (ibid.). A time is predicted when 'there would be no great difference between loving and, say, growing apples or book keeping' (ibid.).

The argument that rationalisation will lead to the end of passionate couple-dom is quite similar, of course, to Weber's argument that it was rationalisation which brought it into being in the first place, in reaction to the 'brotherly love' of salvation religion. If our mass faith in salvation through 'intimacy' really is on the wane, what then will happen to our unruly passions? Perhaps our desire for salvation will soon find expression in new forms of love and religion, and 'passionate coupledom' will indeed become a thing of the past. A second possibility, however, is that, at least for the time being, the contradiction between passion and reason will continue to be contained within the current system of love. The dialectic of resistance and regulation might continue to manifest in the form of serial monogamy, with each new love promising deliverance from a relationship that has become no more satisfying than 'book keeping'. Yet how can love last at all in such a climate? How can individuals fall in love and create a relationship which, according to critics, is inherently conflictual and coercive while at the same time aspiring to one which is equal, reciprocal and contractual? And how, when they are living such a paradox, can individuals continue to 'believe in love'?

Negotiating and containing such contradictions may seem a formidable challenge. However, it can be suggested that this is precisely the activity which characterises modern love and that, notwithstanding the high divorce rate, couples are actually remarkably 'successful' in their attempts to 'make it last'. This effort is visible in the accounts of several researchers, who have noted interesting discrepancies between their own observations and what research subjects actually say about their relationships. Contradictions are also visible between different parts of the accounts of those researched. Mansfield and Collard (1988: 230), for example, found that the newly-wed couples in their study were 'eager' to present their marriages as conforming to the egalitarian ideal, even though what they actually said about their relationships revealed that 'despite the current rhetoric of sexual equality, it seems that husbands and wives frequently experience each other as intimate strangers'. In a study of the domestic division of labour among Dutch couples, Aafke Komter (1989) was similarly struck by the contrast between her own conclusions that these marriages were thoroughly unequal, and the keenness of both husbands and wives to present their relationships as equal. Duncombe and Marsden (1993: 237) also report 'wives in our study who claimed to be happy despite overt evidence to the contrary' and note in particular 'the couples' management of their image to outsiders – including interviewers – so as to present a picture of companionate love'. They suggest, moreover, that this effort may not only be for the benefit of others, and cite Arlie Hochschild's (1983) theory of 'deep acting', whereby a feeling that one believes one should have or wants to have obscures the authentic feeling, even for actors themselves.

It is of significance that the contradictions of love often seem to be most visible in the accounts of women, who appear to put considerable effort into papering over the very cracks which are at once revealed by their own expressions of dissatisfaction. Evidence of gendered patterns further belies the claim that love is becoming chaotic, fragmenting into 'an infinite number of private systems of love' (Beck and Beck-Gernsheim 1995: 180). It suggests, on the contrary, that predominent configurations of love are still very much with us. What has perhaps changed is that where once the relationship between gender, power and love may have been betrayed by formalised modes of deference and institutionalised inequalities, it is now obscured by individuals' own attempts to contain the contradictions in their experience. Those who seek the truth about love must therefore, above all, maintain a critical distance from the new romantic ideal. This is not easy; even theorists who do not deny that power and love are connected are easily 'put off the scent' by the hiddenness of power and their own romanticism. Ethel Person, for example, accepts that male domination can be a problem in love relationships, but is at once blinded by her own faith in the 'power of romantic passion'. She thus observes that 'successful' couple relationships involve 'a workable balance of power, often so subtle and so apparently automatic in its operation that neither the lovers themselves nor outside observers even notice it' (1990: 162). Lapsing into a subjective moral individualism based in the emotion of love itself, she thus concludes that the 'only criterion that can be used to judge them is whether the lovers themselves feel satisfied that neither the one nor the other is being unduly exploited' (ibid.: 163). This, however, may be precisely the criterion which renders the couple relationship an effective and unseen field of governance.

Summary and conclusion

It is thus possible to arrive at a hypothesis which would explain why love has become the focus of such radically different claims in relation to power. That is, while a process of 'democratisation' has indeed made a particular form of love available to all, this kind of love is not in itself amenable to democratisation insofar as this implies a substantive progession towards equal, intimate and reciprocal love relationships. Our society has come to venerate 'deliverance' through romantic passion, and upholds it as the preferred foundation of social arrangements. However, while this appears only to legitimate the freedom of the individual to love and be loved, it in fact legitimates the very means by which the desire for selfish gratification and the coercion of the less powerful may be freely exercised in the guise of 'the most humane devotion'. The 'democratisation of intimacy' promises liberty, equality and togetherness. In fact it is the process by which restriction, inequality and disaffection are merely obscured, facilitating the most insidious government of all: government by love.

Already this hypothesis has some plausibility. It is true that studies of 'marital power' have largely failed to find it, but then they have assumed the very concepts most likely to hide it, and utilised abstraction and commodification to render gender differences in love innocuous. Studies which have looked at emotion have made love concrete and gendered. These have revealed fundamental contradictions in the egalitarian ideal. Such contradictions are sometimes explained as the 'different but equal love styles' of men and women. These explanations, however, are rooted in conceptual dichotomies which merely obscure the relationship between power and love. We may be seduced by the plea that love itself cannot be wrong, because the language of the heart is surely the language of freedom itself. Such romanticism, however, may be precisely what conceals power the most, in theory as in experience. Some may concede all of this, yet claim that this is all the more reason to aspire to the ideal of 'democratic love'. But contradictions within the new romantic ideal reveal it as a most unlikely path to freedom. And while equality is seen to arise from the pursuit of intimacy, men appear not to pursue intimacy at all. Women do, and feel dissatisfied, yet appear keen to portray their relationships as equal anyway.

There is a history of opposition to the equation of romantic love with freedom. Feminists have argued that such beliefs are a form of false consciousness which helps to reproduce oppressive social relations. Falling in love is seen as a *misguided* quest for redemption, based on the delusion that freedom can be attained through bonding with the 'other'. 'Democratic love' theorists have not addressed this challenge, and while no one is claiming that patriarchy is dead, the utmost scepticism must be brought to bear on the suggestion that the fatal blow is to be inflicted through the pursuit of 'intimacy'. Meanwhile, there has probably never been a time when the development of critical analysis was more pressing. If romantic love establishes a domain wherein coercion is exercised, how does this happen? What forms does coercion take? Why is it so invisible? If love has become a method of government, the predominant form of which is the government of women by men, then how is this manifest in the experience of the subject of love herself?

2

ROMANTIC TRANSFORMATIONS

In Chapter 1 we examined some contradictory perspectives on the romantic ideal. On the one hand, love is often portrayed as a rebellious, spiritualised, erotic passion which enables the individual to transcend the limitations of mundane existence and gain a happier and more meaningful life; love, in short, is the expression of freedom itself. On the other hand, critics argue that the experience of romantic love is a delusion which, far from providing an escape from unsatisfactory life conditions, actually helps to bring them into being. This view has been most clearly articulated by feminists, who have viewed women as tragically misguided in their attempts to 'realise themselves' through falling in love. Such endeavours serve only to limit women's freedom and channel their energies into the reproduction of a patriarchal social order. Researchers and theorists offer one predominant approach to reconciling these contradictory claims; the couple is constructed as a site of social progress, implying the increasing redundancy of feminist critiques. In particular, it is claimed that a 'democratisation' of the private sphere means that love is no longer limited by external constraints; lovers are now free to negotiate the terms of their own relationships. This means that if the 'subject of love' is not happy with the terms of her 'love contract', she can simply tear it up and pursue her heart's desire elsewhere. No one has claimed that the couple never was a site of social coercion, merely that love 'no longer serves any political ends' (Beck and Beck-Gernsheim 1995: 172).

Having considered the democratisation thesis, along with evidence which may seem to support it, we concluded that it is unconvincing. It may be true that love relationships no longer involve formal rituals of deference. It may also be true that secularisation, along with legal and social reforms, gives an appearance of greater individual freedom. Certainly, it is increasingly difficult to observe the workings of power. However, this is no reason to conclude that the egalitarian ideal has finally been realised. What if it was never only, or even predominantly, the existence of institutionalised inequalities which prevented love relationships from being conducted in a humane and equitable manner? What if love itself is not, and never was, 'innocent'? What if love takes particular forms, determined by our conditioning, which in themselves bring particular configurations of gendered power into being? What if love cannot be free from the exercise of political authority because love itself is a means of governance?

The aim of the study in which *Revolutions of the Heart* is grounded was to test this hypothesis empirically – to ask: Does romantic love involve the exercise of particular methods of power and control? This question is addressed in respect of the heterosexual couple, and it is addressed through a consideration of the experiences of those who, it has been claimed, are 'subjected to love' within it. Fifteen women with diverse experiences were interviewed for the study (see Appendix). A semi-structured format ensured that basic themes were covered while allowing for spontaneous exploration of issues which arose during the interviews. For an average of about five hours spread over three sessions, each woman described in depth her experiences of establishing, maintaining and in many cases dissolving, love relationships with male partners. The women were also asked for their general views and feelings concerning love. The interviews were intense and stimulating explorations; there was no doubt that this was a subject of great importance to all concerned. The resulting 'data' are rich and fascinating, containing numerous insights into love as lived experience. Moreover, analysis revealed clear patterns across the women's accounts, and these form the basis of a new comprehensive and systematic 'anatomy' of love which is presented over the next five chapters. The account begins here with the experience of falling in love, not simply to conform to romantic conventions but because, if there is 'government by love', it is upon this experience that it is founded. We need to understand 'falling' as both an emotional and a cultural experience – to ask: Why did women in the study fall in love? What meaning did it have in their lives? How were their 'real' experiences related to cultural narratives of romantic love? Did falling in love require that they 'do' anything? What were the risks involved? What did it feel like to be in love? And what convinced women that they had found 'true' love?

Looking for a change

One answer to the question 'Why do we fall in love?' is that the experience constitutes a personal and social revolution; love is a process of change, or attempted change, precipitated by some sense of emptiness or dissatisfaction with life as it is. Sociologists have variously suggested that romantic love constitutes a rebellion against the social order (Weber 1948; Goode 1974; Van den Haag 1974; Alberoni 1983; Beck and Beck-Gernsheim 1995). In Chapter 1, for example, we saw that Max Weber (1948) deemed the eruption of erotic passion to be a reaction to the over-rationalisation of capitalist society – an attempt to reinvest everyday life with enchantment and spiritual meaning. Francesco Alberoni (1983) similarly argues that falling in love is a reaction to profound feelings of emptiness, worthlessness and depression. The predisposition is a general one within Western cultures, but is most likely to happen when we are young or unsure of ourselves and our own worth. The main 'symptom' is not the conscious desire to fall in love, but a sense of inner conflict and an intense desire to enrich our lives, to find a happiness and vitality which eludes us. What makes us fall in love is 'the conviction that we have nothing to lose by becoming whatever we will become; it is the prospect of nothingness stretching before us' (Alberoni 1983: 69–70). Psychoanalysts, too, have argued that falling in love represents an attempt to escape from, and resolve, contradictions within the self. Accounts differ, but all agree that the experience is rooted in some kind of internal conflict, linked to the experience of narcissistic imperfection (Freud 1912b, 1914, 1915a; Bak 1973; Reik 1974; Bergmann 1988; Viederman 1988; Chessick 1988, 1992). Theodor Reik, for example, argues that falling in love is always presaged by a dissatisfaction with ourselves, and suggests that '[w]hen people are entirely satisfied with their actual selves, love is impossible' (Reik 1974: 43).

Feminist analyses of romantic love have addressed the particular reasons why women fall in love, and have similarly cited prior dissatisfaction and self-doubt. This predisposition has been seen as partly the result of patriarchal oppression, which leads women to live stunted lives in the sphere of 'feminine immanence' (de Beauvoir 1988). Falling in love appears as a method whereby a woman can transcend the limitations of her sex and 'recoup her definitional and political losses by fusing with the enemy' (Atkinson 1974: 44). While such theories have yet to be supported by research into 'real-life' love, ethnographic studies of romance reading have found that the stories appeal precisely because they offer women the fantasy of becoming 'somebody', in stark contrast to everyday lives characterised by self-denial and taken up with the care of others (Radway 1984; Christian-Smith 1990). Textual analysis of romance fiction further shows that the narratives promise to heal deep contradictions in women's lives (Modleski 1984; Snitow 1984; Christian-Smith 1990; Belsey 1992). So, whether romantic love is viewed from social, political or individual perspectives, many theories suggest that it arises upon certain conditions: the perception, at some level of consciousness, that one's self and one's life are profoundly unsatisfactory. This painful awareness may be repressed, but may manifest with a vengeance when the individual is confronted with an apparent means of transcendence, taking the form in this case of a more or less intense desire for 'romantic transformation'.

In this study, there was scant evidence that women themselves explicitly understood prior dissatisfactions as being a cause of their falling in love. Rather, in accordance with conventional narratives, some combination of meeting a 'special man' and the 'chemistry' or 'natural attraction' between them were generally seen as the immediate cause. However, when the accounts were surveyed as a whole, patterns of predisposition emerged. These were visible, for example, in narratives of the contrast between the 'before' and 'after' phases of falling in love, and through women's own accounts of retrospective disillusionment. This evidence suggested that intense contradictions and dissatisfactions were indeed the harbingers of romance. In particular, as will become very evident later in the book, feeling extremely disappointed in one love relationship left many women low in confidence and self-esteem, and it was in this context that several described falling in love anew. They used the experience as a way of moving from one relationship to another. A proneness to falling in love was also visible in relation to particular fears about being single, and these accounts provide a revealing backdrop to later experiences of 'romantic transformation'.

Single dissatisfactions

Being in a couple relationship is generally contrasted with the state of being single, something that for women in particular has historically been constituted as a negative identity, connoting undesirability and a useless life. Such attitudes are no longer fashionable and when asked what they thought about being single, most women readily replied that they thought single women could lead satisfying lives nowadays. Women did not need to have a man to be happy, they argued, and ought not to remain in unhappy love relationships. Indeed, some women who were in long-term relationships expressed envy of the freedom and independence which they perceived single women to have. However, many of the things women said about their own lives revealed that being, or contemplating being, single was nevertheless *experienced* with considerable ambivalence. Sarah, for example, was very unhappy at the time of the interviews and felt this to be largely due to her unsatisfactory relationship with her live-in partner, Wayne. She felt like ending the liaison but at the same time believed it gave her some 'security' which compensated for her own lack of confidence. This is how Sarah replied when I asked how she felt about being single:

Sarah: I think it is brilliant. I wish I could do it. I am really envious of, say, Claire because she can do it, and she is really confident, and she believes in herself totally, and it doesn't seem to bother her . . . I just wish that I could be like that. She doesn't seem to get down about it. I'd love to be like that.

Sarah's friend Claire may indeed have found being single to be as easy as Sarah assumes. However, while the 'independent' lifestyle can look desirable to those in love relationships, being in a relationship can seem just as attractive to those who are single. For example, this is how Hannah, the only participant not in a love relationship at the time of the interviews, described her experience:

Hannah: It is ever so *hard* to keep body and soul together when you are working full-time, you know? And who pays the bills? And who tidies the house up? Who does the washing? Who sorts out for the repair man to come, and who gives you emotional support at the end of it all? . . . It is very problematic being on your own as a woman, because you are always by yourself, and that is so draining, *really draining*.

The irony of Hannah's 'single dissatisfaction' is that most of the other women in the study who were currently living with partners, including Sarah, were doing all the things that Hannah describes and often much more besides, but were certainly not experiencing the 'emotional support' that Hannah yearns for.

The practical struggles and frustrations which Hannah experiences in relation to being single may also reflect deeper and more profound fears concerning identity and aloneness. It is in relation to these fears that romantic desire may begin to arise. This is illustrated by another quote from Hannah. While in many ways Hannah enjoys being single and the opportunity it affords her to 'be herself', she also describes how such feelings exist in a growing tension with other feelings:

Hannah: I'm starting to notice that there feels like there's a gap in my life. And I think that gap is like a relationship. I feel that really strongly. Erm [*pause*]
Wendy: What do you think you are missing out on?
Hannah: . . . [I]t's that idea that you're *really* special to one person . . . which is an odd thing 'cause I know I'm special to lots of people, and lots of people are special to me . . . but it's that kind of *exclusivity* [*pause*]
Wendy: So in some ways would you like to have a relationship with somebody now?
Hannah: *Desperately. Desperately.* I think it's also hormonally linked, you know. . . . When my hormones go I think Oh God . . . I yearn for somebody to have that kind of, you know, waking up at three in the morning next to – and just thinking oooh, you know, this is really *intimate*, that intimacy. I really *yearn* for that at the moment . . . I do wonder if I'll ever find anybody to be intimate with [*pause, then sounding sad*] ever again. That worries me. That does worry me. In fact that frightens me.

If no particular meaning were given to her feelings, it could simply be suggested that despite leading a full and busy life, Hannah does not feel as 'special' as she would like, does not feel as close to others as she might, and is fearful that she will be unable to change this situation. Certain questions might then arise. For example, what is it about Hannah's life – about the nature of the job she does, about the kind of social life she has, about the kinds of friendships she has – which leaves her feeling unsatisfied, and leads her to 'yearn' for exclusive intimacy with another person? Such questions, however, can seem irrelevant in a culture where falling in love with a special person appears to be a means of salvation. Given this, it is quite natural for Hannah to articulate the emptiness she feels as representing a 'relationship' which she does not have. Since expressions of the romantic ideal are frequently underpinned by biological determinism, it is also natural for Hannah to assume her powerful feelings are at least in part caused by her hormones 'going'.

As discussed in Chapter 1, the concept of 'intimate' coupledom has become the repository for an ever increasing range of wishes. Existential security, personal identity, emotional satisfaction, sexual fulfilment, companionship, *and* a life which has meaning beyond the round of everyday existence can, it appears, all come through being 'lucky in love'. In contrast, life 'on the outside' is associated with insecurity, emptiness, frustration and loneliness. This dichotomy is reflected in women's accounts and is manifest in two particular ways. Firstly, there is an association between being of value and being in a relationship such that being single is equated with being in some way defective. In the following extract, for example, Ruth replies to my asking her why she has felt ambivalent about being single, even though in many ways she previously enjoyed not being in a love relationship:

Ruth: I think it was sort of a lot to do with not feeling very desirable. I think perhaps I had in my mind somewhere, you know, that if I was *really* a desirable person, you know, attractive or whatever, or nice, then there would be a man around. I mean I wish this wasn't the case, but it is, you know?

Women's painful feelings of not being worthy or valuable in their own right were often contrasted with the wish to feel 'special' to someone, which would be demonstrated by someone wanting them 'for themselves' and wanting them exclusively, as exemplified in Hannah's account, above.

Secondly, alongside the question of personal value, the single–couple dichotomy is manifest in relation to the question of personal competence; being single is associated with fears about not being able to cope with life, while being in a couple is seen to represent the solution to such fears. This assumption, visible in the first two extracts from Sarah and Hannah above, also appears in other accounts in the form of a certain ambivalence about being 'free'. On the one hand 'independence' has many attractions, but on the other it represents the daunting prospect of having no one with whom to share life's burdens. Jenny, for example, left her husband shortly after being interviewed for the study, and agreed to take part in a further 'post-separation' interview. Jenny expressed no regrets about leaving Peter and talked of her relief at being single again. However, her sense of responsibility for the direction of her own life felt frightening; Jenny felt insecure without the marriage which she had previously described as a 'solid rock'. In this extract, Jenny describes how these feelings were beginning to manifest in the form of a growing attraction to a male friend:

Jenny: He's not into control, but I find that really disconcerting, because part of me wants it, I suppose, you know? He just lets me take responsibility for myself, and I find that quite difficult really.

Wendy: What is that part of you that finds that attractive, for someone else to be in control?

Jenny: [*long pause*] Because it's all bound up with . . . need and care and emotion and whatever, I think. I think it's all tangled up together isn't it, you know? If you get emotionally involved with someone, you need them, and that sort of, that seems to take over really, when it shouldn't.

In this way, a fear of autonomy can make the idea of surrendering responsibility and control attractive, and leave women vulnerable to the desire to enter into a new love relationship, even before they have begun to 'recover' from a previous one. Thus, while the women in this study did not overtly associate being single with being 'left on the shelf' and even expressed quite 'romantic' views of 'independence', there was nevertheless a clear tendency to associate personal value and the ability to cope with life with being in a couple. Deep fears concerning personal adequacy and autonomy could easily become, as Jenny puts it, 'all tangled up' with a desire for intimacy. Women's expressions of 'single dissatisfaction' therefore give substance to claims that falling in love arises from an apprehension of oneself and one's life as profoundly unsatisfactory, and provide an important backdrop to the question I will consider next: how does the predisposition to fall in love come to realisation?

Writing herself into love

In Chapter 1, I described how the historical development of romantic love involved the emergence of a new symbolic cultural code which 'encourages one to have the appropriate feelings' (Luhmann 1986: 9). While romance as 'fiction' has often been viewed as distinct from love as a 'real' emotional experience, several writers have suggested that it is precisely as a story or narrative that 'real' love is best understood (Jackson 1993b; Pearce and Stacey 1995; Sternberg 1994, 1996). Pearce and Stacey (1995: 15) suggest that 'the narrativity of romance . . . crosses the common sense boundaries of "fact and fiction", "representations and lived experience", "fantasy and reality". In our relationships as well as in our reading or viewing, romantic scenarios accord to cultural codes and conventions.' Stevi Jackson (1993b: 46) similarly argues that 'We can identify with love stories not because they record some pre-existing emotion, but because our cultural tradition supplies us with the narrative forms . . . through which we learn what love is.' Love may be compellingly real, but it is nevertheless 'socially ordered, linguistically mediated and culturally specific' (ibid.: 39). Robert Sternberg (1996: 71) likewise suggests 'we often enter into relationships with (unconsciously known) ideal story plots with slots waiting to be filled'. So, while falling in love may arise upon a certain predisposition, something more than this is required: the articulation of emotion in relation to a particular narrative structure.

The plots of romance fiction are structured around narratives of transformation. For example, in an analysis of teen romance, Linda Christian-Smith found the typical heroine to be passive, shy, insecure, lacking in confidence and uncertain about her future. Through romance with a special boy, she is transformed into 'somebody' who is mature, self-assured, friendly, outgoing, popular and sensible (1990: 89–91). My analysis of 'real-life' love stories suggests that these too can be understood as women's attempts to 'write themselves into' such a narrative, and thus to transform their own lives along similar lines. A clear feature of women's accounts of romance was that the experience was by no means a passive one. On the contrary, women often appeared to work quite hard at getting a love-story off the ground, actively observing the behaviour of prospective 'heroes', and interpreting their own feelings in an attempt to endow particular encounters with romantic meaning: Is he interested or isn't he? What did it mean when he said that? Am I in love or aren't I? Sharon Thompson (1989) suggests that this kind of construction of the real-life romance is a particularly female activity, a view which appears to be supported by accounts in this study of romances which, at least initially, 'started' without the active co-operation of the man concerned. Here is what Jenny said when I asked her whether she had fallen in love with Peter, her husband of eighteen years:

Jenny: Oh yeah, immediately, yes, I can remember that, the minute I saw him . . . I was totally obsessed with it, totally. Erm, he didn't return it at that time, but like I said the minute I saw him I just sort of fell head over heels. And he was a bit of a catch as well. Erm, I thought this is the man I'm going to marry, erm, you know? Looking back I think perhaps I sort of set my sights on him. I suppose I was, you know, determined, and made it happen in a way, erm, whether that was the right thing to do or not, but that's what happened, certainly. I'd certainly been sort of obsessed, and he was my first boyfriend really.

Through familiar clichés – 'the minute I saw him', 'head over heels', 'a bit of a catch', 'set my sights on him', 'my first boyfriend', 'the man I'm going to marry' – Jenny thus incorporates her initially reluctant hero into a cultural script and constructs herself as the heroine in her own romance. The effort which women like Jenny appeared to put into 'writing themselves into love' and the apparent passivity of their male 'objects' contradicts the popular stereotype of male courtship. This accords with Duncombe and Marsden's (1993) finding that in interviews, women portrayed themselves as having made the 'emotional running', urged on by feelings which included wanting to be in love.

The way Jenny 'writes herself into love' suggests a close and automatic 'fit' between emotion and cultural narrative. In some other accounts, however, the activity of 'romance writing' is more clearly separate from the experience of falling in love; possible plots might be constructed, and an 'emotional interest' in love might be felt, but actually 'falling' involves something more – something that, as I will now go on to explore, is not always quite so automatic as it might at first appear.

Risking it all

While 'writing herself into love' can allow a woman to retain some sense of control, control is precisely what those who fall in love do not have. As many writers on the subject have observed, the whole experience is predicated on risk-taking: '[w]hen someone falls in love, he [sic] opens himself to a different existence without any guarantee that it can be realized' (Alberoni 1983: 32). This is the reason why people generally avoid falling in love: '[w]e say "no" because we have no guarantee that the road to a new life is not the road to desperation' (ibid.: 33). Furthermore, in a society where romantic passion is increasingly free of social conventions and external contraints, there is nothing to 'contain' the unruly and unpredictable emotion; as Beck and Beck-Gernsheim put it, '[t]he lovers have two levers to two trap doors; the end can come very suddenly, on the decision of the other, and there is no appeal' (1995: 193). So, falling in love is nothing if not a gamble, an observation which accords with the theory that we only do it when we perceive the odds to be good, or when we feel we have nothing to lose.

Some writers express no doubt that the risk of love is worth taking. Ethel Person (1990: 350), for example, argues that the reason why romantic love is 'one of life's pre-eminent crucibles for change' is that 'in love the self is exposed to new risks that may result in enlarged possibilities'. Moreover, even the act of risking everything can be empowering: '[p]aradoxically . . . self-surrender can be a form of self-assertion, a kind of giving of oneself that is the ultimate expression of one's will as a free agent' (ibid.: 138). Other writers, however, argue that for women, freedom, empowerment and 'enlarged possibilities' are very unlikely to result from self-surrender and are highly critical of cultures which encourage this. In a content analysis of the hugely successful girls' magazine *Jackie*, Angela McRobbie (1981: 118) concludes that 'the girl is encouraged to load all her eggs into the basket of romance and hope it pays off'. Sharon Thompson (1989: 352) spoke with teenaged girls and similarly concluded that their lives risked being 'ruined by love', not necessarily by what actually happened to them in relationships with boys, but 'by a propensity to stake precious time and lose heart at the gaming table of romance'. Whether writers portray it in positive or negative terms, they agree on one thing: love is a game of chance, and the stakes are very high.

In this study, accounts of falling in love showed varying levels of awareness of, and conscious negotiation of, risk. Some accounts employed a fatalistic 'It just happened and I was powerless to resist' narrative, exemplified by Jenny (above) who, then aged 17, fell 'head over heels' in love with her first boyfriend 'the minute [she] saw him'. Other accounts however, particularly those of older and/or more experienced women, demonstrated more awareness of what might be at stake and even a certain calculation of risk. In some of these accounts, there was clear evidence to counteract the view that people 'can't help' falling in love, and the indication that, at some level of consciousness, 'falling' results from a *decision*. Mary, for example, married to Patrick, had at the time of the interviews recently fallen in love with Barry. One interesting thing about this was that it had not happened before. Mary had felt attracted to Barry for several years, and he had indicated that he wanted them to 'get together'. However, a twenty-five year marriage, material security, the respect and feelings of children and extended family, as well as a whole social network of mutual friends, seemed too much to stake on an uncertain affair with a man who was also married. In this extract, Mary replies to my asking her what eventually caused her to 'fall' at the point she did:

Mary: I think partly because I wanted to, because I decided I was fed up of all the controls that go with mature love, erm . . . I mean I just wonder whether somewhere in your subconscious mind you can . . . protect yourself from falling in love, you don't allow it to happen. Perhaps when you are younger . . . you are more willing to risk it . . . erm and maybe at various stages of your life when you have perhaps reached a crisis (because so many people stick with bad marriages), [you] fall in love, and that's the catalyst that takes [you] off into another relationship. So I think there has to be a willingness somewhere inside yourself to do it, to let go, to drop the control . . . to let yourself be non-adult for a while.

Thus while Mary's love-story was one which she had, in a sense, been 'writing' for a long time, the risk of enacting it had previously seemed just too great. Only when her life felt so difficult that it seemed she had nothing to lose did Mary allow herself to 'let go', to 'drop the control' and let herself be 'non-adult', thus giving herself over to the promise of romantic transformation.

In other accounts, awareness concerning risk is focused less on what might be given up for love, and more on the woman's uncertainty about what she might be 'getting herself into'. A successful romantic transformation depends on something which the heroine is not ultimately in control of: gaining and retaining the affirmation of her chosen 'hero'. Love thus appeared as a difficult and dangerous project for women. It was difficult because of the apparent rarity of 'decent blokes' who were not already in a relationship with someone else, and the competition from an apparent ubiquity of attractive, intelligent and desirable women all looking for the elusive 'decent bloke'. This was a theme throughout women's accounts and the lack of a better alternative was given more than once as a reason for staying with a current or previous partner. Love was a dangerous undertaking because, even when women desirous of love believed that they had located a suitable man, it was hard to be certain that he was 'genuine' and their own propensity to fall in love could make them extremely vulnerable to the attentions of men who 'blew hot and cold'. Skill, self-control and careful judgement were thus required in order to ascertain how far a successful transformation was a real possibility before 'letting go'. This can be a difficult path to tread for those who are 'desperate for love'.

The risk of responding to her prospective hero's attentions was great because once a woman had begun to 'fall' it became ever more difficult to regain any sense of control over her own destiny. Some women described a 'point of no return', a definite moment of being 'tipped over' or 'going over the edge'. That point marked her entry into a phase of intense emotional turmoil which was quite distinct from her previous emotional state. A feeling of things being on a relatively even keel and perhaps rather 'flat' was suddenly replaced by extreme and constantly changing emotions. In the following extract, for example, Ruth describes the danger and excitement of 'falling':

Ruth: It seems to me a time of er *chaos*, you know? Erm, and I think it's much more about your own feelings than actually about the other person. Erm, and it's a very exciting, exhilarating thing to go through. . . . And it can feel so *dangerous* which might be part of the pleasure. Erm, I mean when I've been falling in love, you know, I've had things like I haven't been able to *sleep*, you know, and I've got up in the middle of the night and stared out of the window. And it's all felt like a *knife edge*, you know? *Will* the other person love you back? *When* will they declare their love, you know? It's like living in the middle of a big *drama*! And it's great! I do, I think it's great from that point of view.

This exaggeration of 'normal' emotional life, characterised by extremes of all kinds, is also observed by Alberoni: '[t]he polarity of everyday life is between tranquility and disappointment; that of love is between ecstasy and torment' (1983: 40–41). However, while the turmoil of love may appear, as Ruth suggests, chaotic, the intense emotions women described were in fact quite predictable in the sense of being experienced in relation to an ideal story plot: excitement at the possibility of romantic transformation, bliss at apparently finding 'true love' at last, fear that it would all 'go wrong', and anguish at the prospect of ending up heart-broken. Women's accounts thus accord with Sternberg's observation that 'we feel emotion when we sense a match between an actual or potential story and our ideal one . . . cognition of a match generates positive emotions, the contrary realization leads to negative emotions' (1996: 72).

While falling in love is most often portrayed in positive terms, it has been suggested that this does not necessarily represent experience (Tennov 1979; Alberoni 1983). Certainly, the risk of love can make it an extremely unnerving experience. In some accounts predominant emotions appeared to be fear and anxiety, accompanied by an acute and debilitating self-consciousness. Take the following description from Jane, for example:

Wendy: How did it feel? [falling in love]
Jane: Erm like just butterflies, erm just feeling nervous all the time and, and erm just well feeling a bit sick really . . . I couldn't eat properly and that for a while, I think – because there's the worry about actually eating in front of them. . . .

Another example comes from Hannah. Here, I have asked her to expand on her observation that falling in love is the same as being frightened:

Hannah: . . . I started to shake . . . and part of me felt really kind of [*sharp intake of breath*], you know, terrified . . . on one level I don't like it at all. Quite uncomfortable.
Wendy: How – why does it make you feel uncomfortable?
Hannah: Because I am not in *control*, and I don't *feel* that in this situation I am being natural, or I am being myself . . . it is like being an animal sort of watching out to see if the more powerful animal is going to affect me. And it is almost like I sort of withdraw inside myself . . . it's a worry, that, isn't it?
Wendy: It doesn't sound a very attractive proposition really!
Hannah: Frightened to hell, so I must be in love with him!!

These feelings of 'risk anxiety' underline the fact that while a woman may attempt to retain a sense of control through being the author of her own love-story, the attempt to transform her life through falling in love requires that she relinquish control of the plot. She must render herself an object, lay herself open to the judgement of another and, once having done so, finds herself 'written into' a story in which her destiny, apparently, lies in his hands.

The saved and the damned

To place oneself in such a vulnerable position is not, of course, without purpose: the hope of deliverance from a life which, despite all its apparent advantages, is experienced as dull, lonely and unsatisfying. The attempt is perilous for, as Alberoni (1983: 40–41) observes, 'Everyday life is eternal purgatory. When we fall in love, there is only heaven or hell; either we are saved or we are damned.' Within conventional narratives, the heroine's deliverance, or transformation, commences at the point where the hero recognises her specialness; with one kiss, the princess is awakened from a hundred years of sleep. This pattern was visible, too, in women's accounts in this study. For example, Hannah, whom we saw earlier experiencing a 'gap' in her life and feeling 'desperate' for a new love relationship, describes what happened to her when a man whom she had been 'interested in' for some time paid her some attention:

Hannah: It is *tremendously powerful*. I mean it is like a religious experience . . . that feeling of being lifted out of yourself and er, being somehow transformed. I mean . . . one of the women at work yesterday said to me 'Hannah, you look absolutely radiant', and I am thinking well why, you know? I'm really spotty. And it is something to do with that kind of, you know, er the effect that another person can have on you in the way that you feel about yourself. So it is, it is a, it is like being transformed, and lifted out of yourself.

Wendy: And that's what a religious experience can do for a person?

Hannah: Completely, yeh, can sort of transform you, lift you out of yourself, and also actually make you feel that you are very worth – and very, yeh very erm acceptable as a person, you know? Er that's very powerful, it is powerful stuff.

In this case, the man did not turn out to have any sustained 'romantic interest' in Hannah. Fortunately, she had not completely 'fallen' for him and was thus able to regain her equilibrium, albeit with some loss of dignity. However, the quote illustrates the powerful transformative effects that positive attention can have on a woman who is feeling 'spotty' and not very 'acceptable'.

Hannah's comparison of romantic love with a religious experience was echoed in other accounts, which employed 'spiritual' language to describe the feeling of becoming something higher or better. We saw in Chapter 1 how several writers have compared romantic love to religion (Freud 1930; Weber 1948; Alberoni 1983; de Beauvoir 1988; Beck and Beck-Gernsheim 1995). It has also been suggested, more specifically, that the sudden and dramatic change which characterises 'falling in love' likens it to other experiences of sudden and profound change, particularly political or religious conversion (Averill 1985). The process of 'writing oneself into love' may thus be a particular instance of a wider phenomenon: cultural narratives of transformation. At any given historical moment there may be a number of such narratives, each addressing, and in different ways constructing, contradictions and dissatisfactions within the self and society. Romantic love structures existential 'unsatisfactoriness' as having a very particular meaning which we saw in relation to women's experiences of being single: the absence of a special and 'intimate' relationship which would supposedly provide all that is felt to be missing. So, while on one level romantic love may be understood as a social code which serves to guarantee the reproduction of (heterosexual) coupledom (Luhmann 1986), it should also be understood as a narrative which 'seduces' individuals to invest emotionally in the 'religion of love', through the promise that entry into an exclusive union will deliver them from their 'spiritual' ills.

While romantic transformation may be similar to other narratives of transformation, it is also quite different in that it cannot be undertaken alone, however much the individual tries and however strongly she 'believes in love'. She may 'drop the controls' and open herself up to the possibility of love, but faith alone will not deliver her. Only if her hero responds appropriately and pledges his exclusive devotion can the heroine live out her emotional turmoil as 'true love'. Lucy's hero, for example, fell in love with her and proposed marriage. Her romance was experienced as a joyful and transforming experience. Lucy describes here what being in love was like for her:

Lucy: Quite a romantic feeling and a fluttering of my heart . . . I felt very happy, excited, erm very close to Thomas. Erm walking on air I suppose, yes. On my wedding day I was definitely walking on air. My feet hardly touched the ground that day. That was a lovely, lovely feeling, yes.

Rose, on the other hand, tells a very different story. Falling in love has been, in her words, a 'horrid' experience. She had been involved in a sexual relationship with Ken for some time, but had been consciously determined not to 'fall for him' because of the fact that he continued to live with his partner of many years and their children. However, the intimacy of their liaison and the power of her own longing eventually weakened Rose's resolve. Here, she describes the exact moment when she realised that she had 'gone over the edge', and explains why she has been miserable ever since:

Rose: We was in bed drinking wine, and he fell asleep, and I couldn't sleep, I don't know why . . . And I looked at him, and . . . I *felt* yeah, I really love him. So that sort of panicked me. And from there it got bad . . . I couldn't handle all the change I was going through . . . and I couldn't talk about – cause I can't *tell* him how I feel, which makes it worse because I don't want him to *know* . . . I don't want to lose the little bit of control I've still got in the fact he's not *sure* of me. . . .

Wendy: Are you in love with him now?

Rose: Yeah.

Wendy: What does that feel like?

Rose: Horrid.

Wendy: Horrible?

Rose: Yeah. I mean it's more that I'm not in control of it, him if you like. I can't say 'well I'm in love and it's great because he's in love with me' (which I think he is) 'so we can be together and do all this stuff'. . . . It's not following what I perceive as the natural progression – you have a relationship, you live together and whatever you do, get married or whatever. It's not gonna *do* that. I mean if I *pressured* him, I could get that, I believe. But I *wouldn't* . . . I just want him to look at me and think, she's in love with me and I'm in love with her, and I'm gonna be with the woman, and we're gonna. . . . And that won't happen. But that's what I *want* to happen.

Thus Rose finds herself in the extremely painful position of having fallen in love, yet being unable to achieve romantic transformation. Ken's attentions are not enough – only if he desires her *exclusively* and commits himself to her in complete freedom can Rose's story have a happy ending. Instead, Rose has become one of 'the damned' who suffer the painful longing of a love which will never follow the 'natural progression'. Rose knew that Ken was a 'bad bet', but she took the risk anyway and lost.

Another time, another place

For those who are 'saved', there is the blissful realisation of the 'truth' of the narrative; love really can, it seems, change everything. How this transformation actually occurs remains a mystery, however; most of the women in this study were unable to say much about it beyond describing it as a 'spiritual' experience. One exception was Rose, who was able to give quite a vivid description of falling in love for the first time at the age of 16. Even though the experience occurred twenty years previously, Rose's voice became full of emotion as she recalled how it completely disrupted her normal experience of reality:

Rose: I can't describe how it was. It was just *powerful*, the feeling, and it was hypnotic if you like. Yeh it was kind of hypnotic. He was everything, and I was everything to him. We were just together, just me and him together against the world and all that business. Yeh it was just strange. It was something I had never experienced before, never experienced since. I mean the first time he kissed me I thought – I probably never but – I seen stars. But I probably never. It was like everything was black. It was like spinning in time. That's what it felt like to me. I mean I couldn't hear nothing, I couldn't – nothing around me was happening, just us in the blackness. That was the feeling. That was what it felt like. Obviously it didn't happen like, but that was what it *felt* like.

The power of love made everything else in Rose's life pale into insignificance. Normal life seemed distant and orientation in time altered. The only thing that mattered was to be in the present with her lover. Rose even lost her job because going to work simply seemed irrelevant.

One way of explaining such experiences is that narratives of transformation provide means whereby the individual can arrive at a place outside of normal experience, a place which is free from the constraints of time, space and relationship. Here, 'reality' can undergo transubstantiation, and possibilities may be experienced which lie beyond the limitations of the mundane. Roslyn Voaden argues that for the contemporary woman, romantic love thus offers a way to experience a 'threshold moment', a moment when she can transcend the normal rules and roles which limit her life:

> For once in her life, she is the heroine; she has achieved a position of power in a culture which habitually denies power to women. It is a brief moment of glory, evanescent and enchanted – made so by the very limits set upon it. Even if it is only temporary, she is watched, she is listened to, her exploits have significance.
>
> (Voaden 1995: 80)

Also drawing a parallel with religious conversion, Voaden makes an interesting comparison between modern romance fiction and the erotic visions of medieval women mystics. The appeal of both genres is a narrative structure which extends this 'liminal' moment, enabling the woman to be 'forever poised on the threshold between the potential and the actual, where she is always the lover and never the wife' (Voaden 1995: 78).

The sense that love happens at 'another time' and in 'another place' was a theme in many women's accounts. Here, for example, Mary talks about falling in love with Barry:

Mary: It was an out of reality experience and even when it was happening I knew it was out of reality. . . . But it was empowering because I knew there were other possibilities, that life did not have to stay the same as it was.

Paradoxically, however, at the same time as love being 'out of reality', its reality is more compelling than anything else. Few experiences can compare, for example, with the sheer physicality of being deeply in love. Lovers describe a dramatic coursing of energy through the body which is quite apart from the merely sexual, and an almost unbearable feeling of a power that 'tears at the innards' (Goodison 1983: 51–52). Here Mary, for instance, expresses her sense of amazement at the fact that while her experience was like a story, it was nevertheless so absolutely and undeniably 'true':

Mary: I sound like a 14-year-old schoolgirl . . . but never mind [*laughter*]. It worked at *every level*: intellectually, emotionally, sexually, and everything, you know? It just worked. It shouldn't, you know, it didn't ought to have worked. Basically you know these things only happen in films, and there it was happening to me. And it was *romantic*, you know? It was all of these things happening at once. . . . The most special part of it actually [was] intimacy, the absolute *comfort and security*. It was *very very strange*. I have never experienced it before.

Mary thus echoes the observation that falling in love feels like 'getting to star in your own movie' (Brunt 1988: 19, quoted in Jackson 1993a: 212). Suddenly and irrevocably, love is no longer just a story.

True love at last

At the centre of women's dramatically altered sense of reality was an existential experience of intense bonding or even 'merging' with the beloved, a feeling of finding their 'other half', of becoming 'whole':

Jenny: There was a very strong spiritual bond . . . a very strong emotional bond.

Diane: It was lovely. It was erm, it was like a oneness, you know? A feeling of two pieces of a walnut together making a whole, you know what I mean? Like that . . . it felt really whole.

Hannah: . . . just this really sort of intense feeling of being really close to somebody. And this sort of feeling of erm almost being unseparated from them.

The feeling that the beloved had become 'everything' or the 'whole world' was accompanied by a more or less complete withdrawal of interest from the 'other world'. Parting felt like a painful wrench and time spent apart an ordeal to be endured, while time together seemed to pass all too quickly. Women spoke of becoming completely absorbed in a world of intense verbal and physical communication characterised by emotional openness and powerful feelings of connection. One particular feature was the loss of sexual inhibition. Jane, for example, had a history of intense anxiety and dissatisfaction concerning her body, experiencing herself as fat and unattractive. Sexual relationships had often felt upsetting, and even abusive. At the time of the interviews, however, Jane and Paul were 'very much in love' and she was experiencing sex as passionate, tender and sensitive. In the following extract she speaks with unrestrained enthusiasm about her sex life:

Jane: This is what I have been looking for all these years. This is definitely sexual fulfilment. This is *it. I have arrived!* And yeh, it is great! . . . and there's no embarrassment there . . . I don't think twice about walking round with no clothes on or whatever, you know? . . . There's just no way I can imagine improving on it really.

Rose gives another account of sex in the context of 'true love':

Rose: Sexually it was great. We used to just spend days in bed, days and days and days, and never get up.

Another feature of being deeply in love was a sense of being completely 'in tune' with the other person, and of experiencing a level of communication and understanding which was 'beyond words'. While 'evidence' of such communication is by its very nature impossible, its existence seemed to be confirmed by 'normal communications' which revealed that lovers were apparently thinking the same thoughts or sharing the same feelings. Ruth, for example, is animated as she recalls the early days of her relationship with her ex-husband:

Ruth: I can remember when I was out with Colin, and we were walking down the street together, and we both started singing the same song at the same time, and I just felt like *God* . . . this is so wonderful! It felt like such a connection . . . like there's this tremendously *deep* level of connection, and you've got so much in common, you know?

For women who believed they had found 'true love', the risk of 'falling' seemed only to have replaced dissatisfaction and loneliness with an intense, joyful and spiritualised world, where the boundaries of self and other had dissolved into a lake of communion and deep understanding.

There are probably few people who 'in the cold light of day' really believe that it is possible to find emotional security, sexual fulfilment, perfect companionship, personal identity and the meaning of life in a single relationship with another human being. It seems improbable. But women's accounts of finding 'true love at last' suggest that this is exactly what they experienced. Even if they did not 'believe in love' before, now they *knew* that romantic transformation was possible because it had happened to them. Thus they had no doubt that their whole future life should be founded upon this experience. In the words of Kate, who found 'communication and security and total acceptance' with Harry: 'I thought *this is it*. Love. This is it forever.'

Summary and conclusion

We can see, then, that women's experiences of falling in love can be understood as cultural experiences. Through 'writing herself into love', the individual can attempt to escape from dissatisfactions which appear to be caused by her being single or by being in a loveless relationship. This unhappiness might be overcome if she is willing to chance her heart at the 'gaming table of romance'. There is no guarantee that salvation will be hers, but with self-restraint and a little careful 'risk management', she might shorten the odds against being damned in the hell of unrequited love. If she is wise and lucky her chosen hero will notice her, and her transformation will begin. The transformation itself happens 'somewhere else'. In a state of extreme emotional turmoil, the heroine finds herself standing in a 'threshold moment' where everything is suddenly transcended and her troubled past melts away. Enveloped in a spiritual bond that is oneness beyond words and glowing with a sense of wholeness and well-being, she realises that love is no longer just a story. Thus is the heroine reborn into a new and magical world with a life of happiness stretching out before her.

Here, of course, the story usually ends, and what a place to end! For the heroine's own sake, however, we must resist the 'happy ever after' closure. We have undertaken to investigate some very serious allegations concerning her love: that it is a delusion that will lead her to 'humble herself to nothingness' before her lover (de Beauvoir 1949: 653); an 'emotional rationale' for the submission of her ego to that of her lover (New York Radical Feminists 1971: 442); 'a special psycho-pathological state of fantasy' which will ensure her collusion in a patriarchal society (Atkinson 1974: 43); a 'frenzied passion' which will compel her to 'submit to a diminishing life in chains' (Dworkin 1976: 105); and a mere pretence of 'humane devotion' which will lead to 'the most intimate coercion' of her very soul (Weber 1948: 348). In the light of such claims we cannot afford to take 'true love' at face value, however seductive the plot.

There are already some worrying signs. We have seen the heroine struggling with some great difficulties: her lack of confidence, her fears about her worth, her unhappy marriage, her ambivalence about her 'freedom', her loneliness, her worries about the repair man, the mortgage, and the meaninglessness of life. Now all these fears and worries are gone! We have also seen her weighing up the risks of love and trembling with fear and feeling rather sick as she placed her heart on the line. Thank goodness it has all turned out perfectly. Or has it? What if the heroine's love is indeed a delusion, a fantasy of escape rooted in self-deception? If it is, however, how can we explain why it feels so utterly convincing? If not 'true love', what else can account for her sexual satisfaction, the strength of her emotions, the authenticity of her communication with her beloved, and her powerful experience of transcendence? Perhaps romantic transformation *is* a spiritual experience: beyond words, beyond time, beyond rational thought, beyond all social conditioning – simply beyond? Too much is at stake, however, to abandon the quest for a more 'down to earth' explanation and in Chapter 3 we will dig a little deeper into women's 'romantic transformations'.

3

ANALYSING LOVE

From a rational perspective, women's 'romantic transformations' may well appear illusory; everybody *knows* that falling in love does not resolve all of life's dissatisfactions. However, the whole point of romantic love, as we saw in Chapter 1, is that it is a profound and irrational rebellion of the spirit. And as we saw in Chapter 2, the experience involves deep and powerful emotions and subliminal perceptions which, when experienced in relation to a cultural narrative, render this narrative compelling. To ask someone in the grip of such a passion to deny that she is truly 'in love', with all that this implies, would be to ask her to crush all hope and even to doubt the reality of her own existence. Yet we cannot afford to abandon the possibility of critical analysis, for it has been suggested that it is precisely the irrational and rebellious nature of romantic love which makes it an effective hiding place for the exercise of power. In order to progress further, then, we need an approach which can embrace the contradictions of love and account for its paradoxical appearance. Love needs to be addressed as both reality and illusion, as both 'otherworldly' and yet very much of this world, and as both liberating yet possibly at once constraining. We need to explain how romantic transformation can take place 'somewhere else', while at the same time accounting for how the journey there arises upon certain conditions and is imbued with particular cultural and psychological meanings. The account should not deny the 'subject of love' her feelings of excitement, well-being and confidence, for they are clearly real enough. It should acknowledge her experience of 'transcendence', and the faith it has given her in the possibility of a happier and more meaningful life. But it must also allow for the possibility that the fundamental basis of her feelings and perceptions may not be what it seems and may even, if critics prove correct, be productive of her demise.

Of the few existing attempts to understand romantic love in any depth, psychoanalysis has particular utility in respect of these criteria. For a project which aims to understand how women's experiences of love might be connected to the reproduction of social power, this might seem a surprising claim. Psychoanalysis remains undeveloped as social theory and the neglect of women's experience by Freud and many of his followers, along with a persistent blindness to issues of power, has made it subject to cogent criticism. However, as my analysis of women's accounts progressed, I found myself being increasingly drawn to psychoanalytic theories by their power to explain the predominant patterns which were emerging. The development of a 'sociopsychoanalytic' account of romantic love is by no means straightforward. Although Freud himself was clearly interested in love, his published thoughts are fragmentary and contradictory, and neglect of the subject by his followers means that there is certainly no coherent theory which can be readily applied. What has proved possible is the employment of a number of different psychoanalytic approaches to shed light on particular aspects of love which were prominent in women's accounts. The insights gained contribute to a systematic 'anatomy' of love which emerges over the remainder of this book. My first task, in this chapter, is the integration of a psychoanalytic approach with the story so far. This task is realised through a preliminary Freudian 'analysis' of the 'subject of love' which endows her 'romantic transformation' with a radically different set of meanings to the ones which conventionally prevail.

Freudian transformations

We have seen that the fundamental aim of falling in love is to change one's life for the better, to rise above the dissatisfactions and disappointments of mundane existence. Transcendence is attempted, and sometimes 'realised' through experiencing deep and powerful emotions and altered perceptions in relation to a particular 'narrative of transformation'. Our critical understanding of this transformatory experience is greatly limited by the difficulty in accounting for its authenticity other than by recourse to the 'romantic' meanings endowed by a particular narrative structure: if love is not what it appears to be, why is it so compelling? In this respect, psychoanalysis presents itself as particularly pertinent. The reason for this is that the discipline itself was partly born out of Freud's own attempt to account for the same phenomenon that I have termed 'romantic transformation', an attempt which gave rise to a very 'unromantic' explanation of love.

One of Freud's great breakthroughs, in the course of the treatment of his 'neurotic' female patients, was his 'discovery' of 'transference love' and its therapeutic potential. Transference love initially presented itself as an embarrassing difficulty for the analyst, whereby 'a woman or girl patient shows by unmistakable allusions or openly avows that she has fallen in love . . . with the physician who is analyzing her' (Freud 1915b: 377). Terminating the treatment and referring the patient to another analyst proved no solution. The therapeutic situation itself seemed to provide optimum conditions for the development of the patient's impulse to fall in love, and she would simply develop her 'transference' on to the next analyst, and the next. Freud's assumption of a male analyst and female patient is probably not simply evidence of a prejudice. History has confirmed this as the typical case of transference love. Neither does this indicate that women are simply more susceptible to falling in love; 'counter-transference' in which male therapists fall in love with their female patients is also far more common than where female therapists fall for male patients. These patterns simply reflect a general tendency for women to be drawn to those in a more powerful position and men to those over whom they have a power advantage (for discussion of gender and transference love, see Lester 1985; Person 1985).

As transference love emerged as a regular and predictable phenomenon, Freud began to wonder whether the patients' propensity to 'fall' might have a direct and important relation to their psychic distress. If this were the case, and the analyst could begin to understand the origins and aims of the patient's compulsion, this might actually be of help in her treatment. Thus, through close observation of his patients, Freud came to develop an explanation for the transference. He concluded that the patient's experience was neither original nor arbitrary; it was, like all other loves, 'entirely composed of repetitions and rechauffés' (Freud 1915b: 387). The reason why love occurs is twofold. Firstly, in response to the inevitable disappointments and dissatisfactions of infancy, the developing child suffers injuries to its self-esteem. Secondly, and crucially, the child blames its parents for having inflicted these wounds upon it. Knowledge of these painful 'events' is repressed into the unconscious mind, where there persist feelings of resentment and indignation towards the parents, and the conviction that they were the original cause of feelings of inadequacy that constantly threaten to undermine the ego. Driven by an unconscious wish for reparation, the adult is compelled to 're-create' the object relations of infancy through falling in love. The upswelling of desire for each new love object is for the parent substitute who, it is hoped, will make up for the failure of the first and thus restore the individual to a state of lost perfection. In short, love is a purposeful attempt to reach a different resolution of the past.

The theory that falling in love is an attempt to rework the dramas of child-hood led to a classic case of redefining a problem as an opportunity. Instead of the patient's transference on to the analyst being viewed as an obstacle to a cure, Freud came to see it as the very means by which the cure could be brought about. Whereas in the normal course of events the aim of falling in love remains unconscious, leading to an inevitable repetition of past disappoint-ments, the transference allows a unique opportunity for change. The coming to the surface of the patient's 'substratum' of love makes available a rich source of psychic material which can be analysed, enabling 'the discovery of the infantile object-choice and the phantasies woven around it' (Freud 1915b: 387). With this knowledge, the patient can be freed from the grip of the regressive wishes and desires which cause her to repeat neurotic and harmful patterns. Equally important is the powerful motivation which accompanies falling in love and the considerable energy that is unlocked. Such is the strength of transference love, Freud remarked, that 'one has the impression that one could achieve any-thing by its means' (ibid.: 388). For this reason 'the patient's desire and longing are to be allowed to remain to serve as driving forces for the work and for the changes to be wrought' (ibid.: 383–384). Convinced of the crucial importance of this redirection of desire, Freud is adamant that on no account is the patient's transference and the therapist's counter-transference to be enacted as a romantic falling in love. If such restraint is not practised, 'all the inhibitions and pathological reactions of her love-development would come out, yet there would be no possibility of her correcting them, and the painful episode would end in remorse and a strengthening of her tendency to repression' (ibid.: 385). Only a prolonged and unrequited relationship between patient and analyst allows for the possibility of a cure.

In effect, then, psychoanalysis was in part developed as an alternative to romantic love. While Freud's patients attempted to escape from their psychic distress through romantic transformation, Freud aimed to 'hijack' their attempts and harness the energies and processes involved for ends other than the foundation of a conventional love relationship. While the 'religion' of romantic love promises to save individuals from their 'spiritual' ills, Freud's 'science of love' aimed to cure them of their neuroses. Moreover, while Freud was clearly a physician and not a social theorist, nowhere does he suggest that 'neurotic' love is of a fundamentally different kind to 'normal' love and there is clear evidence that he took a very critical and anti-romantic view of attachment love in general, seeing it as unlikely to bring the happiness and security that individuals long for (see Freud 1922, 1930). Unfortunately, Freud's thoughts on love have remained undeveloped; followers in the psychoanalytic tradition, if they have looked at love at all, have rarely touched on social or cultural perspectives and have neglected entirely the question of power.

However, while a coherent critique of romantic love has never emerged from psychoanalysis, psychoanalytic perspectives have much to offer in developing sociological models of love. Largely constructed through the analysis of thousands of individual 'love histories', each giving new meaning to the wishes and desires manifest in the transference, psychoanalysis is a body of knowledge which explores how subjectivities and social identities come to be constituted through particular patterns of 'love'. Even the language and concepts of psychoanalysis, such as 'attachments', 'cathexes', 'object relations', 'fusions' and 'identifications' refer to those very features of experience which outside of psychoanalysis are understood as 'love' (Gaylin and Person 1988). Psychoanalysis remains a controversial and contested collection of theories and practices. The point here is not the status of these as ultimate 'truth' or their utility in the cure of neuroses. Rather it is their usefulness in developing a critical perspective on 'revolutions of the heart', one which reveals the nature of the relationship between love and power. With this aim in mind I will, over the rest of this chapter, revisit women's 'romantic transformations'. Drawing on psychoanalytic theories, I will suggest that the reason why love is so compelling is that it is underwritten by older, deeper narratives of which the individual may not be even dimly aware.

Losing herself

In popular culture, the formation of a couple through romantic love is often portrayed as involving a loss of separate identity; two individuals become 'an item', their wedding car displays 'U2R1' number plates and partners are referred to as 'other halves'. Such sentiments may be far from superficial; in Chapter 2 I described how, for women in this study, romantic transformation was characterised by a powerful sensation of merging with the object of desire:

Diane: It was lovely. It was erm like a oneness. . . . It felt really whole.

Hannah: . . . this sort of feeling of almost being unseparated from them. . . .

Jenny: I just absorbed myself into him completely.

It was this loss of self, accompanied by such perceptions as having the same thoughts as the beloved and feelings of being 'out of reality' which gave the experience an 'otherworldly dimension'. This was reflected in some women's claims that falling in love was a 'spiritual' experience, claims which give depth to the view that romantic love functions as a 'secular religion'.

A spiritual interpretation of love was powerfully contested by Freud (1930) who developed his 'scientific' theory in opposition to the views of those who favoured religious explanations for the 'oceanic' feeling of 'oneness with the universe'. Freud argued that all such experiences originate in a repressed desire to re-create the original bond with the first love object. At this time, the ego is not yet formed and the infant experiences itself as being one with the mother. Falling in love reproduces this irrational sense of merging because it involves the regression of the ego so that '[a]gainst all the evidence of his senses, a man [*sic*] who is in love declares that "I" and "you" are one, and is pre-pared to behave as if it were a fact' (Freud 1930: 66). We may think of falling in love as an 'adult' experience, but according to Freud 'a child suckling at its mother's breast has become the prototype of every relation of love. The finding of an object is in fact the refinding of it' (Freud 1905: 145).

Freud's theory of love as a 'refinding' of the mother's breast has proved a pop-ular explanation with psychoanalysts interested in the subject (Bergmann 1971; Bak 1973; Kernberg 1974; Altman 1977; Verhulst 1984). Martin Bergmann (1971: 35), for example, suggests that the ability to fall in love at all and thus 'exaggerate the difference between one person and another' may be dependent on the exclusivity of the mother–child bond. Common features of love such as the extreme dependency on the beloved, the preoccupation with their face, and the emptiness, anxiety and longing which accompany separa-tion, may draw on imagery and sensations from the very earliest stages of ego development when the infant first becomes aware of its dependency on the all-powerful mother (Bak 1973; Verhulst 1984). 'Spiritual' dimensions of falling in love, such as the experience being 'beyond words', may reflect its origins in the pre-verbal stage of the mother–child bond (Altman 1977; Verhulst 1984). Disturbing 'symptoms' such as the loss of ability to structure time sequentially, an incapacity to objectify and an inability to distinguish between past and present loves may be further evidence that the normal functions of the ego are transcended (Verhulst 1984). In this study too, features such as women's experience of unusually spontaneous sexual expression accompanied by a sudden disappearance of self-consciousness and inhibition might similarly be accounted for by the regression of the ego along with its usual defences.

Such experiences are generally seen as positive and auspicious – signs of intimacy and caring which demonstrate the special nature of the bond between persons in a couple. This is certainly how they were interpreted by the women in this study. For Freud, however, they are evidence of a regressive psychic disturbance with a 'compulsive character which borders on the pathological' and which is 'more like abnormal than normal mental phenomena' (Freud 1915b: 387, 388). Such a radical view would have found little favour in the emergent 'intimate culture', perhaps accounting for why Freud appears to have modified his position somewhat by 1930 (p. 66), when he deemed falling in love to be 'admittedly an unusual state, but not one that can be stigmatized as pathological'. Certainly, critical observations of love have remained few in twentieth-century society, where it is seen as one of the higher human experiences and lamented only in its passing. Exceptions are Johann Verhulst's (1984) view that it has structural similarities to radically altered states of mind induced by depression, psychosis and drug addiction and Ti-Grace Atkinson's (1974) conviction that women in love are suffering from 'hysteria' and are in 'a pathological state of fantasy'. While such views may seem extreme, it is worth remembering that before the 'democratisation' of love the phenomenon was often believed to be a kind of sickness or madness (Bergmann 1971, 1987; Stone 1979).

Women in this study certainly did not see themselves as being mad or hysterical when in love. They did however, as we saw in Chapter 2, describe love as a risky and nerve-wracking undertaking – one which could make them feel sick and extremely frightened. Given this, it is striking how rarely love is acknowledged to be other than a universally pleasant and positive experience. Few writers comment on the negative and disruptive effects that 'falling' can have (for exceptions see Tennov 1979; Alberoni 1983). Freud's theory of ego regression, however, does offer an explanation for why falling in love induces deep fear and insecurity. Before individuals can hope to be transformed by love, they must be prepared to let down their defences and allow the boundaries of their ego to 'melt away'. Only by risking herself in this way can the heroine of our story return, as it were, to the beginning of love and attempt to heal the hurts of the past. But what does she hope to gain by such an adventure? What is the prize that she aims to win by 'losing herself'?

Finding herself

After the risk of the fall, it is no wonder the 'winners' feel fortunate. Having been prepared to enter what Francesco Alberoni (1983) terms 'the nascent state', those lucky in love may indeed feel 'reborn' into a new happy and meaningful life. But how could this experience follow simply from an individual 'losing herself'? The answer is revealed in the following extract from an interview with Mary. Here, I have just asked her whether she thinks it is possible to 'love somebody too much', the implication being that self-surrender might be damaging to the subject:

Mary: Although falling in love is about losing your identity, in a perverse sort of way it is also about confirming it . . . I suppose if it's unreciprocated being in love then it's too much. If it's reciprocal then it's great because you are getting this wonderful feedback where somebody's telling you that you are the most wonderful person on earth, so you can feed off that. And it – you know it can be quite empowering. But unrequited love, you know, that – that would be too much, especially if it went on and on and on forever, because that's just a total denial of who you are.

As Mary observes, then, while 'falling' involves 'losing oneself', this only appears to be a problem where the fall is one-sided. Then the subject's loss of identity becomes painfully compounded by the 'total denial of who you are'. If the fall is mutual, however, there is no sense of loss; identity is not only 'confirmed', but the subject undergoes the 'empowering' experience of becoming 'the most wonderful person on earth'. She can at last leave behind her imperfect self who struggles with confidence, autonomy and mortgage repayments. Through the act of giving up herself, she has found herself – this time her perfect, powerful and wonderful self.

If we are to persist with the theory that romantic transformation is illusory we need, at this point, to account for its compelling nature. We cannot simply deny the subject's experience. When she and Barry fell in love, Mary *really did feel* like 'the most wonderful person on earth'. Why? And why is this transformation, and the attraction which precedes it, accompanied by another change, this time in perception of the 'love object'? The latter phenomenon is commented upon here by Sharon:

Sharon: People that don't really look anything suddenly become extremely handsome! There must be something released into your bloodstream, you know? [*laughs*] . . . you'd never really noticed him, you know, and then it's 'ooh isn't he lovely', you know?

For Freud (1914, 1917, 1922), it is no mere chemical in the blood that turns the frog into a prince. This magic, together with the heroine's own transfor-

48

mation, is brought about by an altogether different means: a sudden and profound investment of psychic energy in a particular object, a process sometimes termed 'cathexis'. Once again the story is one of repetition; even if the subject should be certain that this is her 'first love', it is not in fact the first time that she has given up her (imperfect) self for the sake of an apparently better one. According to Freud, this is precisely how every infant reacts to the discovery of its narcissistic imperfection, a discovery which arises inevitably upon the apprehension of itself as separate from, and dependent upon, the parent. In an attempt to heal its wounded narcissism, the infant withdraws psychic energy from itself and invests it in the idealised parent figure with whom it then identifies. Disappointment is inevitable, but seeing no other way to respond to his or her existential predicament, the developing individual is compelled to try again and again.

The attempt to secure oneself through concentrating psychic energy in objects is one which may be repeated numerous times with many different objects. Falling in love, however, is generally the most profound of such attempts; 'in the state of being in love ... the subject seems to yield up his [sic] whole personality in favour of object cathexis' (Freud 1914: 33). This can explain why the subject's experience of 'losing herself' and 'finding herself' is so compelling, and also begins to tell us something about the relationship of love and power. Here Freud describes how the original process of empowerment repeats itself:

> [T]he ego becomes more and more unassuming and modest, and the object more and more sublime and precious, until at last it gets possession of the entire self-love of the ego, whose self-sacrifice follows as a natural consequence. The object has, so to speak, consumed the ego. Traits of humility, of the limitation of narcissism, and of self-injury occur in every case of being in love.
>
> (Freud 1922: 74–75)

'Self-injury' will not be apparent to the subject, however, nor indeed the faults of her lover, for her critical functions will have ceased. The reason for love's blindness is that while the ego has been lost to the object, '{t}he object has taken the place of the ego ideal' (ibid.: 75). The 'ego-ideal' in psychoanalysis is that part of the psyche which is produced out of, and stands as a substitute for, the infant's original narcissistic perfection. So in other words, just as the infant attempts to overcome the discovery of its own imperfection through identifying with the 'perfect' parent, so the 'subject of love' becomes 'one' with the lover who, in her unconscious mind, represents her own ideal self. Thus her love, like all loves, is a search for identity 'realised' through the illusion that empowering the object has restored her to perfection.

While object cathexis constitutes a basic mechanism of empowerment, however, substantiation of the proposition that there exists 'government by love' requires the development of a far more complex and particular theory. This theory would need to demonstrate exactly how individual 'empowerments' are related to systematic patterns of social power. Again, we can usefully draw on Freud's work, for while many of his references to love are quite generalistic, his observations of transference love reveal each person's repetition to have a very particular character:

> every human being has acquired ... a special individuality in the exercise of his [*sic*] capacity to love – that is, in the conditions which he sets up for loving, in the impulses he gratifies by it, and in the aims he sets out to achieve in it. This forms a *cliché* or stereotype in him, so to speak (or even several), which perpetually repeats and reproduces itself as life goes on, in so far as external circumstances and the nature of the accessible love objects permit.
>
> (Freud 1912b: 312–313)

This study does not focus upon the uniqueness of love. However, it does aim to understand how individual love-stories are embedded within, and possibly productive of, social processes. Given this, a particular question can be asked: are there features of women's accounts, perhaps less specific than a 'special individuality' of love, but at once more precise than a simple sense of 'becoming onself', which might give us some indication of how women's romantic transformations in particular might be linked to social power relations? More specifically, how exactly were the new 'selves' which women became different from the ones which they gave up?

Women who could do anything

In Chapter 2, I described how the background to women's romantic transformations had certain features. Despite expressing the view that women do not need a man to be happy, women's accounts suggested that this confidence was not necessarily experienced at an emotional level. On the contrary, being single was associated with fears concerning attractiveness, desirability and the ability to 'cope', and with a certain ambivalence concerning freedom and autonomy. It was precisely these kinds of fears, fears which are widely claimed to be particularly associated with the 'attainment' of femininity, which were dispelled through 'successful' love. Jane, for example, spoke of how she suffered from a deep lack of confidence and a tendency to see herself as fat and unattractive. She had developed eating problems during her previous unhappy marriage to Keith. At the time of the interviews, however, Jane had recently fallen mutually in love with Paul. Suddenly, her fears had evaporated and her eating problems had disappeared. Love had changed everything:

Jane: What a difference it has made, just, it is just this confidence building, erm, actually believing in myself, believing I can do it. I can – I can do whatever I set my mind to. And that I look alright the way I am.

Another example comes from Sarah who, again, talked of being very unsure of herself and of not knowing what to do with her life. Sarah admitted that she found it hard to contemplate 'being without a man', an admission which she clearly found painful. Her struggles can be contrasted, however, with how she felt at the time she and Wayne fell in love, eighteen months prior to the interviews:

Sarah: I was really happy. I could do anything because I was in love with him, basically. I mean I managed to get another job, I was having a good time. . . .
[Being in love] just makes me feel like – like I can do anything. Whatever happens . . . I can handle it.

A particularly striking feature of women's accounts was that although they attributed this new sense of confidence to being in love, it was nevertheless experienced as the arising of independent selfhood. Mary, for example, had been very unhappy for many years in her marriage to Patrick. She had not felt able to leave, however, until falling in love with Barry provided a 'catalyst':

Mary: I was no longer *afraid* of being without a husband. Not because I thought I was going to another partner, but [because of] something I found inside me.

Love, then, seems to have a certain contradictory logic; through gaining the recognition of her chosen 'hero', the subject comes to feel happy, attractive, competent and independent. Paradoxically, falling in love enables her to feel that she can 'manage without a man'. Our cultural context does not encourage us to subject the benefits of love to critical examination. Certainly, women in this study simply felt lucky. They had fallen in love with someone special and this, quite straightforwardly, was the reason why they had found the confidence to achieve things, take risks, make changes and 'be themselves'. We must ask, however, *why* love made women feel they could 'do anything'.

As we saw earlier, love appears as fundamentally rebellious in character (Weber 1948; Goode 1974; Van den Haag 1974; Alberoni 1983). In Chapter 2, we saw how women in this study attempted to transform their lives through 'writing themselves into love', emulating the fictional heroines who rise above their limitations and become 'somebody' through romance. Here, romantic transformation is further seen to involve the arising of a self-confident and independent attitude and a rejection of dependency. Support for, and explication of, these findings comes from Freud's (1915b) own detailed

51

observations of transference love between female patient and male analyst. Freud describes how initially the patient is 'docile'; she accepts the analyst's explanations for her condition, and appears willing to submit to the treatment. Coincident with developing her transference on to the analyst, however, a dramatic change occurs which 'always comes over her just as one had to bring her to the point of confession or remembering one of the particularly painful or heavily repressed vicissitudes in her life-history' (ibid.: 381). At this point the patient becomes, in Freud's words, 'stubborn' and 'rebellious', and loses all respect for 'the physician's well-founded judgement' (ibid.: 386). Indeed:

> No matter how amenable she has been up till then, she now suddenly loses all understanding of and interest in the treatment, and will not hear or speak of anything but her love, the return of which she demands; she has either given up her symptoms or else ignores them; she even declares herself well.
>
> (ibid.: 380)

Here, then, begins a power struggle between doctor and patient to define the meaning of her attempted transformation. The patient's experience is that her psychological distress has evaporated because she has fallen in love, and all she needs to secure her new-found well-being is the analyst's reciprocation. For the analyst, the patient's 'resistance' cannot be a path to well-being since, if allowed to take its 'natural' course, it will simply compound her neurosis.

Freud's account of his female patients' rebellion thus implies something more particular than the resolution of conflicts within adult identity; it suggests that women's transformations result from the eruption of resistance to adult *feminine* identity. It can thus be suggested that the reason why women in this study suddenly felt they could 'do anything' was partly because falling in love enabled them to 'transcend' the aimlessness, submissiveness and lack of self-confidence – as Freud puts it, the 'docility' – which characterises embodied femininity.

Men who were not men

The view that falling in love does not have a homogeneous character and will reflect the particularities of conditioning draws further support from what women had to say about the men with whom they were involved. When describing their experiences, especially where they were in love at the time of the interviews, women said they felt extremely lucky because their lover was exceptional; indeed he was unique. This, in itself, may not be suprising; love is, after all, based upon idealisation. However, if we ask *how* men were seen to be unique, interesting patterns again become visible. Through surveying the accounts as a whole it could be seen that firstly, the 'unique' qualities of individual men were actually quite similar and that secondly, these qualities were contrasted either with a previous partner or with what 'men in general' were normally like. Women consistently complained that 'most men', and especially male partners in established relationships, were self-centred, indifferent and emotionally distant. In contrast, men who were in love with them were described as loving, devoted and emotional. For example, here are some of the things Jane said about Paul, with whom she was mutually in love at the time of the interviews:

Jane: I am amazed. He is quite different. He has just got a natural kindness to him, you know, putting you first. A lot of men, a lot of the other ones I went out with . . . all put themselves first . . . where he is totally unselfish, Paul.

He is always saying that . . . the number one thing in his life is to make sure that I am happy. And if I am not he wants to know why, and he's going to do something about it, you know? . . . So it's quite a change for me, I feel spoilt.

When he found out I loved carnations, he'd turn up with five bunches at a time . . . [and] just the way he talks to me, just constantly show-ing affection. And he knows if I am not feeling very well or anything like that and he is just extra concerned.

Jane's examples of Paul's loving and attentive behaviour were so numerous that it was certainly very easy to appreciate why her previous doubts and fears about relationships with men had melted away, to be replaced by the certainty that she had finally found 'Mr Right'. Here seemed evidence indeed to support Jane's conclusion that her previous disastrous marriage had been due to her 'picking the wrong man'.

However, what could be seen through having access to all the women's accounts was that Jane's was by no means the only description of a 'unique' man. Another example is provided by Jean, who describes here how, after twenty years of marriage to Ron, who she complains shows no interest in her 'as a person', she finally found recognition and acceptance in a love affair with Frank:

Jean: He was very interested in what I had to say, extremely interested, not just sort of pretending to be. Erm, and sort of er, full of praise, you know, like *'God are you working and doing voluntary work and doing a course? . . . it's amazing'*, you know? And he really meant it. I mean I – I wasn't doing anything that *I* felt was amazing, you know? But it was quite nice for somebody to say that, and actually to sort of think: oh he thinks I'm amazing, you know?

So unusual was this kind of attention in Jean's experience, and so powerful its effect on her, that every few weeks she would engage in considerable subterfuge to make the secret plans and preparations necessary to make a 500-mile round trip just to spend two hours with Frank, while her husband was at work. While Jean's admission that *she* did not see herself as amazing is clearly highly significant in accounting for the fact that she would go to such lengths for affirmation, it is nevertheless also significant that Frank's praise and approval of Jean as a capable and worthy woman *was* experienced as unusual, and thus as highly seductive. Jean's experience of being praised for her competence was reflected in other accounts. Kate, for example, was a single parent when Harry fell in love with her. Kate described how Harry praised and admired her self-sufficiency and her ability to cope with her four children at the same time as doing many other things in her life.

It was not only recognition and admiration which proved gratifying for women. They also remarked on their lovers' 'unusual' capacity to be tender and emotionally 'open'. Here, Kate reflects on the early days of her relationship with Harry:

Kate: [H]e was incredibly open and generous, and I mean *very* open emotionally, and we spent a lot of time communicating, talking, just being. . . . [H]e actually appeared to accept *whatever* I said and still loved me. . . . He was just so *gentle*.

Another example of the unusual emotionality shown by men in love comes, again, from Jane's description of Paul:

Jane: [W]hen we got engaged, [Paul's parents] gave us £350 to start us off with the wedding . . . and Paul, he just cried his eyes out. And his Dad was saying like 'hey behave yourself' sort of thing, you know, thinking I'd be embarrassed. But I [wasn't]. I thought oh, you know, how lovely, because he was just – he was genuinely showing how he felt.

Jane expresses considerable pleasure as she tells the story of how Paul displayed this 'unmasculine' behaviour in front of his parents. This, along with other similar examples, indicates that what women found most gratifying about being in love with a man was that in some senses he was not behaving 'like a man' at all.

This emerged as an explicit observation in two accounts. Kate, for example, had described previous love relationships which involved violence and extreme alienation. In seeking to account for her experiences Kate expressed the popular view that men in particular have difficulty with 'intimacy'. She was also conversant with feminist arguments that a socially constructed heterosexuality helps to ensure the control of women by men (see e.g. Atkinson 1974; Rich 1980; Wilkinson and Kitzinger 1993). All this had led Kate to the 'rational' view that she would be better off confining herself to relationships with women. However, she still experienced a strong heterosexual desire. Kate's dilemma appeared to be resolved when she met Harry:

Kate: I can remember when I fell in love with Harry actually saying 'I can love you' (because I had actually made a decision not to have another relationship with a man), erm, 'I can love you because you are not like a man, so I see you as a feminine man' – which was the next best thing to being with a woman.

In time, Harry's atypical behaviour was revealed as a temporary phenomenon. He turned out to be a very 'masculine' man. The observation that men in love are 'different' from other men, along with the insight that this is indeed temporary, is also made here by Mary:

Mary: Well he was *listening*. He wasn't talking, he was listening. He wanted to hear my ideas, and what I thought and how I felt, erm which I know always wears off. That – that is a man in love. That is not a *man* you know? There's a huge difference.

So, at least part of the 'uniqueness' of male lovers stemmed from women's experience that *a man in love is not a man at all.* This observation reflects analyses of romance fiction which suggest that part of the appeal for female readers is that the hero, initially arrogant and indifferent, is transformed by his love for the heroine into an affectionate and devoted lover. In this way the reader is offered the fantasy of reconciling men's difference and dominance (Modleski 1984; Snitow 1984). Women's accounts of 'men who were not men' suggest that real men too undergo 'romantic transformations' which facilitate the expression of characteristics that are normally repressed by the embodiment of masculinity. In this study there are no direct reports of how men experienced their 'unmasculine' rebellions, but women's accounts suggest both that they found love deeply gratifying and, as we have seen, that they readily expressed pleasure and admiration at their partner's apparent ability to 'do anything'. Thus it can be suggested that for women and for men, love's rebellion involves, among other possible aspects, the experience of breaking through particular constraints and limitations produced by gender conditioning, and the liberating disruption of 'normal' gender relations. Yet how can this proposition be incorporated within a model of love which allows for the possibility that romantic transformation may turn out to be *productive* of social relations characterised by gendered power?

Gender, love and the 'missing self'

To develop a model which might contain such contradictions and, should they emerge, be able to account for their specific manifestation, we need a more sophisticated explanation of love than the imperfect 'infant's' idealisation of the 'perfect parent'. My analysis of love already indicates the possibility of particular gendered patterns. But why might members of particular social groups have a tendency to become attracted to members of other particular social groups and why might their love for each other manifest in particular ways? Here we can turn to another of Freud's theories. This seeks to explain why an unconscious wish to repair losses involved in the process of becoming who we are might manifest as desire for a particular object. Desire can take a number of forms, causing a person to love '(a). What he [sic] is himself (actually himself). (b). What he once was. (c). What he would like to be.' or '(d). Someone who was once part of himself' (Freud 1914: 47). When the sexual object is seen to approximate the ego ideal, it may 'enter into an interesting auxiliary relation to the ego ideal' (ibid.: 38). The object is not loved for its own sake; rather 'whoever possesses an excellence which the ego lacks for the attainment of its ideal, becomes loved' (ibid.). The key mechanism involved is projection: weak, repressed or unrealised aspects of the self which are unconsciously experienced as a lack are projected on to the object, towards whom a powerful attraction is then experienced. The love object may or may not actually possess some of the desired qualities. The point is however, as Theodor Reik (1974: 43) puts it, that while we think we love a real person, '[t]he love object is . . . a phantom to a great extent, a peg on which we hang all the illusions of ourselves which we long to fulfil'.

In our 'romantic culture', sexual attraction is seen to need little explanation in itself, and if explained at all is usually reduced to a simplistic notion of 'hormones' or 'chemistry'. This lack of awareness or understanding of the specificities of attraction is not seen as a problem. On the contrary it is romanticised; love is deemed to be inevitably mysterious, a matter of fate or destiny. The concept of 'projection' is, however, present within the culture. In the following extract, Hannah uses it alongside a more usual biological narrative to reflect on her own attraction for a man who she sees at work:

Hannah: I kind of endow him with *loads of characteristics* which I then feel attracted to, and feel very kind of, you know, I mean my – the last week or so my hormones have been just through the roof, and I've been – I can't concentrate, you know? . . . Feels very out of control, which I don't like at all, which is why I try and squash it. But I realise that that reaction is very much based on what I perceive he might be like.

Hannah does not suggest that her 'endowments' are denied aspects of herself, knowledge which generally remains unconscious. Nevertheless, the concept of projection allows her to conceive of herself as an active agent in causing the attraction she feels, rather than explaining this simply in terms of her body being beyond her control or as the result of her being pulled by some strange and irresistible force. This demonstrates the potential usefulness of the concept of projection in reflecting critically on sexual/romantic attraction.

Identity in psychoanalysis is complex and individually unique, and the desire of 'infant' for 'adult' may represent the object relations of any period of development or all simultaneously. Patterns may be discernible however, and the theory of 'narcissistic object choice' has clear potential for developing sociological models. It may be suggested in particular that prevailing imperatives of masculine and feminine conditioning will produce dominant patterns of repression and dominant unconscious configurations of the 'desired other'. These in turn may produce particular patterns of attempted reparation and therefore particular manifestations of attraction and love. The theory has been taken up by few writers since Freud, however. Where a link has been made with gender identity, it has also sometimes been suggested that only women attempt to 'find themselves' in this way. Freud (1914) himself was of this view, portraying desire for the narcissistic object as primarily a means by which women attempt to undo the trauma of 'castration', and compensate for their injured self-esteem (see also Reich 1953). While Freud and many of his followers are infamous for their attachment to the myth of male completeness, it is interesting to note that feminists too have tended to assume that only women seek themselves through falling in love, implying that men already *are* themselves, and 'really do' possess what women desire.

Some psychoanalytic writers have alternatively placed the emphasis on gender polarisation, stressing the way in which both masculinity and femininity are always defined in relation to the absence of the other, and constituted in identity through repression of the other (Jung 1931; Reik 1974; Bergmann 1988). While this should not be read as a normative model of heterosexuality – questions of desire and identity are much more complex – it importantly allows for the explanation of both female *and* male heterosexual desire since femininity is not defined only as an absence, a lack, but as something which, like masculinity, can be experienced as something lacked.

Theodor Reik (1974), for example, argues that it is precisely the apprehension of their own defectiveness, along with the perception that women possess a 'completeness' which they do not have, that underpins male heterosexual desire. Taking up Freud's observation that an intensification of female narcissism at puberty produces an apparent self-sufficiency and inaccessibility which is particularly attractive to men, Reik stresses the narcissistic nature of this desire: '[w]hile the admirer is dissatisfied with himself, full of dissonances, split and stirred up, the object seems to remain cool, self-possessed and self-contained' (Reik 1974: 48). The woman's apparent independence is thus experienced as a challenge by the man, making him more aware of the discord within himself, and producing mixed emotions of excitement and resentment which make 'an excellent mixture for the preparation of love' (ibid.: 49). When the man falls in love, the envy and jealousy which are 'the secret forerunners of love' (ibid.: 50) are converted into admiration for the woman's apparent independence and self-sufficiency which, once he has 'merged' with her, he can then experience as part of himself (ibid.). Reik's analysis certainly accords with the accounts of women in this study whose own transformed experiences of confidence, competence and independent selfhood were most gratifyingly affirmed by the admiration of male lovers for these very same apparent qualities.

Individuals' apprehension that they have become more complete and more integrated through 'merging' with someone of the other gender may further free them from the need to repress counter-gender wishes, a need which is integral to all embodiments of masculine or feminine identity. Evidence in this study of women's powerful feelings that they could 'do anything' when in love, along with their descriptions of tender and emotionally expressive partners, indicate that this liberating effect may be equally true for both sexes; for both women and men, the bliss of being in love may be at least partly accounted for by the freedom of a fuller expression of self than is possible within the constraints of gendered identity. Thus, through the mechanism of projection and the investment of the greater portion of their psychic energy in each other, two individuals can collaborate in the project of 'creating' a new and better self for each. These transformations manifest as the realisation of a special wholeness and efficacy which sets the individual apart from other men and women, a 'fact' blissfully confirmed by the admiration of each for the other. True love at last!

The trouble with love

Within our romantic culture, even those writers who regard love as a narcissistic illusion nevertheless tend to portray it only in positive terms. Psychoanalyst Milton Viederman (1988: 10), for example, stresses that this 'gratifying and powerful illusion' is 'the closest thing to ever-elusive happiness'. Viederman's conclusion expresses a common belief that falling in love is as near as the individual can get to the elimination of psychic tension and the attainment of a more complete, cohesive and conflict-free self (see also Bak 1973; Bergmann 1988; Chessick 1988, 1992). Psychologists too have endorsed the 'self-expansion' which comes through falling in love with someone who is different from ourselves (Aron and Aron 1986, 1996). Love, it is stressed, leads to very positive feelings about oneself which can result in a real, if temporary increase in self-efficacy (Aron et al. 1995). I would certainly not dispute that being in love can produce a profound sense of happiness and well-being which often contrasts absolutely with the life 'before the fall'. Some women in this study seemed to 'come alive', even when describing love which had occurred many years previously, and we have already seen how love generated empowering feelings of confidence and self-value.

If we could simply enjoy the 'special effects' of love's illusion as the temporary product of our own mind, perhaps there would be no more to be said. However, falling in love cannot be considered only as an 'intrapsychic' phenomenon. The whole point of romantic transformation is that it is the 'realisation' of love in the world. Once two people 'declare themselves', love is no longer simply 'in the mind' but always already involves each acting upon, and reacting to, the other. These actions and reactions, moreover, will have a particular determination, for no sooner is our desire for transcendence 'realised' than a new desire quite naturally arises: the desire to remain attached to that which we perceive as the cause of our good fortune. We aim, that is, to make permanent our new sense of self through securing our relation to the object. As Kate said of her love for Harry: 'I thought *this is it*, love, this is it *forever* (second emphasis mine). In contemporary Western culture, Kate's aspiration may be seen as optimistic, but not unreasonable. After all, a lasting and committed sexual relationship which is the focus of all our most important needs and desires, and around which our life is based, is an almost universal aspiration. Rose, who we met in Chapter 2, termed this the 'natural progression' of love, and other women in the study had similarly hoped that such a relationship would follow on from their 'falling'.

I want to suggest, however, that in the light of the analysis made in this chapter, the project of lasting love is ambitious indeed. Grave dangers can already be seen lurking amid the joy of love. We have seen that women in the study 'became themselves' through 'losing themselves', something which is only possible because, as Martin Bergmann (1988: 65) puts it, lovers 'temporarily or permanently, forfeit the autonomy of their intrapsychic structure by exchanging their ego-ideal for another person'. Quite paradoxically, each lover has supposedly attained to individual selfhood through ceasing to be an individual at all. It could be suggested that this situation, though difficult, is not entirely hopeless. Perhaps mutual co-operation and commitment can secure the 'selfhood' of both lovers? Such a proposal merely deepens the contradiction, however, for what both individuals require in order to maintain their respective 'resolutions' is that the beloved should continue to embody the lover's ideal self. What kind of freedom can be realised through a contract where, in exchange for the conditions which allow each to 'be themselves', each must approximate the other's unconscious fantasy of perfection? In the beginning, of course, dissonance may be imperceptible and love is experienced as simple and undemanding. This is because no contradiction is as yet apparent between the subject, the object and the ideal self. They appear to be one and the same. The man praises and admires the happy, confident and self-sufficient woman, and she feels happy, confident and self-sufficient. The woman praises and admires the happy, sensitive and emotionally open man and he feels happy, sensitive and emotionally open. Everything seems resolved.

If we look a little closer at each lover's position, however, the inherent instability of the whole situation becomes more apparent. For the women in this study, feelings of confidence, self-sufficiency and independence may well have arisen upon the 'realisation' of an internal fantasy, but this realisation in turn *depended upon* its being 'confirmed' by their 'hero'; it was his attention and affirmation of them that triggered women's romantic transformations. We saw, for example, how Mary felt 'empowered' by Barry telling her that she was 'the most wonderful person on earth'. Here she describes the intersubjective dynamic upon which her love depends:

Mary: It's like seeing yourself through his eyes. He's in love with you so you're in love with yourself.

But what would happen to Mary's new and exalted sense of self if Barry was to stop telling her that she was the most wonderful person on earth, or even if he began to tell her this a little less often, or with a little less enthusiasm? And how would Mary feel about Barry and how would she behave towards him if, in the process, he became a little less 'open' and a bit 'more of a man'? Equivalent questions can be posed concerning Barry's love for Mary. While, like Mary, the typically 'feminine' subject aims at securing selfhood through being recognised as an object, the typically 'masculine' subject aims at securing selfhood by assuming the position of subject in relation to an object whose own selfhood appears *not* to depend upon such recognition. Desire and admiration arise in relation to the woman who, as Reik (1974: 48) puts it, appears 'cool, self-possessed and self-contained'. It is the love of such a woman which triggers the man's transformation, allowing him to be emotional and to reveal his vulnerabilities. But what would happen to the man's new sense of self if his lover began to appear a little less independent, a little less 'cool', a little less self-possessed? And how would he feel about her, and behave towards her, if she became a little more unsure of herself – a bit more 'needy', a bit more 'feminine'? Love might last, it seems, if the woman can remain a 'woman who can do anything'. Her partner will then be able to remain a 'man who is not a man', enabling her in turn to retain her new identity. Yet how can the lovers collaborate in such a scheme when her desire for him depends upon his desire for her, but his desire for her is dependent upon her being independent of his desire for her?

The 'trouble with love' is only intensified by the fragility of the lovers' 'new identities'. Born from the eruption of wishes repressed in a long forgotten past, new ways of being are at this point incipient. In Freudian terms the new self is literally in its infancy. The integration and self-expansion which lovers experience does not result from a gradual process of maturation, involving the testing out, consolidation and growth of confidence in the new self. On the contrary, the new self is arrived at much more easily – by simply giving up struggles and responsibilities. As Mary observes in a quote we looked at in Chapter 2, falling in love arises precisely from the desire 'to let oneself be non-adult for a while'. Deliverance is achieved when the subject assumes the position of infant in relation to a fantasised parent, and depends entirely upon this 'parent' not disappointing or frustrating as previous parent(s) have done. The task of building lasting love is thus a task indeed: each partner, themselves

60

an 'infant' with a nascent and untested identity, must take on the task of 'parenting' their also 'newborn' partner in a way that will enable them to 'grow up' differently from the first time around. At first, of course, love does not seem difficult; the powerful unleashing of repressed energies can make anything seem possible and lovers promise that they will 'do anything' for each other, that they will 'go to the ends of the earth'. Such sentiments may be sincere and deeply felt, but we must not forget that worship and adoration of the beloved are aimed ultimately at the self. Nobody falls in love out of a desire to be somebody else's perfect parent.

Were the contradictory, unstable and fragile constitution of 'true love' not disquieting enough, yet further dangers inhere in the lovers' powerlessness and their vulnerability. The mutual surrender of adult identity appears to dispense with any desire to exert power or control over the other, to limit their freedom. Power appears only to be given away. Indeed, as Freud (1917: 418) observes, falling deeply in love involves so radical an emptying of the narcissistic cathexis of the self that the object becomes *supremely powerful* (my emphasis). With neither lover apparently interested in controlling the other, it is no surprise that several women in this study described falling mutually in love as a profoundly equal experience. Moreover, the acute sensitivity and vulnerability which follows on from submission can be gratifying indeed when one is subject to admiration and devotion. And in turn, the expression of admiration and the giving of pleasure are easy enough when one feels blissfully happy. However, we should not forget that this outpouring of positive emotion flows forth upon certain conditions: the unconscious experience of 'refinding' the perfect parent and the perfect self. Before we fall in love, a very different situation usually prevails. Reik reminds us that our initial motivation towards the love object may be anything but kind and giving, and stems instead from unconscious feelings of envy and resentment towards that object for appearing to possess something which we lack. Love may well be a rose, says Reik (1974: 47), but it 'springs from a soil which is fertilized with evil-smelling manure'. When we fall in love, this underlying hostility is transformed into positive emotion, but this transformation may be just as easily reversed. What will happen if love's illusion threatens to turn into *dis*illusionment? What will happen if the lovers begin to 'smell the manure'? Will they still be content to merely submit to the 'supremely powerful' object?

Summary and conclusion

In Chapter 2, we saw how women articulated their experiences of falling in love through a cultural narrative of 'romantic transformation'; loneliness and the struggles of single life or a loveless partnership were made history by the appearance of 'true love'. From a rational perspective, this 'transcendence' may appear ephemeral and illusory. Yet the sheer power of a love that feels like an insurgence of the spirit itself can endow even the most unlikely romance with

61

a seemingly irrefutable factuality. In this chapter, I have drawn on Freudian ideas to subject love's mysterious power to 'scientific' analysis, arguing that romantic transformation is compelling because it involves the repetition of older, deeper narratives of salvation. Women's accounts of 'losing themselves' and 'finding themselves' may be dressed up in the hearts and flowers of romanticism, but they are rooted in other long-forgotten attempts to give up an imperfect self in exchange for existential security and lasting satisfaction. Sexual love may be an 'adult' phenomenon, but it is at once the expression of a tiny infant who, in terrified apprehension of a changing, frustrating world and its own insubstantiality, takes refuge in the blissful illusion of a perfect and all-powerful parent. Love's redemption is a fantasy, but in our minds it is real. The symptoms are irrational, but they make perfect sense. It happens here and now, but it also happens there and then. And while we remain who we are, we become someone else.

Our search for a 'complete' and integrated selfhood can take many forms. Romantic love is one in which cultural legitimation is given to the desire to seek completion through attachment to a sexual object. As we struggle to repress the painful knowledge of our own incoherence and the unsatisfactoriness of life, one apparent solution is the idealisation of someone who appears to be what we are not. Consciously, our only experience may be one of a compelling attraction to that person which, if it grows to eclipse any perceived risk, may cause us to 'fall in love'. When we fall, all the psychic energy employed in the struggle to prop up the imperfect self is invested instead in the perfect object with whom we 'merge'. Inner conflicts disappear and we feel that, at last, we have 'become ourselves'. New ways of being suddenly seem possible as our repressed longings and undeveloped potentials erupt in rebellion against all that our conditioning has led us to become. Conditioning has many aspects and the identity we do not possess may have many unconsciously imagined forms. Fundamental, however, is the shaping of the self in relation to a more or less polarised opposition of masculinity and femininity. This may produce an unconscious conviction that what we lack in ourselves is possessed by someone who represents our 'opposite', most likely, although not necessarily, someone of a different sex. It seems that by loving them, we can finally become 'ourselves'. Certainly in this study, love appeared gendered in important ways; narratives concerning 'women who could do anything' and 'men who were not men' suggest that, for both sexes, the attempt to 'become oneself' may involve a rebellion against the constraints of a gendered subjectivity.

'Becoming oneself' through romantic love can be deeply gratifying and it may be argued that this in itself is not harmful, even if it is based upon an illusion. It might further be suggested that for women in particular, it is no bad thing to throw off the shackles of femininity. However, love's rebellion is no manifestation of independence. On the contrary, love leads us to believe that our 'liberation' depends crucially upon the establishment of a 'permanent' relationship to the object. Love may be illusory, but it is no mere illusion when we attempt to actualise it in the world; 'true' love, by its nature, will have consequences. At this stage in the story, with the 'subject of love' standing enraptured in the 'threshold moment', we do not yet know what these consequences will be. We have seen, however, that the seeds of trouble are already germinating. Both lovers have surrendered their desire to control, given up their defences, and opened their hearts to the healing power of a love which is benevolent and empowering, a love which will not let them down. It is faith in such a love which has transmuted pain into pleasure, sorrow into joy, envy into admiration and resentment into affection. But what will happen if this faith becomes tinged with doubt? What will happen if love threatens to reveal its contradictory and unstable constitution? Whether coercion and subordination will ensue and what form(s) this might take we do not yet know, but 'analysis' clearly does not augur well for the development of 'democratic love'.

4

EVERYBODY'S MUMMY

One striking feature of romantic love is that while it appears as a coherent 'life narrative', perhaps especially for women, this coherence is at once everywhere disrupted by a hiatus. This intervenes, for example, in the form of a popularly assumed distinction between the 'falling in love' stage and some later stage of love. One is never quite sure how the latter arises from the former, except that 'you have to work at it'. The dislocation is present too in romantic fiction, which almost invariably leaves the heroine poised at the 'threshold' of her new life. This convention in turn reflects the 'happily ever after' closure of fairy-tales. Meanwhile, established love relationships are generally considered quite apart from romance. There have been, for example, numerous sociological studies on marriage and couple relationships, but while the origination of these in a mutual falling in love is always assumed, it is never explored. Evidence points to pronounced differences between the couple in love and the established couple, yet the processes through which this change comes about are yet to be explained.

In Chapter 3, we countered the view that 'romantic transformation' is an inexplicable phenomenon. Now we face a second 'mystery of love': the mystery of exactly how 'true love' in turn undergoes transmutation into a more mundane relationship typically characterised by particular gendered dynamics. A few writers have inferred such a process, even if they have not detailed it. These, moreover, are the very same writers who have also pointed to a close connection between love and power. Max Weber (1948: 348), for example, has argued that it is precisely within the bliss of the romantic union that 'the most intimate coercion of the soul of the less brutal partner' originates. Feminists too have claimed that it is woman's 'transcendence' through love which implicates her most inexorably in a system of oppressive patriarchal social relations. What is proposed is that romantic love is not a phenomenon which is distinct from the later phase of established coupledom, but one which, on the contrary, *determines* it. Falling in love, that is, brings into being a very particular kind of relationship which is deeply and inherently problematic. It is the 'analysis' of this coming-into-being which is developed over the next three chapters.

In Chapter 3, I proposed that the bliss of love depends upon the coincident arising of fragile, paradoxical and mutually contradictory unconscious fantasies. Motivated by a search for the 'missing self' and 'realised' through a massive investment of psychic energy in a new 'parent', these fantasies disrupt adult gendered identity and trigger an outpouring of positive emotion. This produces a profound sense of intimacy and mutuality. Since there exists no integrated or coherent psychoanalytic theory of love, exactly how this scenario begins to change as the lovers 'settle down' is not easily predicted. However, Freud's premise of the 'repetition compulsion' offers us a basic model and begs a certain question: if falling in love can be explained as the unconscious 'resolution' of the past, then perhaps 'falling out of love' may equally be explained as the unconscious realisation that the past is not, in fact, resolved at all. Just as the compelling bliss of love may be rooted in infantile illusions, so the all too ordinary disappointments, frustrations and dissatisfactions which follow may similarly be underpinned by past *dis*illusionments. We will return to a detailed consideration of this theory later in the chapter. Firstly, however, we need to find out how the 'subject of love' fares as she 'steps over the threshold' into her new life.

The abandonment

It was certainly the case that dissatisfaction and disappointment were prominent themes in women's accounts of current and previous love relationships. This in itself is unsurprising; it would be unlikely indeed that any relationship could measure up to the kinds of hopes and expectations which are liable to be placed upon it. What is interesting, however, is the particular character of women's dissatisfactions and their perceptions of how and why things changed. Accounts were imbued with a sense of mourning for a lost world of intense verbal and physical communication, emotional closeness and a deep sense of connection. While some relationships enabled occasional glimpses of this lost world, in others the loss seemed complete and irrevocable. Women's perception, moreover, was that it was their partners who were responsible for this change. They spoke repeatedly of how the central problem in their love relationships was that they wanted to be more 'intimate', but that male partners did not and resisted all attempts to close a gap that opened up between them.

Women's dissatisfaction with a 'lack of intimacy' has been the predominant finding of other studies of heterosexual relationships (see Chapter 1). What this analysis particularly highlights is the processes of change involved. Women would remark with frustration that the whole reason they had 'got together' with their partner in the first place was that, unlike 'other men', he *was* able to engage in intimacy. We saw 'evidence' of this in Chapter 3. However, sometimes suddenly and sometimes more gradually, this initial intimacy disappeared – a change precipitated, according to women, by the unilateral 'withdrawal' of their partners. The following extracts from Diane and Kate describe the typical pattern:

Diane: We used to plan to go here, there, and everywhere, you know? We used to laugh and joke. And then it has just been a gradual pull away . . . [On the part of John].

Kate: The first three or four months were idyllic . . . about communication and security and total acceptance. But that changed when I wanted to get married. . . . What he did was initially withdraw from me, totally, well withdraw all his – everything that had been previously in our relationship . . . I'm disappointed that . . . erm, I lost the man, that erm – *communicating* man. . . . He's just not there now, and . . . there's a great gap for me. It's like the mundane everyday stuff, whereas I know there's something else. I know there's a deeper, more loving man.

However the change occurred, women were generally at a loss to explain it and struggled to find reasons. One possible precipitating factor was felt to be the woman's desire for 'commitment' from her partner, as in the case of Kate (above). Other apparent 'causes' of the man's withdrawal included the birth of a baby, or, as in the following quote from Mary, the woman's pregnancy:

Mary: There was this *huge* – it wasn't just a physical withdrawal, it was an emotional withdrawal. I mean I can rationalize it that there is this 23-year-old man suddenly confronted with a wife and a child on the way. He was going to have to support them. But even – I mean at the time I wasn't sure what was going on, and even now I am not sure what was going on. I think – I think there was something going on that was being denied at the time. It was absolutely nothing to do with the situation, but I honestly don't know.

While women looked for explanations for their partner's disengagement, however, the exact relationship seemed unclear. In some accounts there seemed to be no particular causal event, yet the change happened anyway.

Analysis showed that women experienced two particular changes in their partner's behaviour. Firstly, he seemed to lose the ability to be emotionally open and spontaneous which he had demonstrated in the beginning, becoming more 'distant' and 'unemotional'. Coincident with this was an apparent loss of interest in the woman; whereas early in the relationship the man openly demonstrated that he liked his partner, admired her and enjoyed being with her, he now seemed increasingly indifferent. Other things became the focus of his interest and attention. Examples included leisure activities, DIY, socialising with other men, getting involved with another woman, pornography, and especially work. These changes led women to experience powerful and painful feelings of *abandonment*. Moreover, when they tried to talk to their partners about what was happening, they met with little success. On the contrary, women's efforts seemed only to compound the problem in that, paradoxically,

the more they asked for recognition of their hurt feelings, the more their partners were liable to 'back off'. Furthermore, instead of acknowledging that there
was a problem, men – like those in Mansfield and Collard's (1988) study –
often seemed completely baffled as to why women were so upset. They would
increasingly react by maintaining their 'distant' and 'unemotional' stance,
while becoming angry and defensive if women 'pushed the issue'.

She's so demanding

As their love relationships became established, then, a growing disjuncture
appeared between women's hopes of living 'happily ever after' and their experience. Initially, partners had been loving and devoted, and women could look
to the relationship for a feeling that they were 'special' and loved 'for themselves'. Now their desire for attention and affirmation was ignored or, even
worse, reflected back to them as unreasonable. This would lead women to feel
not only hurt, but confused. On the one hand they wanted to assert the
validity of their expectations of what a love relationship *should* be like, but on
the other, this was difficult when their partner's reaction, and sometimes that
of others too, cast doubt upon the legitimacy of such expectations. Kate, for
example, has felt hurt and dissatisfied ever since Harry's sudden 'emotional
withdrawal' from her. She wants the attention that Harry used to give her, but
others see her desire as being the problem:

Kate: I think he is very patient with me, tremendously patient, because I
am demanding. I know I am demanding, erm, because people have
told me so.
Wendy: Why do you think you are demanding?
Kate: Erm [*pause*] yeh, well [*pause*] er [*pause*] because I expect attention.
But I don't always get it, but erm, er, but I don't really know why I
am demanding.

This construction of women's desires for attention as lacking legitimacy was
common in the data, sometimes associated with a corresponding sympathy for
the man, who was seen as long-suffering. Kate, for example, further recounted
how both her present and previous partners had been described by others using
the prefix 'poor', as in 'poor Harry' and 'poor Steve', referring to Kate's supposedly unreasonable demands for attention. Another example comes from
Ruth who talked of years of unhappiness with Colin, who was distant and cold
towards her. In this extract, she tells the story of how Colin's mother responded
when she heard that Ruth had decided to end their marriage:

Ruth: I can remember my mother-in-law ringing up with this 'why are you
doing this?' business, you know? And she says 'well Colin says it's because you don't feel he loves you. So are you *really* ending your marriage

just because you don't feel he shows you any affection?', like this was really ridiculous, you know? Why would you end your marriage over a petty thing like this – like it was putting the milk bottles out at night or something, you know? And I *always* felt he didn't love me.

Ruth's glowing account of her early relationship with Colin (see Chapter 2) is testament to the fact that she did not *always* feel unloved. Her point was, however, that everything seemed to have changed. Like other women who had undergone 'romantic transformation', Ruth had hoped that Colin would at least continue to demonstrate affection and show that he cared about her. Now her hopes were dashed. She was deeply hurt, and nobody else seemed to think that her feelings were legitimate.

One thing which some women found extremely puzzling about the 'abandonment' was that, when pressed on the question of whether he still loved her, her partner would answer that 'of course' he did. Yet, she reasoned, how could this be true if he constantly ignored her, did not seem to care how she felt, and responded by getting quite 'ratty' if she demanded reassurance? It was as though he did not expect there was anything he needed to *do* actively in order to demonstrate that he loved his partner; the fact that he had told her so should be quite sufficient. If the woman tried to explain that this was not how she saw 'love' and listed the needs for attention, affirmation and emotional support which she had hoped her partner would meet, he would simply appear mystified or criticise her for being 'insecure' or 'demanding'. He might further feel attacked by her demands for reciprocity and defend himself, for example, by comparing his own behaviour favourably to that of 'other men' or by citing efforts he had made to please her. Some women complained that, insofar as their partners could not see any 'reason' for their unhappiness, they would simply not accept that there were any substantial grounds for grievance.

Women, as we have seen, did feel aggrieved. Indeed, the most frequent sentiment expressed during the course of the interviews was some form of anger, frustration or resentment towards male partners. The data revealed two particular ways in which women attempted to deal with such feelings. In the first place, they might attempt to deny or suppress their feelings while attempting to convince themselves that they 'ought to be happy' – perhaps the problem *was* with them? Perhaps they *were* being unreasonable? Perhaps they *did* expect too much? In the following extract, for example, Mary adopts an 'absence of negatives' narrative to question the validity of her own feelings of dissatisfaction:

Mary: He doesn't beat me up, doesn't spend all the wages down the pub. To be with a partner who . . . not only does none of these things, but, you know, works incredibly hard to give you a good standard of living, you feel ungrateful, because – and unworthy because you want something more, you know? What right have you, you know? Who the hell are *you* to want more than this? Who do you think you are, you know?

Kate, too, experiences a contradiction between feeling abandoned and unloved and the lack of any 'legitimate' reason to expect anything different:

Kate: Well I am struggling internally with the fact that I know that I *should* feel loved, because actually he's a very good man. He does all the right things, doesn't really beat – well he doesn't beat me, doesn't touch me, doesn't mistreat me, doesn't emotionally abuse me.

Kate's and Mary's accounts echo those of women in Duncombe and Marsden's study (1993: 26) who also compared their relationships with the worst possible scenarios and stated that their partners 'were good providers, didn't drink, weren't violent and so on'. However, women's attempts to 'reason themselves into happiness' in this way did not work. It was clear from the way they expressed themselves in the interviews that hurt feelings and resentment remained and undermined any attempts they made to reconcile themselves with the reality of their relationships.

A second way in which women attempted to deal with the contradiction between their hopes of lasting love and the disappointing reality was to resist the view that they were overly 'demanding' and to insist on upholding their 'right' to emotional reciprocity. In the following extract, Hannah, for example, relates a conversation with a woman friend on this issue:

Hannah: Something I've had said to me quite often is, you know, 'You're too demanding. You're too demanding', which really drags you down after a while because you think oh my God, maybe I am, you see? But . . . [a] friend put this in perspective, because she had the same thing said to her, and . . . she said 'Yes I am. I am more demanding than a sofa!' (and that's too demanding for most men!). She said: 'You would give a cat more attention than you give me'. . . . Yes, in the eyes of the men who said that to me, I'm too demanding. But . . . I'm not too demanding in terms of what I actually *should be getting* from somebody and what I am prepared to *give* in a relationship. But yes I'm more demanding than a doormat, or something you sit on. Existing is almost too much for some men, isn't it?

In another example, Ruth also articulates resistance to the negative connotations of the term 'demanding':

Ruth: I think I'm demanding because I think I *should* be demanding, erm, because I feel like well I'm not going to let a man walk all over me, and if I'm not demanding, that's what most men will do.

Thus Hannah and Ruth both utilise feminist discourse to assert resistance to what Shere Hite (1988) terms the 'unequal emotional contract' of heterosexual love. They attempt to uphold their expectations that love relationships should be both intimate and reciprocal.

This approach, however, brought its own problems. Relationships could come to feel like a constant 'battleground'. While women themselves felt that they 'couldn't have spelled out more clearly' why they were dissatisfied, their partners remained puzzled. Men appeared to alternate between making 'efforts' which women complained were 'hopeless' and 'pathetic' and getting angry and defensive, complaining that *they* felt unappreciated. Thus there seemed to be no way for women to resolve their anger and disappointment at their partner's withdrawal. Accounts suggested a tendency for them to oscillate between the two unsatisfactory positions outlined above: either fighting for a 'better deal' which meant constant struggle and frustration, or giving up the struggle. This enabled a greater degree of 'harmony', but stifled feelings of dissatisfaction and resentment which did not go away, and did nothing to assuage the growing sense of alienation which women had come to experience.

Holding it all together

One solution to this dilemma was to consider ending the relationship. This, however, was in complete contradiction to women's own powerful desire not to lose the love in which they had invested so much hope. The solution to this contradiction therefore seemed to be for women to channel their efforts into trying to 'make the relationship work'. This strategy, however, brought further problems. Faced with a partner who himself appeared disinterested in 'making it work' in the way she wanted, a woman could easily come to feel that the only way to 'keep things going' was to take on that responsibility herself. Such was the extent of this that several women described themselves as more or less singlehandedly 'providing a relationship' for the man to 'be in'. In the following extract, for example, Ruth replies to my asking her whether, in her experience, she had found her partners to be as concerned with love relationships as she has been:

Ruth: [*breaks into laughter*] You're joking! [*laughter*] Oh well really, are they ever? *No*, of course they haven't. They *never* are, *never*. I can say that *absolutely, absolutely* across the board. No. It's always been me *looking after the relationship*. I sometimes like envisage it like a little garden, you know? I'm the one who does all the gardening and the men come out and sit in it [*laughter*]. I do. That's how I imagine it. They sit in it, and I'm pulling the weeds up, pruning the roses [*laughs*]. That sums it up for me.

70

Ruth's experience was echoed throughout the study; whereas, initially, the woman experienced the relationship as a 'joint project', her partner's emotional withdrawal left her feeling that it was 'all up to her'.

The irony of women's supposed 'neediness' and 'demandingness' was that within their accounts it appeared to be *men* whose 'needs' and 'demands' were increasingly met, while women felt abandoned and devalued. Moreover, as the couple became more established, so this pattern of emotional responsibility for 'the relationship' was extended. Gradually, women came to assume responsibility for other areas such as housework, household budgeting, shopping, childcare, arranging holidays and organising family occasions such as Christmas celebrations. Responsibilities could come to stretch way beyond the 'front door' to include the maintenance and support of wider family and social networks. One woman, for example, described how she had come to take responsibility for remembering her husband's relatives' birthdays, and buying, wrapping and sending presents and cards to them. She also reminded him when he should telephone his parents and even on occasions did this on his behalf if he 'couldn't be bothered'. In addition to the lack of intimacy, women's other major area of complaint about men was their selfishness, laziness and expectation that their female partners should be responsible for 'everything'. The gendered division and organisation of domestic and relational labour has been extensively discussed elsewhere. The point I want to make here is that while these gendered patterns are clearly mediated through a host of social, economic and cultural factors, they appeared in this study to 'grow out of' love itself. The assumption of these responsibilities was rooted in processes of change which, so far as women were concerned, appeared as their partner's unilateral 'withdrawal' from an initial intimacy and mutuality.

Women's claims that they were responsible for 'everything' did not necessarily imply that men did nothing. Most male partners *were* prepared to contribute to some extent. However, women complained that what men would not do was to take domestic responsibility or show initiative. Even where both partners were in full-time employment, men were reported as assuming their contributions to be 'helping' the woman and deferring to her overall organisational responsibility. This was experienced by the woman as very hard work, since each time she wanted her partner to do something, she would need to give him specific instructions. He might then carry out the task, often with some degree of grumbling or procrastination, but would then return to his irresponsible position and do nothing more until a further instruction had been issued. A typical example comes from Ruth, who describes here how this pattern operates in her relationship with Nick:

Ruth: I'll say 'Oh didn't you put the washing in the dryer?' And he'll say either 'I was just going to do it', or 'I didn't realise it had to be done', or 'Oh I didn't realise it had to be done; why didn't you tell me?', you see? And I must seem a right old bag saying these things but that just *infuriates* me, because I mean nobody ever comes along and says to me 'Oh look Ruth, get that washing out of the washing machine and put it in the dryer' or 'Sort out the children's shoes for tomorrow'. Nobody ever says that. I just do it, you know, because I look round and I think what's got to be done and I *do* it. And sometimes I say to Nick 'Right, you do this', and I resent that. It's not that he never does anything – it's as I said before, the buck stops with me . . . I mean it may seem terribly mundane, but in my life it assumes *massive* proportions.

The responsibility which women carried often led them to feel constantly tired and overburdened. Again, however, there seemed no way to resolve the problem and they would find themselves oscillating between two equally unsatisfactory positions. Sometimes women would fight for a more equal distribution of responsibility. However, the constant struggle involved in this, on top of all they were doing anyway, could seem like hard work. Moreover, the constant 'nagging' they might have to engage in to resist being 'put upon' could itself seem to be the cause of a discordant atmosphere which women themselves wanted to avoid since they felt responsible for maintaining a 'happy home'. Even in the interviews, women were reticent about 'going on', as exemplified by Ruth's concern (above) that she would seem like 'a right old bag' for complaining about 'mundane' issues. The other alternative, described here by Mary, was to give up this painful struggle:

Mary: It's *so draining*. It takes *so much energy*. And fighting it takes so much – in fact giving in to it is so much easier than fighting it, because it is very easy to give half your awareness to somebody and say 'The shampoo is so and so . . .' and 'Your clean shirts are so and so' and 'If you get your red top out – it's on the top shelf of the wardrobe'. It's all too easy to do that. It is much harder to say 'No. I am not going to do it', and resist it . . . that is probably why I am much more angry at the moment than I've ever been.

As Mary makes clear, however, while putting up with things can result in the appearance of greater 'harmony', women's stifled feelings of resentment do not go away, and undermine the 'happy couple' still further.

What was implicit in the dynamics which women described was made explicit in many accounts: as men 'withdrew', women came to assume a 'maternal' role in relation to their partners who, correspondingly, assumed a position of childlike irresponsibility with regard to personal and family relationships and domestic life. Repeatedly, women told the story of their love relationships in these terms. Diane and Ruth, for example, sum up the general feeling:

Diane: Basically, I'm just the Mother of the house, you know? . . . I think of myself as having three children, three people to look after. It is just that one goes to work and the other two don't.

Ruth: I feel like I've got three of them to sort out, you know? I feel like I'm everybody's Mummy, you know?

The following extracts from Mary's interviews give some examples of what such 'mothering' might involve:

Mary: Even as to packing a bag, or deciding what to wear when he is going out . . . it will be 'What shall I wear?'; 'What do you think would be the right thing to wear?'; 'What shall I have on my sandwiches for work tomorrow?'; 'What shall I . . .'. This constant refusal to make the decision, you know? . . . I even say to him 'Now you're a big grown-up boy, make your own mind up.'

No matter what you are doing . . . there is these constant demands for attention. . . . It is always 'Have you got a minute?' 'Can you just help me with my CV?' or 'Can you tell me what to wear tonight?' or 'Can you tell me where the shampoo is?' It is always there, this constant battering, this constant demand for attention.

Repeatedly, women talked about their partners 'refusing to grow up', being 'immature', 'acting like a big kid', etc. One extreme example was Sharon's ex-husband who, she reported, would become progressively scruffier and smellier, apparently oblivious to the effect on all around him, unless Sharon reminded him to wash and shave. Even then, she related, he would moan and say 'Do I have to?'

The power puzzle

The processes of change through which the newly formed couple moved as they 'settled down' certainly appeared detrimental to the women in this study. On top of the painful experience of the emotional withdrawal of their once-keen partners and the frustration of needs and desires they hoped would be fulfilled, they ended up experiencing themselves as 'responsible for everything'. Women felt hurt, angry and devalued as they grappled with the contradictions that these changes entailed. The relational dynamics which emerged appeared to facilitate women's disadvantage within their love relationships. Through withdrawing interest in their female partners, focusing their affirmation on other things and by 'opting out', men appeared able to benefit from a dominant pattern of gender relations characterised by an unequal division of labour, and to ensure that their own needs and desires were met while those of their partners were rendered illegitimate.

This analysis, however, emerged from a long process of piecing together the many insights, observations and descriptions contained within the women's accounts. Certainly, none of the women interviewed presented her story as a straightforward narrative of her own subjection. This is not to say that the exercise of male power was entirely invisible; when talking about their frustrations at being 'responsible for everything', some women did apply varying degrees of feminist analysis on topics such as economic inequality, the domestic division of labour and motherhood.

However, the relation of these issues to love itself remained a hidden and fragmented story within the accounts. Moreover, where the operation of male power was visible to women, this was not usually in respect of their own current relationships. Several women, for example, talked about how other women they knew were dominated by male partners, sometimes speaking very critically about the woman concerned in the vein of 'I don't know why she stays with him. I wouldn't put up with it'. Women were also much more likely to see themselves as having been subordinate in their own past relationships. With the benefit of hindsight and the comfort of having 'moved on' from a painful situation, it was perhaps easier to admit that they had been 'naive' or 'stupid' and allowed a man to 'get the better of them'. They might stress, however, that they certainly would not let this happen now.

All of the women were explicitly asked who they thought had the most power in their current relationship. There were three answers to this question. The most common was that the relationship was equal, with one or two women adding that they and their partners had 'different kinds of power'. The second most common answer was that the woman had *more* power than her partner. A woman was least likely to claim that her partner had more power. Moreover, even where women saw the relationship as equal, they tended to place more emphasis on their own sense of power when describing their relationships. So, not only was there a general invisibility of power in relation to women's own understandings of their relationships but the power of their partners was *less* visible, while their own power was *more* visible.

This finding is not a new one. Pat O'Connor (1991), for example, also carried out a study where women claimed to feel more powerful than their male partners. In Chapter 2, I pointed to the problems in taking such claims at face value. However, some crucial questions are begged: Why do women feel powerful? What do they understand this power to be? And how do their claims square with my analysis which suggests a clear process of subjection as love relationships became established? To answer these questions, let us look at two women's accounts of why they saw themselves as more powerful than their partners. Firstly, here is Helen:

Helen: I think I have probably got more power in an awful sort of a way. I mean erm Jonathan obviously earns the money, erm, but I am sort of quite a powerful person. And he just bobs along with whatever I am doing. I organise what's going on, what we are going to do . . . I mean I just seem to organise it. It is not that I want to. It is just if I didn't organise things we wouldn't do anything. And I sometimes think I can be overpowering, definitely overpowering.

> I seem to be a bit more the dominant partner in the relationship, the *stronger* partner in the relationship . . . I am the one who sort of keeps everything bubbling along day to day.

If we look closely at Helen's account, we can begin to see the paradoxical nature of her 'power'. On the one hand, Helen sees herself as powerful because Jonathan 'just bobs along' with whatever she organises. At the same time, however, she tells us that 'It is not that I *want* to. It is just if I didn't organise things we wouldn't do anything'. Also of note is Helen's slippage between being 'the dominant partner in the relationship' and 'the *stronger* partner in the relationship'. A second account of women's power comes from Kate:

Kate: I feel I have more power in the relationship because I determine what we are like, I determine the way we are. Therefore if I *choose* to count, to block him out of my life he has no choice, because he has already chosen to do that with me in some ways. Erm, I don't know *why* – I don't know why I say this, but I feel like I have the power to reject him, far more than he does me. Probably because I feel like I live with a certain rejection anyway, but I don't feel he feels that of me. Erm I *bring in* I think more to our relationship than he does.

Again, a paradox is visible in that Kate's 'rejection' by Harry leads her to feel that *she* has more power. The fact that she 'bring[s] in more to [their] relationship' makes Harry dependent on Kate and she is aware of how this makes him vulnerable. Thus it can be seen that women's feelings of power were rooted in the *very same relational dynamics* about which they complained so consistently, and which appeared as the source of their disappointment and dissatisfaction. On the one hand they were hurt by their partner's emotional abandonment and were resentful that they had become 'reponsible for everything'. On the other, the fact that this was the case could lead them to feel strong and capable. It was in this sense that women felt powerful. They lamented the fact that they had become 'everybody's Mummy' and wanted to resist it and assert their own needs. Yet the processes of change that brought this situation into being nevertheless gave women a sense of power and control in their relationships.

Good boys, bad boys

The paradoxical nature of the feelings of power which women can experience through 'feeding egos and tending wounds' is something which has also been observed by Sandra Bartky (1990: 115):

> A source within the woman has been tapped and she feels flowing outward from herself a great power of healing and making whole. She imagines herself to be a great reservoir of restorative power. This

feeling of power gives her a sense of agency and of personal efficacy which she may get nowhere else.

Bartky warns, however, of the treacherous nature of such feelings for women. They may, she argues, constitute some compensation for women's powerless-ness, but they are only *feelings* of power, and should not be mistaken for real power to act in the world on one's own behalf. Is Bartky right? Had women in this study been seduced by a mere *feeling* of power?

To an extent, I think Bartky is right. However, things are perhaps more complex than this in respect of love relationships. Some women in this study not only claimed to *feel* powerful, but gave examples of how they *were* powerful in the sense of being able to get their partners to do things they wanted them to. Most typically, women claimed they had a kind of 'emotional power' over men which enabled them to get their own way. A typical statement to this effect comes from Sarah:

Sarah: I think I was more in control emotionally, because I just, I knew he would do anything for me.

I found these kinds of claims puzzling at first because they were in such sharp contradiction to women's complaints that men were selfish and would not 'do anything' at all. Indeed, several women made both kinds of claims about the same relationships. However, closer analysis revealed that the claim that 'he would do anything for me' related only to certain kinds of things. Mary gives an example of the sense in which her partner would 'do anything':

Mary: Within that domestic sphere I have had a great deal of power . . . which I know I could have abused if I, and I was aware of it – that if I really wanted the wallpaper changing every week, I could have had that because that's what men do for their wives.

Generally speaking, then, men would only 'do anything' in certain narrowly defined senses. This would mainly involve supporting the woman in her 'Mother' role by doing practical tasks 'for her' such as DIY jobs, washing up, getting her car serviced and so on. Sometimes it would extend to supporting women's outside activities. Examples included giving her lifts to evening classes and making tea and coffee if she had a group of people round to the house for a meeting. Indeed, it seemed that some men were very keen to do these things, and were sometimes quite amenable to being 'bossed around' by their female partners.

However, the 'anything' that men would do generally did *not* include all the things that women claimed they really wanted men to do, such as taking domestic and relational responsibility and giving emotional support. Moreover, women complained that men expected them to be pleased and grateful for anything they did and wanted to be praised for their efforts, especially where traditionally female activities were involved. Indeed, they might sulk and become disgruntled if this appreciation was not forthcoming and complain that the woman was ungrateful. Women's 'ungratefulness' was certainly visible in the interviews. Some women complained that what men did actually amounted to very little or that it was not what *they* wanted anyway. So while women were able to exercise power over their partners, this was largely in respect of requests for certain kinds of practical 'help' which were determined by a quite strictly defined set of gender roles, and negotiated through a 'mother–son' dynamic.

A second sense in which women felt they could exercise power was in respect of acting as a judge of their partner's behaviour. Paradoxically, although men seemed very reluctant to do what women wanted them to do, this did not mean that they were necessarily unconcerned about women's approval. On the contrary, according to some accounts, men appeared to be quite anxious about what their partners thought of them, especially as to whether they were 'good'. In the following extract, for example, I have just asked Ruth whether she thinks there are any ways in which she exercises power over Nick:

Ruth: Yeah, I do in some ways – I think, erm, in this role of like moral policewoman. His experience of that is that it's quite powerful and quite frightening sometimes, you know? . . .

Wendy: You mean like you've got more power to judge him?

Ruth: I don't think I have. I'm really thinking of how he experiences it, and I think he – I can tell he finds me very powerful then, you know? Erm, and he feels at a disadvantage in that moment, you know?

However, although men sought women's approval, this did not generally mean that women had the power to determine the criteria by which the man was to be judged. On the contrary, so long as a man did not indulge in excessive 'bad behaviour' (drinking, gambling, womanising, wasting money), 'did his best' in terms of the traditional male role, and especially if he did something 'extra' such as 'helping' around the house, he expected to be seen as a 'good boy'. Indeed, he might be quite indignant and defensive if, despite all of this, he still did not meet with his partner's approval.

Men's attempts to avoid being 'in trouble' featured in some accounts. One woman, for example, described her partner's failed efforts to find inventive places to hide his porn magazines. Another said she always knew when her partner had been for a 'crafty' drink after work by the smell of mints and the 'inane grin' on his face when he arrived home. Where men had obviously 'behaved badly', they might feel guilty and be prepared to 'grovel' to the woman. A particularly extreme example of this comes from Kate, who spoke of how she gained a sense of control over her ex-partner Phil after he had committed a violent attack on her:

Kate: He was always on his best behaviour from then on. He was always having to prove to me that he was all right, and I suppose I was in quite a powerful position for me, erm, in many ways.

This example perhaps highlights more than any the paradoxical nature of women's power. Phil had failed to live up to his own ideal of being a 'decent bloke' who does not hit women and felt very guilty about what he had done. Because of this, Kate found that she could exercise control over him by maintaining the moral high ground. The fact that Kate had this 'power' at all, however, was rooted in the fact that Phil had caused her physical injury, and her motivation to exercise this power was partly rooted in the fact that she was frightened of him.

A third way in which women claimed to exert power over their partners was through withholding 'services' which the man wanted, as a way of punishing him or controlling his behaviour. In the following extract, for example, Jackie explains how, when dating her ex-partner, she would use the withdrawal of sex as a way of ensuring that he showed some interest in her and treated her 'like a lady':

Jackie: I think with Brian I had more power when it came to the sexual side of the thing. . . . If we'd been out for the evening and if he'd got up my nose, I'd just say I wasn't going back to his flat for the night. . . . I mean if we are going out for the evening, then we go out. . . . I don't want to be sat in the lounge with all the ladies, while he's in the bar with all the – saying 'Oh we'll go back', and we'll just go to bed, you know? . . . If we were going out for the evening, we were going out as a couple . . . not just send a drink over every time he saw an empty glass.

Once again, women's exercise of power is seen to be paradoxical. Jackie's 'sexual power' is rooted in her own lack of sexual subjectivity; sex for her appears as a method of rewarding Brian for showing an interest in her which he clearly does not feel, since he would rather spend the evening with his mates.

It seems, then, that the benefits of the power that women could wield over their partners were dubious indeed. Exercising control in the ways that they did appeared merely to confirm women in the 'maternal' role which they resented. If this was the case, however, why did women's resistance to their 'maternalisation' appear so weak and ambivalent? What prevented them from exercising a greater awareness of the contradictory character of their 'power' and the realisation that it was rooted, in a sense, in their own powerlessness?

Maternal compensations

What women really wanted, as we have seen, was to retain the new sense of themselves which their romantic transformation had brought into being. They wanted to be 'somebody', somebody who mattered, somebody whose thoughts and feelings counted. However, this 'new self' was easily undermined by their partner's emotional withdrawal and, as we have seen, women found that their attempts to 'stick up for themselves' were hard work and produced a conflictual atmosphere. A dilemma was produced: women had 'become themselves' through falling in love, yet as time went by they experienced a growing tension between the possibility of 'being themselves' and their remaining in the relationship. There seemed to be two possible choices: either to give up hope of resolving this conflict and end the relationship altogether, or retain the hope of 'making it work' by finding ways to negotiate the painful contradiction which this choice entailed. It is as a response to this dilemma that women's habituation to the maternal role can be understood. Becoming 'everybody's Mummy' allowed women some gratifying, if highly problematic, compensations for not being themselves. We have already seen, for example, that while women felt hurt and disempowered, maternalisation enabled them to exercise control. Albeit in strictly limited and paradoxical ways, women could boss men around, exercise moral superiority and 'punish' them by 'withdrawing their privileges'.

A second and related area of 'compensation' can be identified in the data. Although women's self-confidence and sense of worth declined in response to men's emotional withdrawal, there was also a sense in which their assumption of the maternal role allowed them to see themselves as strong and capable in comparison with male partners who were frequently described as 'hopeless' and 'useless'. In the following extract, for example, Helen, whose 'responsibility for everything' includes managing the family finances, is laughing as she describes her frustration at husband Jonathan's financial incompetence:

Helen: My Jonathan's hopeless, yeh he's hopeless [laughs]. . . . If I wanted to I could probably draw it all out and spend it [laughs], and he probably wouldn't say anything. He's pretty clueless. He thinks the chequebook means he can just write cheques, and I, erm, you know, have to sort him out a little bit. . . . That's the little boy in him, that he doesn't want to be responsible. He doesn't want to be responsible for money.

Sometimes women described efforts they were making to try and teach their 'hopeless' partner to do new things. Here again, for example, is Helen:

Helen: I don't do everything. I don't think that it would be fair to say that I do everything. Erm, I've even taught him to iron. I said I wouldn't iron another shirt for him, so he does all his own ironing now. . . . He will do the hoovering and, you know, if he cleans the bathroom, he cleans it really well. But he doesn't think about where he drops everything, just – it's like having another child really. He just drops, you know, takes his clothes off and leaves them in a heap, and, and this sort of thing. He just doesn't think about it.

Within such narratives, women's frustration at being overburdened is mixed with evident pleasure in their own maturity and competence. These qualities are implied through the presentation of men as 'hopeless' and themselves as indispensable. Men are portrayed as needing to be propped up, organised and patiently encouraged towards adulthood – a goal that is somehow never quite attained. Meanwhile, although women complained bitterly about men's laziness and immaturity, they were also at times keen to demonstrate that they wanted to be fair to their partners, presenting them in a good light by praising them for 'trying hard' or being 'helpful'.

A third way in which maternalisation compensated women for their 'lost selves' was that it allowed them to get their own way by deceiving or manipulating their partners. Men might like to believe they are in charge, the thinking went, but we women know better. Mary, for example, explains how she overcomes her husband Patrick's tendency to be controlling *and* has the last laugh in the process:

Mary: [Y]ou plant an idea and leave it for a week or two, and let him think it was his idea in the first place, and go along with it being his idea, and *praise* him for having such a good idea. It's awful isn't it? [laughs] *So* manipulative!

Another example is Kate's secret fund:

Kate: Well at the moment he does have more control over the money . . . I have set up my own private little – and he doesn't generally know what I've got in that. . . . In a way it is my sort of subverting, you know, I am subverting our system. I'm just syphoning off [*laughs*]. It's awful!

It was very noticeable when transcribing the interviews that women laughed a lot when describing how 'hopeless' their partners were and how they were able to trick them. It may be suggested that such humour allowed an outlet for feelings of frustration and powerlessness and served to bolster the consoling fantasy that men's domineering behaviour was an obstacle which could easily be surmounted by their own cleverness.

While this study does not address men's experience directly, it is important to note here that the mother–son dynamic did not appear to be straightforwardly beneficial to men. There appeared to be a price to pay in that it could undermine men's own feelings of importance or competence. Helen, for example, described a recent crisis in her marriage. Her husband Jonathan had become increasingly 'distant'. Helen had become correspondingly resentful at having to 'hold it all together' while Jonathan involved himself more and more heavily in his work. Eventually he also started an affair with another woman. When the crisis erupted, Helen and Jonathan went to 'Relate' for counselling.

Here, Helen describes her exasperation when Jonathan blamed the breakdown of their relationship on the fact that she did everything:

Helen: I am such a capable person, and everybody expects me – and Jonathan expects me to be capable. And I mean that was the *big thing* that came across when our relationship broke down, was that he said that, erm, he felt that I didn't *need him*, that I was capable. I ran the house, and I was doing my degree, and I looked after the children, and I – he just wasn't needed. I was capable of doing everything. And that *really hurt* because I thought well *Oh God! The only reason I am doing it is because nobody helps me.* I mean you have got to be capable because you just can't let it all fall down.

Other accounts also suggested that while men appeared to enforce the mother–son dynamic, they were not at all happy in the role of 'son'. The emotional dependency could make them feel vulnerable and powerless and their own distancing could, paradoxically, make them feel unwanted and unappreciated. Several women thought that their partners experienced them as threatening, and while women themselves understood their partner's emotional withdrawal as being the cause of the difficulties in the relationship, men's avoidance of intimacy could also be seen as defensive. One woman, for example, observed that in order to exert control over her partner she had to 'make him stand there and look at me'. If he managed to evade eye contact, there was nothing she could do.

It can be concluded, then, that the paradoxical nature of women's 'power' and the way that its exercise implicated them in a pattern of exploitative gender relations was partly obscured by the compensatory pleasures which women could experience in their 'maternal' control and competence. Moreover, it may be suggested that this obscuration might be furthered by men's own experiences. While being a 'little boy' might bring structural advantages, these may be accompanied at the emotional level by feelings of powerlessness and incompetence. But how can we explain *why* such dynamics emerged as couples 'settled down'? Why did men withdraw emotionally and appear to lose interest in their partners and in the relationship? Why did they seem baffled at women's complaints and unable to understand their distress? Why were they so discomfited and defensive in the face of women's requests for attention and emotional support which, given the cultural primacy of the ideal of caring coupledom, do not seem unreasonable?

Mummy's Boy

The general picture which emerged from this study of women appearing to want greater intimacy and men appearing to want less is no surprise. It has been a predominant finding in sociological studies (Hite 1988; Mansfield and

Collard 1988; Duncombe and Marsden 1993). More specifically, several psychologists have observed how heterosexual relationships are characterised by a particular gendered dynamic whereby men avoid women's demands for intimacy and connection, while women alternate between approaching men and coping with the pain and frustration of being 'shut out'. This has been variously termed the 'pursuer–distancer' pattern (Fogarty 1976), the 'rejection–intrusion' pattern (Napier 1978), the 'demand–withdraw' pattern (Wile 1981) and the 'approach–avoidance dance' (Rubin 1983). The analysis presented here, however, features three particular aspects which have not been highlighted in other studies. Firstly, this gendered pattern appears embedded within, and characterised by, a 'mother–son dynamic' which is visible and at times quite explicit in women's accounts. Secondly, this dynamic has a particular and paradoxical relation to gender hierarchy. Thirdly, and crucially, the dynamic is one which 'grows out of' an initial situation in which love appears to have a quite different manifestation.

One theoretical approach which seems particularly useful in explaining the first two of these aspects is Nancy Chodorow's (1978, 1989) account of how the phenomenon of male dominance is rooted in the male infant's defensive reaction to maternal omnipotence. Chodorow's fundamental thesis is that the differential pre-Oedipal treatment of boy and girl infants by their mothers, consolidated in the Oedipal phase, means that masculinity and femininity are constructed in relation to fundamentally different patterns of object relations. Seeing her daughter as like herself, the mother does not feel a strong need to encourage her separation and individuation and because the girl's Oedipus complex is not firmly resolved, her unconscious tie to her mother remains important. The result is that the girl will tend to retain her desire for connection with others at the expense of seeking autonomy. Seeing the boy as different from herself, the mother tends to encourage his separation and individuation from the outset – a process consolidated by the firmer resolution of his Oedipus complex. This, combined with a 'positional' rather than personal identification with his father, leads the boy to lack a felt need for closeness with others. Moreover, because masculinity is predicated on being 'not-feminine', and because intimacy and relationality remain associated with pre-Oedipal femininity and merger with the mother, males tend to adopt a distancing and dominating stance in order to defend their ego boundaries against what is unconsciously experienced as a threat of engulfment.

The deep contradictions in the mother–son relationship mean that where men involve themselves in heterosexual relationships, 'it is likely to be with the ambivalence created by an intense relationship which one both wants and fears' (Chodorow 1989: 77). Heterosexual men desire women, but they are at once likely to display defensive behaviour in response to women's desires for connection. Women do not experience the same ambivalence because women were never 'merged' with the absent father. Thus while men and women may be 'meant for each other', they will not be able to fulfil each other's needs. The theory that men and women are 'psychically incompatible' and at their most comfortable in different kinds of 'object worlds' is a credible explanation for some of the general difficulties which characterise established couple relationships (Rubin 1983). More specifically, it helps to make sense of some of the particular puzzles and contradictions highlighted in this chapter. It sheds some light, for example, on why men claimed that 'of course' they still loved their female partners, while at the same time appearing distant and disinterested. It helps to explain why men complained that women were 'needy' or 'demanding' in the face of what appear to be quite reasonable expectations of care and attention. It offers a plausible explanation for why women were intensely frustrated and did not get what they wanted, while at once experiencing themselves, and apparently being experienced, as powerful in relationships. And it would further account for the 'compensatory' pleasures that women experienced in their maternal role; men's 'hopelessness' and dependency at least ensured a certain kind of relationality which confirmed them in their feminine identity, even if this was also disappointing and not the kind of 'intimacy' which women had in mind.

Chodorow's theory thus helps to explain both the 'mother–son dynamic' and its paradoxical relation to gender hierarchy. However, although it enables a useful juxtaposition of the bliss of 'true love' with the strains and contradictions of socially conditioned coupledom, it also has important limitations as a theory of love. Insofar as it explains relationships in terms of relatively fixed patterns of interaction between individuals with relatively fixed personality types, arrived at through the more or less successful attainment and consolidation of gender identity, it succeeds at the cost of recognising how the unconscious 'constantly reveals the failure of identity' (Rose 1987: 184). The whole point of psychoanalysis is that identities are fraught with contradictions, and only ever provisionally and precariously 'achieved'. In Chapters 2 and 3, we saw how love itself arises out of the 'failure of identity'; contradictions within the self find expression as desire which, if enacted, enables the subject to break out of the limitations and dissatisfactions of their 'comfortable' existence and 'realise themselves' differently. In other words, love cannot be explained simply in terms of who we have already become, since its driving force is precisely the attempt to become someone different. This attempt, of course, is not the resolution it appears, and in this chapter we have begun to explore the form that love's 'counter-revolution' takes. What this has made most clear is that love's 'failure', like love's 'realisation' is not simply a result, but a *process*.

At the beginning of this chapter, I proposed Freud's theory of the 'repetition compulsion' as a basic framework for a model of love which is both comprehensive and dynamic. If falling in love can be explained as the unconscious 'resolution' of the past, then perhaps 'falling out of love' and the relational patterns which emerge may equally be explained in terms of an unconscious realisation that the past is not, in fact, resolved after all. If the bliss of 'true love' is rooted in infantile illusions, perhaps the disappointments and dissatisfactions of 'love gone wrong' are similarly underpinned by past *dis*illusionments. In other words, the forms which love takes may not be the outcome of processes of becoming which our infantile conditioning once produced, so much as the repetition of those processes – leading us to *re-become*, in spite of ourselves, that which we have already become. Certainly, stories of 'hopeless' men and 'powerful' women, who appeared through processes of male emotional withdrawal and female 'maternalisation', substantiate the proposition that coupledom does not simply involve the expression of identities long established. It involves the *reconsolidation* of identities disrupted by romantic transformation. The drama of 'Mummy's Boy' is not simply the story of a failed revolution, but the story of how the revolution failed.

The counter-revolution part 1: his story

Since, in this chapter, it is women's partners who have most obviously appeared in an 'infantile' role, I will end by advancing a provisional explanation of the typically masculine 'counter-revolution', asking: How did the hero's first attempts at love 'go wrong'? How did these attempts lead to the development of his adult identity? What form is taken by his unconscious fantasy of resolution? How is it realised? What experiences threaten to undermine his illusion? How is he inclined to respond to such threats? And how might his response be a repetition of the past – a repetition which contributes to the failure of love?

While the precise course of 'successful' masculine identity formation remains subject to debate, there is agreement that the boy's experiences of separation and individuation from the mother occur in conjunction with his coming to terms with a fundamental difference from her. At each successive stage in this process, the boy experiences new hurts, frustrations and disappointments as he repeatedly tries and fails to 'secure himself' through loving his mother. Matters come to a head at the 'Oedipal crisis' when the boy 'discovers' that his mother is 'castrated'. He must abandon all hope of securing himself through identification with her and accept that, due to his own 'inadequacy', he cannot satisfy her either. Repressing his desire for the mother, the boy switches course and invests his efforts in the task of 'measuring up' to his father, with the aim that once his manhood is consolidated, he will be able to satisfy his mother and thereby resolve his love for her. The wounds 'inflicted by' the parents persist in the unconscious mind and determine future experience. For the male, relationships with women are imbued with a compound and deep-seated anxiety and hostility, rooted in 'fear of the pre-Oedipal mother of infancy who abandons/engulfs; of the phallic-narcissistic mother who confirms/denigrates masculinity; of the Oedipal mother who cannot be fulfilled, who rejects and falsely seduces, and who prefers the father' (Person 1990: 280). The male's fear and hostility, however, exist in tension with an equally powerful, compound and deep-rooted fantasy of the mother who has the power to heal all the hurts that have ever been caused and restore him to narcissistic perfection. A central aspect in male psychology is the wish to split off the benevolent mother from the malevolent one (see Dinnerstein 1976).

This conflict in the male unconscious finds heterosexual expression in a powerful desire for a 'mother' who will both confirm his identification with her and at once make manifest her complete sexual satisfaction by him, thus enabling him finally to 'transcend' his inadequacy. The risk of enacting this drama is immense however for, like his heroine, the male subject must be prepared to 'lose himself' if he is to 'find himself'. Only by giving up his defensive and controlling masculine identity is there the possibility of resolution, yet in so doing he at once puts himself at the mercy of a woman who might, after all, turn out to be the overwhelming, castrating, insatiable and fickle 'mother' of his worst fears. It is the sheer depth of this male fear and the fact that love inevitably reinvokes a pre-Oedipal terror of 'feminine' merger and connectedness which is stressed by feminist Object relations theorists (Dinnerstein 1976; Chodorow 1978). It is no wonder then that most of the time, the risk of falling deeply in love is experienced as too great. However, reparation through love always remains a powerful possibility in the unconscious, and the desire to risk a 'fall' intensifies when certain factors are present: the awareness of inadequacy and dissatisfaction pressing itself upon consciousness, the existence of a cultural narrative of transformation, and the availability of an object who appears both like and crucially unlike the first love object.

For the heterosexual male, as Wilhelm Reik observes, the desire to fall seems to become particularly strong in the presence of feminine narcissism when an extreme tension is experienced between the apparent self-sufficiency of the object who 'seems to remain cool, self-possessed and self-contained' and the subject who is 'dissatisfied with himself, full of dissonances, split and stirred up' (Reik 1974: 48). The crucial question is: Why is the man's compulsion to repeat the past intensified by the appearance of *this* object? The answer, it may be suggested, is that loving this woman appears to be a relatively 'good risk', and this feeds the fantasy that the good mother can be split off from the bad one. Her apparent boundedness and self-containment suggests that she will not force him into a painful withdrawal in order to defend himself against a boundless and insatiable femininity. Her self-love marks her as a source of love who will not disappoint. Her self-possession suggests that she will not be dependent on being satisfied by him and therefore will not find him lacking. And being apparently complete unto herself, neither will she compel him to turn away from her in disgust at her lack. If the woman has a certain vulnerability, being perhaps younger than himself or in a less powerful social position, so much the better. This also helps to assuage his fear of the 'new mother' who, being so supremely powerful that she may grant him all that he desires, might alternatively inflict upon him every hurt that he has ever felt. It is *this* 'mother' who is the object of the male subject's transformation, brought to blissful realisation when his idealisation of her is reciprocated by a woman in love who, as we saw in Chapter 3, appears precisely as self-confident, independent, sexually satisfied and absolutely delighted with her 'unmasculine' partner. Finally he can be 'himself'.

Seeing the nature of the delusion upon which the hero's 'transcendence' is based, the contradictions which inhere in 'true love' could hardly appear to be greater. The female subject's transformation begins with the 'affirmation' of her hero, an affirmation which *bestows upon her* a coherent, potent and radiant subjectivity. For the male subject, however, the heroine *already possesses* such a self and his 'affirmation' is merely an expression of his own 'self-seeking' admiration. No wonder he is discomfited when the heroine begins to appear dissatisfied and requests more attention and emotional support. This may seem all too reasonable an expectation given the ideal of intimate coupledom, but to the unconscious 'infant' male it triggers a deep foreboding. The illusion that his 'mother' is independent, self-sufficient and wants nothing from him – other than that he 'be himself' – is threatened by the fact that she *is* now asking for something from him, something that he does not understand. The male subject's idealisation is based on the fantasy that the heroine will bestow everything upon him. She, however, once believing herself to have been rescued from the lonely struggle of 'keeping it all going', expresses a deep ambivalence at being 'responsible for everything' and cannot hide her resentment at his expectations. Thus no sooner is the male subject blissfully merged with his benevolent mother, and thereby restored to narcissistic perfection, than there appears the spectre of someone else: the evil mother who would frustrate him and taunt him with demands which he cannot satisfy.

Insofar as the man attempts to resolve his existential situation through following the path of love, there are two fundamental possibilities. He could give up the illusion that his current partner is, or can ever be, his perfect parent and let his desire lead him in an endless search for a 'mother', who will not disappoint him. Alternatively, he could pursue his search by remaining with his partner, clinging on to the hope that having once given him everything she might do so again. To this end he will develop ways to negotiate the growing disjuncture between this fantasy and the reality of the relationship in which he now finds himself. For example, if his partner complains that she 'wants more from the relationship', he might appear baffled or mount a counter accusation that she is 'too needy'. If she demands more intimacy, he might 'back off' in an attempt to control the threat he perceives. He might 'shut off' to her criticisms in order to defend himself against the painful feelings they arouse. He might try to mollify 'bad mummy' by being a 'good boy' and hiding things which might 'get him into trouble'. He might simply engage in denial and appear oblivious to his partner's distress, hoping that if he carries on behaving in accordance with his fantasy, everything will be all right. And if his partner succeeds in breaking through all his defences, his fear and hostility might erupt in more overt aggression towards her.

These strategies, all of which are visible in women's accounts, can thus be understood as manifestations of typically masculine counter-revolutionary love, a love which has one aim: to protect the subject from the pain of disillusionment, and thus enable him to cling on to the illusion of deliverance through revolutionary love. Through his defensive actions, the man helps to shape the inherent instability of 'true love' into a particular and intensifying dynamic. Fearful that his partner is a subject with desires which he is expected to satisfy, he withdraws emotionally, leaving her disappointed and hurt. She keeps trying to 'make it work', but her frustration grows and her resentment becomes manifest. His fear grows and he withdraws still further, taking with him all signs of tenderness. In this way, the 'man who was not a man' disappears and love's counter-revolution (re)turns him to more familiar ways of being. Here he is more 'comfortable' but empty of something supremely precious which, once grasped, melted into the air.

Summary and conclusion

Some way into the relationship, then, clear processes of change have transformed the world of the 'subject of love', leaving her disappointed and dissatisfied. She had entered into this liaison precisely because her partner seemed able to be 'intimate', but the longer they are together the more he withdraws from her, and the more she tries to close the gap the more he tries to open it. The more she feels hurt and abandoned the more everybody else's needs and demands become the focus of her attentions. Romance had transformed her into a 'woman who could do anything', but stepping over the threshold has led her to become a 'woman who does everything'. Once love seemed like a shared project with shared goals, but now the heroine finds herself deciding what the hero should have in his sandwiches while he shows more interest in his computer. Some women did try to resist these changes. Love, they argued, should be equal, reciprocal and negotiable. They too were individuals with needs and desires of their own. But struggle and conflict ensued and, in the face of partners who did not seem to understand what they wanted, even women who were relatively determined not to 'give in' found themselves to some extent submitting to their 'maternalisation' while containing the resentment which accompanied it. Overall, women's resistance was weak and ambivalent. Perhaps surprisingly, they placed more emphasis on their own sense of power over their partners. This 'maternal' power provided certain 'compensations' for women's disadvantage but its exercise was paradoxical. It merely compounded the dynamics about which women complained most and was rooted ultimately in women's own domestic overburdening, sexual objectification and fear of male violence. Maternal power certainly offered no means whereby women could change the dynamics of their relationships with men.

While these relational patterns may be explained in terms of 'gender incompatibility', it is crucial to realise that this is never fixed or final. It is powerfully disrupted when a mutual falling in love renders a man and woman 'compatible', if only temporarily, and is thence reproduced by processes which are born in this very disruption. Falling in love enables men to rebel against the constraints and limitations of adult masculinity, but it also returns them to the distant and frustrating position that facilitates the maintenance of male structural privilege. Falling in love enables women to rebel against the constraints and limitations of adult femininity, but it also reconciles them to the role of 'everybody's Mummy'.

We saw in Chapters 2 and 3 how love's revolution is underpinned by the 'realisation' of unconscious fantasies. In this chapter we have seen that love's counter-revolution is simply the continuation of the same transformatory processes; 'true love' is tragically and paradoxically destroyed by individuals' attempts to defend themselves against the pain of disillusionment. Looking in particular at the typically 'masculine' position, we have seen how the man's withdrawal and his partner's 'maternalisation' are in part driven by his attempts to retain the illusion that she is the all-giving, all-healing mother of his infantile fantasies. We may sympathise with the heroine. What woman wants to look after a disinterested partner who ignores her distress and leaves her to pick up his dirty underpants? The 'treacherous pleasures' of maternal power seem little compensation for the loss of her dream that she was 'some-body'. No wonder women were critical and resentful and complained that their partners were 'hopeless' and 'pathetic'. We may feel, like some women in the study, that women should indeed 'demand a better deal'. But we must also spare some compassion for the hero. While counter-revolutionary love and the social structures it helps to reproduce endow certain privileges upon him, all this is partly underpinned by his own narcissistic demise and the fact that for all his attempts at manipulation, self-deception and control, he cannot prevent his partner from smashing into pieces his precious fantasy that she could grant him everything while wanting nothing for herself.

5

THE DAUGHTER'S SUBMISSION

Given the depth and extent of many women's dissatisfaction and disappointment in love, a particular question comes readily to mind: Why did they stay in these relationships at all? Historically, of course, relationships appear less a matter of choice; social, legal and economic imperatives overrode individual misery, and institutionalised gender inequalities could make escape from a brutal and exploitative marriage almost impossible for women. Moreover, to suggest that relationships today are free from such constraints would be misleading; the decisions of women in this study to stay in, or leave, particular relationships were often deeply embedded in a complex web of gendered financial, practical and family considerations. Nevertheless, it was equally clear that these considerations were not always salient and even where they were, did not in themselves prevent women from leaving. Fundamental although certainly not separable from other considerations was women's own desire to keep on trying to 'make the relationship work', despite their partner's 'psychic desertion' and their own unhappiness. What compelled women to make this choice?

The analysis presented in Chapter 4 provides a partial explanation: 'maternalisation' habituated women to a role which their feminine conditioning rendered familiar and which offered some 'compensatory gratifications'. Certain forms of pleasure and control were manifest in women's presentation of themselves as mature, clever and capable in comparison with male partners who were immature, inept and easily manipulable. Feelings of strength and pride could be attached to the ability to 'hold it all together' in spite of everything. This, however, is not a sufficient explanation for women's relative acquiescence since, as women became 'maternalised', they also felt abandoned, deeply hurt and devalued, and came to practise a self-denial which produced internal contradictions and persisting resentments. Given that it is precisely the painful contradictions inherent in adult femininity that are blissfully 'healed' when women become 'somebody' through romantic transformation, why is there not more evidence in the study of stronger and more sustained resistance to the process of maternalisation and a more sharply critical view of the 'benefits' which it offered? While the answer to this question is far from self-evident, it is clearly rooted in the powerful desires and deep compulsions which women themselves experienced as 'love' but which were otherwise difficult to account for. So what does 'love' mean for women?

In Chapter 4 the focus was on men's love. Emotional withdrawal was explained as the man's attempt to protect himself from the painful realisation that his 'revolution' had failed. The question that arises here, therefore, is how might the failure of women's love be similarly explained? How might women's determination to 'make it work' be underpinned by the attempt to avoid the pain of disillusionment? Women's own past is less obviously visible in their accounts than that of their partners. In contrast to the usage of 'mother–son' language, there was almost no evidence of women consciously positioning themselves as a child in a parent–child dyad. In psychoanalytic terms this is not surprising; the whole point is that the events of infancy remain as an *unconscious* foundation of adult identity, and that a good deal of effort is employed in keeping knowledge of our past repressed. Given this, it is clear that if we want to understand the nature of the love which underpins women's relative acceptance of their 'maternalisation', we need to look beneath the sense of power and competence this afforded them. We need to identify any particular sensitivities and insecurities which the 'mother' might be covering up. 'Unearthing the daughter' in this way will allow us to look more critically at the nature of 'maternal' power. At the same time, we also need to look beyond women's presentation of their partners as 'hopeless boys'. We saw in Chapter 4 how this presentation gives male behaviour something of an 'innocent' air; men are seen to gain advantages, but only through 'opting out' in a childish and frustrating sort of way. This view is left unquestioned by a theoretical emphasis on 'maternal omnipotence', leaving open the possible conclusion that patriarchy is simply reducible to a form of male hysteria rooted in infantile fears that it is really women who are in control. This chapter, then, explores the 'other half' of love by focusing on two questions: What particular forms did 'paternal' power take in women's accounts? and What is the process of the 'daughter's submission'? I will start with the first of these questions.

The power of silence

In Chapter 4 I described how, when asked who had more power, women in the study most often presented their relationships as equal, and also tended to be more aware of exercising power over their partners than vice versa. This, however, was often in sharp contradiction to how women actually described the dynamics between themselves and their partners. Not only did men's withdrawal leave women feeling frustrated and deeply upset but it was repeatedly described as having an oppressive effect; one woman, for example, said it felt like 'having your personality squashed'. One explanation for this contradiction is women's attachment to their 'maternal' power; it can be 'comfortable' and reassuring to experience oneself as being 'in charge'. Another factor, however, may be that a systematic understanding of male power is obscured by certain presuppositions about the nature of power. When asked, for example, *how* their partners exercised power over them, most women's answers revealed the assumption that this would involve men telling them what to do, exercising overt limitation or prohibition on their movements and behaviour, or using threats or physical violence against them. Women had at times experienced men behaving in these ways towards them, and readily identified such behaviour as controlling. However, most men, most of the time, did not exhibit such behaviour. Therefore most men, most of the time, were not seen to be exercising power. Indeed, the assumption that exercising power involves 'doing something' meant that men's behaviour was particularly *un*likely to be identified with the exercise of power. The reason for this is that women's complaints about their male partners precisely concerned what men were *not* doing: not talking, not listening, not 'showing their emotions', not caring, not taking an interest and not taking responsibility. A number of questions therefore present themselves: What, more specifically, did men's 'doing nothing' consist of? Why did it have such destructive effects on their female partners? And how did it enable men to benefit from women's maternalisation?

I will explore these questions by looking in turn at three different aspects of men's withdrawal. Firstly, and fundamentally, men appeared able to exercise control through silence. Repeatedly in the interviews, women spoke of how their male partners would reveal very little about themselves in the relationship. They would simply not talk about their personal feelings or experience, and this meant that as far as the women were concerned, men were distant and unavailable:

Helen: It was like being in the same house with a stranger really.

Jean: There is still a great big gap between us . . . I can't fathom him.

Jenny: He's a totally closed book on that level.

Some women gave examples to illustrate what they saw as the quite remarkable extent to which their partners were able to 'hold everything in':

Diane: He put the phone down and he said, erm, 'oh my father has died, he has just died'. And I said 'oh', you know, 'I'm *so* sorry', you know? And he said 'Oh well, I suppose the funeral will be so and so and so and so. Eh, look at the time, I'd better get back to work. I'll see you later', and went. He never . . . talked about it or anything. . . . And then his Mum died and he was the same.

The extent of men's 'silence' varied within the women's accounts. Some women said that there were times when their partners would 'open up', even if this was only in a crisis, while others described relationships where men *never* revealed their feelings. Diane said her husband showed so little feeling that he was 'like a psychopath'.

Men's silence was experienced by women as disturbing in that it created uncertainty, and this uncertainty had an undermining effect on their confidence. In the following extract, for example, Jane describes how she has experienced this difficulty in previous relationships:

Jane: You don't know where you are with them. They are not being one hundred per cent honest, because they are not telling you how they feel about things. They are always holding back. . . . So you can't judge how to – how to react or how to behave in a situation, because you don't really know what is going on inside their heads . . . I think you have to have a fair idea of how they feel about things in order to actually handle the situation yourself.

This kind of uncertainty over 'where they stood' in relation to a partner with whom they were 'supposed' to be on intimate terms led women to feel anxious and to lose confidence in the relationship in which they had invested so much. Fearing that there must be 'something wrong', they would become increasingly concerned to try and work out what 'the problem' was so that they could 'sort it out'. In this extract, for example, we can see how Hannah is highly motivated to try and work out what might be going on behind her partner's silence:

Hannah: I don't think I would *actively* think their feelings are more important than mine. But in certain situations I know I will spend time thinking, erm, or talking to friends, and saying 'I wonder what he's thinking? I wonder why he's acting like this? I wonder what he's feeling?'

Because women tended to respond to their partner's withdrawal in this way, they would develop an increasingly exaggerated sensitivity to what they *thought* he felt and what they *assumed* he wanted. Meanwhile, they would easily lose sight of what *they* felt and what *they* wanted, since the corollary of romantic transformation was the assumption that the best way of ensuring their own well-being was to put their efforts into trying to 'make the relationship work'. Men themselves may not have even known what they felt or what they wanted, but if they did, this dynamic made it much more likely that they would get it; emotional withdrawal, as was suggested in Chapter 4, may well be a defensive reaction motivated by fear, but it nevertheless enabled men to gain control in relationships.

The more complete the man's silence, the more effort the women might expend in carrying out what has been termed 'emotion work' within the relationship (Duncombe and Marsden 1993). Some women described themselves as going to very great lengths indeed in an attempt to produce some kind of evidence that they were on intimate terms with their partners. Mary, for example, describes here how she tries to communicate with her 'very quiet and very withdrawn' partner:

Mary: I have got to drag it out of him. I have actually got to, I have actually got to second-guess, I have actually got to work out what is going on in his life to find out what is upsetting him, so I can ask him the right questions to get him to tell me what is wrong in his life. Erm [*pause*]

Wendy: How does he respond when you do that?

Mary: He will *admit* there is the problem but then he won't go on any further from there. He will, he will not talk about his internal life whatsoever.

Although little is actually revealed regarding Patrick's subjective experience, the sheer effort that Mary feels she has 'got to' expend in 'dragging it out of him' demonstrates how her response to his silence produces her maternalisation. By such efforts, women sought to overcome the contradiction between their partner's silence and the 'intimacy' which had once prevailed.

The power of evasion

Women did not always respond to a partner's withdrawal by trying to 'work him out'. Sometimes they would challenge his silence more overtly, saying that they were unhappy and they wanted to 'talk about the relationship'. However, according to women, their partners were almost invariably reluctant to respond to such approaches. Several women described how, whenever they attempted to initiate a 'talk', their partner would immediately find excuses to avoid this or put it off until 'later'. Examples included going to mend the garage door, going to put petrol in the car, and going to see someone on 'urgent business'. Some men were observed to have developed particular strategies of avoidance such as pretending to be engrossed in a television programme, claiming they were 'too tired to talk now', or falling asleep whenever the subject was broached. Here, for example, is what Kate said when I asked her if she had tried to communicate with Harry 'on a deeper level':

Kate: He'd ignore me, and he wouldn't – he just wouldn't engage in any – anything that would expose him emotionally, anything that would make him vulnerable. He would – well his best tack on this one was to fall asleep. I would mention emotions or in some way us, relationship, commitment, anything, I could guarantee within two minutes . . . he would be *fast* asleep, absolutely fast asleep, out like that [*snaps fingers*]. And – well you can imagine the frustration. I wanted to *kill* him [*laughs*], and I just felt totally rejected. I just felt you are not interested, great, you know, fine.

While Kate is laughing as she says she 'wanted to *kill*' Harry, her frustration at her lack of success at getting her feelings on to the agenda is clearly real enough. In the interviews, women would often become quite agitated as they described such scenarios.

The build up of frustration and resentment could cause women to 'blow up' over things. However, while this allowed an emotional release, it did not change anything since the man concerned would usually continue to avoid engagement, often remaining calm and apparently unruffled. In the following extract, for example, Helen describes what happens if she 'has a go' at Jonathan concerning his 'lazy' or 'selfish' behaviour:

Helen: Well he just sort of ignores me. I jump up and down and say *'this is just typical of you, typical'*, and it just sort of, just sort of goes over his head. He doesn't get drawn into any sort of arguments. He knows that I'll calm down, you know, and ten minutes later I'll be holding his hand. . . . If I think – if I sit and think about it, he doesn't really get drawn into arguments at all really.

While, like Helen, other women saw such behaviour as being 'typical' of their partner as an individual, the analysis of many similar accounts showed that this kind of gendered dynamic had a much more general typicality.

In some couples conflict did not surface at all. Rather, the relationship was characterised by a notable degree of harmony; everything seemed to run smoothly, relations between partners were polite, everyday practicalities were successfully negotiated, and other people, so it seemed, even perceived the couple to be happy. But this 'official' version of the relationship was no indication that all was necessarily well. For example, this is what Diane told me when I asked her whether she and her husband John have arguments:

Diane: Erm, we have done, terrible arguments, but it has been me arguing at him, and I don't get anything back . . . I get more and more upset, and . . . you know, it doesn't make an iota of difference to him, one iota. . . . It is like arguing with yourself really, and er that's no good.

Wendy: So if there are things you are unhappy about . . . you wouldn't try and have it out with him at all?

Diane: No, because there wouldn't be any point. No, there wouldn't be any point in sort of having it out with him really.

So while Diane and John maintain a facade of amicability, their relationship bears little resemblance to their early days of intimacy and companionship. John has withdrawn to such an extent that he evades Diane completely. Diane does not know how John feels and has given up trying to tell him how she feels since such attempts simply result in her 'going round and round in circles' in a frustrated attempt to be heard. Diane described her marriage to John as continuing amid a 'festering atmosphere'.

In comparison to this state of hostile alienation, descriptions of arguments and rows between women and their partners appear to be relatively intimate. While conflict may not be enjoyable, it seemed that if a woman's partner entered into an open disagreement with her she could at least feel that her point of view had some recognition, which was better than being ignored. Fights, even if not constructive, might also 'clear the air', enabling a relationship to continue on a more comfortable and friendly footing, at least for a while.

'Rational' man/'emotional' woman

Even if women did succeed in 'breaking through' their partner's evasiveness, this did not mean that he would necessarily recognise their point of view as having any validity. A commonly described scenario was one whereby, if a woman insisted on being heard, her partner would claim that he was 'more than happy' to discuss her concerns. However, while this apparently meant that both points of view would be on the agenda, there was a condition: the man would only agree to communicate so long as the discussion was conducted 'rationally' and that his partner explained exactly what was troubling her in a calm and 'reasonable' way. Then he would be prepared to consider what she had to say. The problem here, however, was that when women attempted to explain why they were hurt and dissatisfied, their partners – as we saw in Chapter 4 – often appeared to be baffled. They seemed unable to understand, even when they tried. Recognising the same old pattern, the woman would feel frustrated and begin to get upset. As soon as she began to show these feelings her partner would then refuse to carry on the conversation on the grounds that she was getting 'too emotional'. In the following extract, for example, typical of many of the women's narratives, Jackie describes how her 'very controlled' partner will only listen to her once she stops being 'emotional':

Jackie: I'll blow up over something, and Dave won't understand why on earth I'm blowing up, it's just me . . . Dave will not argue back, which makes me even worse. He sits there and doesn't say a word. That winds me up even more. Erm, but when I have calmed down – it maybe a day or two . . . he'll say 'can we talk about this rationally now, now that you've calmed down? Can we talk about this quietly and rationally?'

This kind of response left women in a double bind. In order to be able to insist on being heard, they needed to feel upset enough to force their way through their partner's 'stonewalling'. However, if they became 'emotional', their partners would then refuse to communicate with them until they had 'calmed down'. Once women had calmed down again, however, they no longer felt able to force the issue, and in any case it did not seem possible to convert all their upset and confused feelings into the kind of 'rational' account which their partners demanded. Moreover, because the experience of trying to be heard was distressing and emotionally draining, women themselves might feel exhausted and relieved to return to the relative 'harmony' of the status quo, while their dissatisfactions remained unexplored.

The way in which men appeared to block women's attempts to communicate can be understood as a reinforcement of the more general defensive strategies of silence and evasion. Sensing, we might infer, that his partner's point of view was not one which he would find comfortable, the man appeared to prefer not to know what it was. If she insisted on expressing it anyway, a further attempt to side-step the challenge which this posed could be made by declaring the woman's perspective to be 'irrational'. The accounts of the majority of women in the study contained examples of male partners overtly refusing to listen to them, or to take seriously what they said on the grounds that they were 'emotional', 'irrational', 'mad' or 'illogical'. On occasions this was explicitly linked to gender, as in the following quote from Hannah:

Hannah: He'd get you to a point where you'd sort of actually complain about something he'd done, and he'd say: 'You women, you're all mad. You're all completely mad. You're just so illogical. Look at what you're doing.'

Such attempts to 'delegitimise the opposition' could be quite effective. Even if, consciously, a woman believed quite firmly that her own point of view was a legitimate one, her self-confidence could be undermined by deeper doubts: she certainly felt emotional – perhaps she *was* being irrational, illogical? In psychoanalytic terms these apprehensions are, of course, entirely correct since the unified, rational subject is a fiction created by the ego. The point is, however, that unless she also challenged her partner's attempt to undermine her point of view, a woman could easily fall into the trap of problematising only her own perspective.

The privileging of male 'rationality' appeared as a successful strategy of control insofar as what it actually consisted of remained unexamined. The reason it remained unexamined, so it seemed, was because it was a fundamental assumption rather than an overt claim. That is, men's accusations that women were 'irrational' implied a deviation from a norm which was assumed to be manifest in men's own point of view and which therefore, paradoxically, did not require examination or rational explanation. Analysis suggests, however, that employment of a rational/emotional dichotomy was generally no more than a device whereby men attempted to get their own way. The following extract, for example, comes from an interview with Diane where she describes a row between herself and her husband John over the fact that she had decided to withdraw from sexual relations with him:

Diane: I didn't want to have sex with him or anything like that, and ... I said 'I feel so and so and so', and he just turned around to me and said 'That's nothing but emotional crap'. And that was it, just *emotional crap.*

It was clear from Diane's account that she was indeed acting upon her emotions. She told me she had felt hurt and abused because she felt that John did not care about her and was simply using her for his own gratification. It seems equally clear, however, that if John had such a powerful desire to have sexual relations with Diane that he was willing to behave aggressively towards her, and attempt to render her resistance invalid, the basis of his behaviour was no less emotional than hers. So how should we understand the emotional life of 'rational man' with his silent, evasive and hostile stance?

Power of the fathers

In Chapter 4, we saw that in the male unconscious, heterosexual love is a drama which can have two outcomes. In the first, everything is resolved; the man's lover is the 'mother' he has longed for all his life – the always-loving, ever-giving woman who confirms his narcissistic perfection by being completely satisfied with him and by him. This 'outcome' corresponds to the state of being in love, where the most grandiose illusion manifests as the profoundest truth. In the second outcome, the hero's hopes are dashed; his lover turns out to be the always-desiring, ever-needing 'mother' who is never satisfied, who undermines him and who only loves him for her own ends. In the beginning the man's love may not seem to be self-seeking, for he praises and admires his lover, appearing to recognise both her intrinsic worth and her independent subjectivity. In fact he does neither. Paradoxically, his 'recognition' of her is entirely conditional upon her correspondence to his unconscious ideal, and in so far as she is revealed as the 'wrong kind of mother', he will be reluctant to recognise her at all. In Chapter 4, this non-recognition was manifest as an 'emotional withdrawal'. Here we have seen that the withdrawal may consist of a variety of defensive strategies, including silence, evasion and derogation of the 'irrational' other. During love's revolution these defences fall away, made redundant by the appearance of the 'good mother'. The merest sign of the 'bad mother', however, and the man will begin to defend his precious illusion by 'shutting out' all that would contradict it.

The disappearance of the sensitive and vulnerable 'boy' may seem tragic, but we must look beyond any tendency to imbue the counter-revolution with a simple innocence. The 'reconstruction' of male defences may be rooted in infantile fantasies, but they have an actual and demoralising effect upon the women who are 'loved'. When it becomes apparent that his lover has needs and desires of her own which he may not understand and cannot meet, a man may respond with reticence and silence. If his partner's dissatisfaction becomes apparent he may 'avoid' her, ignore her and employ methods which discredit her point of view. If she continues to make 'demands' and makes manifest her hurt and frustration at his 'failure', he may take to patrolling his psychic fortifications with the vigour of a man possessed, willing now to display overt hostility or even, as we shall see in Chapter 6, to act violently towards her, all in the effort not to hear what she has to say. In this way, men who during the 'fall' were not 'men' at all underwent a process of *paternalisation*, whereby their initial openness and sensitivity gave way to a rigid and frustrating masculinity. Through this they came to exercise a considerable degree of control over their female partners and contributed to the destruction of intimacy, in so far as this implies the mutual recognition of two subjectivities.

There were several accounts of relationships in this study where 'fortress man' appeared to have become completely impenetrable; there simply seemed no way for the woman to 'get through' her partner's defences. In such relationships, the woman's subjectivity appeared to have been overridden to such an extent that the 'relationship' was conducted entirely in accordance with the man's wishes and perceptions. Jane, for example, tells here of how she simply gave up trying to have a point of view in her marriage to Keith:

Jane: He just wasn't interested. He thought I was being a silly emotional woman, and he didn't want to know anything. . . . He just shut his mind out and decided that we were happy, and just carry on as we were sort of thing. . . . Something wasn't right inside me. . . . But I am sure he thought everything was hunky-dory. He didn't dream there was anything wrong, you know? He couldn't see past the end of his nose. As far as he was concerned, he was getting what he wanted out of the relationship . . . that was the end of it really.

We might guess that underneath Keith's hopeless attempt to 'decide' that his relationship with Jane was happy, there probably lurked a terrible apprehension that things were in fact very far from 'hunky-dory'. Meanwhile, the reduction of Jane's resistance to a mere feeling that 'something wasn't right inside me' testifies to the great extent of her submission to Keith's ego and exemplifies the complete alienation of a couple who were once on intimate terms. Jane did eventually leave Keith and she described how, even then, he initially put this down to her being 'silly' and deemed her complaints about the relationship to be 'petty' whilst at the same time attempting to persuade her to return.

When partners became extremely controlling, women *did* see that they were being subject to domination. Jane, for example, reflected on how, by the end of her marriage to Keith, his expectations that she existed to please him had become overt. They took the form of demands that she should wear the kinds of clothes that he liked, that she should behave in a particular way in front of people he knew, and that she should have sex with him whenever he felt like it. However, while, like Jane, women might readily identify patterns of control that were the 'end result' of changes in the relationship, the nature of the processes through which such dynamics had come to emerge from the bliss of true love remained largely invisible: *why* was a man who was once loving and devoted now cold and abusive? Jane's only way to explain this was that Keith had conned her and only shown his 'true colours' once he had 'got her where he wanted her', and that she herself had been stupid not to have 'seen through him' in the first place. It was even more difficult for women to find an explanation in cases where male control did not take the more actively aggressive forms, but remained as a silence defended by evasion. Most commonly, the man's behaviour was put down to a kind of emotional backwardness which was 'typical' of men. This, however, did not explain why male partners had manifested such 'atypical' behaviour in the beginning.

Whether women came to see their partner as a 'bad lot' or simply as 'emotionally inept', one thing was clear: it was he who was generally seen as the cause of their dissatisfaction and frustration. Several women expressed the feeling that they had done 'everything they could' to try and 'make the relationship work', and yet still their partner persisted in his indifferent, irresponsible and frustrating attitude. What they wanted did not seem so much to ask, they argued – just a bit of consideration now and again, a bit of support, some acknowledgement of how they felt. Having entered into the relationship in 'good faith', and being prepared to put a great deal of effort into it, women expressed a deep sense of injustice at their partner's 'abandonment' of them. Several women stated that even though 'underneath it all' they still loved their partner, they could not see the relationship lasting unless he changed – why should they 'keep it all going' when he showed so little regard for them?

In women's accounts, the 'power of the fathers' thus appears to be immensely frustrating and difficult to challenge. This is not to suggest, however, that women's experiences of abandonment and maternalisation were simply effects of male power, or to imply that women themselves did nothing which contributed to these processes. To argue that men behave in ways which render women's exploitation possible is not to argue that male behaviour, in itself, is a sufficient explanation for women's subjection. So what else contributes to the counter-revolution? Of crucial significance is the invisibility of male power. As I noted in Chapter 4, in so far as women equated male behaviour with the exercise of power at all, this tended to result from reflection either upon their own past relationships ('I must have been stupid not to see it at the time') or upon the relationships of other women ('I don't know why she stays with him. I wouldn't put up with it'). In women's own current relationships, it tended only to be where a partner's behaviour had become extremely and overtly hostile that women would recognise it as 'domineering'. Even here, the tendency might remain to put this down to his simply being 'difficult' or 'childish'. What, then, makes women relatively blind to male power, and especially so when they 'love' the man concerned? Given that men's 'paternalisation' was a process, why did women not recognise its implications and challenge it more forcibly in the early stages? Meanwhile, just what was the 'everything' that women did to try and 'make their relationships work'? It may be clear that women did not 'deserve' their partner's indifference, but does that mean that they played no part in the counter-revolution? And why, even though they claimed to be continually on the point of leaving, did some women stay; what did they hope to achieve by 'sticking it out'?

With these questions in mind, we will move on now from considering the exercise of 'paternal' power, and focus on the second important question addressed in this chapter: What is the process of the 'daughter's' submission? Perhaps this will help us to explain further the contradiction between women's all too evident disappointment in love, and their equally evident determination to 'make it work' nevertheless. In particular, might women's efforts to surmount this contradiction, manifest as the process of 'maternalisation', have a similar basis to men's 'paternalisation'? That is, might maternalisation also be rooted in the formation of defensive strategies which cover up fears and insecurities at the heart of feminine identity? Might women's 'counter-revolution' also be understood as the attempt to avoid the repetition of past disappointments? To find out, we need to look beneath the 'mother' who featured in Chapter 4, and beneath the sense of power and competence which this identity affords the 'subject of love'.

Feeling 'so small'

In Chapter 4 we saw that women's reaction to men's withdrawal and their own assumption of 'maternal duties' was characterised by an oscillation between resistance and complicity. On the one hand, they would challenge their partner's indifference and fight for a better deal. On the other, they would be frustrated by his stonewalling and repress their disappointment and resentment at being 'responsible for everything'. I remarked that women's expression of resistance often seemed to be weak and ambivalent, and while this is perhaps unsurprising now that we have seen just how difficult it was for women to break through their partner's defences, women's complicity nevertheless remains a problem to be explained. We have identified counter-revolutionary tendencies within the male subject, tendencies which are there at the very beginning of love. Now we need to identify whether corresponding tendencies in the female subject also play a part in undermining women's resistance.

In Chapter 4 we saw that women's narratives of loss and abandonment were characterised by the expression of frustration towards, and disappointment with, their partners. Underlying such expressions, however, were deep feelings of hurt; women felt wounded by their partner's apparent loss of interest in them. Moreover, and crucially, women reacted to this hurt in a very particular way: they experienced their partner's emotional withdrawal as a reflection of their own value and importance. This meant that the more he appeared to lose

100

interest, the more likely women were to lose confidence in themselves. In some narratives this sense of devaluation, like the man's withdrawal, appeared to occur slowly, perhaps imperceptibly, over time. In others, however, it was described by the woman as a sudden realisation. In the following extract, for example, Ruth describes a scene where, in response to her challenging Colin's 'distancing', he confesses that he has transferred his interest and affirmation on to another woman:

Ruth: It was so humiliating, because – I mean I'll just never forget this. It was my twenty-seventh birthday and I was nine months' pregnant, and we went out for a drink, and he was very quiet. And I was saying: 'What's the matter? What's the matter?', as you do. And in the end I managed to get it out of him, and he said 'Well I don't love you any more. I love Karen'. [*pause*] And I mean the hurt – I can still feel the hurt actually now when I tell you – but mixed with that was *total* humiliation, total. To think, you know, I was nine months' pregnant and this was going on, you know? I felt *so* small.

Ruth's feelings of hurt at Colin's betrayal are not surprising. What I want to draw attention to, however, is the way this hurt was 'mixed with . . . *total* humiliation'. Ruth was not merely wounded but lowered in status, rendered '*so* small'. These kinds of feelings were strongly characteristic of women's experiences of their partner's withdrawal, whether or not there was any obvious 'rival' for his attention. So why did women feel so devalued by their partner's behaviour?

It is not that women simply blamed themselves. On the contrary, as we saw in Chapter 4, they tended not only to see the relationship problems as caused by the man's withdrawal but, at least on the 'rational' level, to see this as being his problem. He might be seen as 'too immature' to cope with commitment or fatherhood, or simply 'emotionally illiterate' due to his membership of the male sex. Women certainly blamed men for avoiding 'the problem' and expressed a good deal of frustration at such behaviour. This, however, was not the whole story. Alongside women's attempts to explain and deal with what they saw as their partner's failings was another tendency, a tendency to attach a particular meaning to his withdrawal which was experienced very powerfully at an emotional level. This is exemplified in the following extract where Mary has been telling me about how she tried to challenge her partner's withdrawal:

Wendy: How did you confront him?
Mary: By demanding to know what was wrong with me. Why do – you know, why do you not value me any more?

Thus despite believing at a conscious level that they had 'done nothing wrong', and despite being very critical of their partner, at another level women seemed to react as though his withdrawal might have been precipitated by some fault or deficiency in themselves. Like Mary, they would try and pinpoint what this supposed fault or deficiency might be, and a growing anxiety and sense of insecurity would only be deepened by the man's failure to offer any explanation. It was this anxiety and insecurity which formed the crucial emotional basis for women's 'maternalisation' and undermined their resistance to the 'power of the fathers'. To substantiate this observation, I will go on to outline how women's accounts revealed two particular processes which paralleled the emotional withdrawal of male partners: 'self-objectification' and 'self-silencing'.

Self-objectification

We saw above how Mary responded to her partner's withdrawal and her own feelings of devaluation '[b]y demanding to know what was wrong with me'. Through such assumptions, which were only 'confirmed' by a partner's deepening 'silence', women would begin to apprehend themselves as an object in an attempt to perceive themselves and evaluate themselves through their partner's eyes. Once engaged in this practice, a practice embedded in a whole personal history and cultural milieu of ideas about what they, and women in general 'should' be like, women would indeed find fault with themselves. This seemed often to involve a *re*activation of various pre-existent fears about their personal adequacy which had temporarily subsided through romantic transformation. Self-objectification appeared as a direct response to the powerlessness which a woman felt in the face of her partner's silent withdrawal. If she could only work out what it was that had led him to withdraw, the assumption went, perhaps she could attempt to remedy the situation and thus win back his approval. One particularly clear insight into the aim of self-objectification is enabled by Hannah's own reflection on the dynamics of a past relationship in which she attempted to 'win back' the admiration of the man:

Hannah: The initial reaction I got from him was a positive one. He was just delighted with me, everything about me. He couldn't have enough of me. He couldn't say enough nice things about me. And as time went on . . . he backed off you see. And I wanted more of the same. So I kind of thought ooh what can I do now to get it back, you see? And you kind of get into very convoluted twists to get back what you've had, which was quite nice. It means that you stop thinking I want to be myself, and you start thinking what do I have to do or be to get this person to react in the way I want him to react in, and the way he was reacting initially, because it was nice.

Self-objectification did not generally appear as an overt and conscious strategy in women's accounts, but as a response based upon underlying assumptions about the nature of love relationships. And what motivated women to act upon these assumptions, and to focus upon themselves as an object of desire, was that it represented the apparent possibility of regaining some sense of control in a situation where they felt they had lost it.

It is not surprising that women in this study actively sought to construct themselves as objects of their partner's desire. At the cultural level, this appears simply as a manifestation of a more general imperative that, for women, love and approval are to be won and retained through regimes of beautification and the self-conscious construction of a pleasing 'personality', the evaluation of which lies ultimately with others. The familiarity and apparent utility of this strategy is dangerous indeed, however, for it may obscure how self-objectification simply undermines women's already vulnerable sense of self. To illustrate this, here is Hannah again, describing her attempts to work out what might make Leon regain interest in her:

Hannah: I bent over backwards so much to try and be and do what he would think was appealing. . . . When we were at college he went out with someone who had very short hair, you see . . . [so] I had my hair cut really short, and I'm sure that in some way that was influenced by what he would think was attractive – this independent, carefree woman image which he was quite attracted to . . . I just became so much not like myself that I disliked what I was doing, and I lost all sight of me as a person, and me as an individual.

Through engaging in self-objectification, Hannah thus became implicated in a process of losing 'herself' which was motivated, quite paradoxically, by the desire to regain the feeling that she was loved 'for herself'. Thus the relationship between women's romantic transformation and their subsequent demise begins to become clear. Once having interpreted a particular man's desire for her as his 'recognition' of her, his loving her 'for who she really is', his withdrawal simply produces the corresponding effect. Just as the woman 'found herself' through true love, now she begins to 'lose herself'. Both the 'finding' and the 'losing' have the same cause: the pre-existing propensity to seek identity through the objectifying gaze of another.

To focus on women's *self*-objectification is not to imply that their partner was blameless in this respect. On the contrary, in some accounts men did appear to assume a right to sit in judgement. It may also be suggested that for men who were reluctant or unable to account for their own part in the counter-revolution, women's tendencies towards self-blame might have proved convenient. However, there is no simple causal relation between men's objectification of women and women's loss of self-confidence. Two women in the study, for example, spoke of how their current partners actively challenged their tendencies towards negative self-evaluation and sought to offer reassurance. One thing was clear, however: women's propensity for self-objectification rendered them acutely sensitive to any criticism. Some women reported that their partners had complained they were 'over-sensitive' because they would be reduced to tears over 'nothing'. Certainly, in some accounts, hostility from partners appeared to have a potent effect in activating women's insecurities. In the following extract, for example, Ruth sounded hurt and upset as she described an incident which had actually occurred many years ago, in her previous marriage:

Ruth: I saw this ad for a magazine. It was on monetarism, that's right, and I said 'I think I'll get that because I'd like to find out a bit more about it', 'cause I did do economics 'A' level, and I was quite interested in it. And he sort of *rounded* on me, you know, and said 'who do you think you *are?*', you know? And that was really humiliating because you feel like you see yourself at that moment through the other person's eyes, and they see you as somebody who's *very* insignificant and rather stupid, but thinking – having like delusions of grandeur. Er, and that's really horrible actually, you know? It's like seeing a photograph almost of yourself. You see what they're seeing, and it's very unpleasant.

Ruth's account gives a clear illustration of the self-deprecation which is made possible by a self-objectifying disposition. Once Ruth's sense of herself had become dependent upon Colin's recognition and approval, a hostile remark from him was enough to 'humiliate' her, to render her 'insignificant' and 'stupid', to suggest to her that even to think her point of view was important was to have 'delusions of grandeur'. In that moment, Ruth felt that she had become what she imagined Colin's image of her to be: 'like seeing a photograph.'

Self-silencing

The desire to try to regain a partner's affirmation through self-objectification automatically involved an associated process; women would silence their own desires where they supposed these might displease their partners. Again, there is no suggestion that men were blameless in this respect. As we saw in Chapter 4, male partners readily complained that women were 'needy' or 'demanding' if they expected to be listened to and given attention. However, like objectification, silencing was not a process simply imposed on women by individual male partners, but one in which women themselves played an active part. Indeed, there were even examples of women actively silencing their own needs and desires in an effort to pre-empt a partner's feared displeasure, before there was any concrete evidence of this. Maureen, for example, entered her current relationship with Bob when she was particularly vulnerable and insecure, having recently left a very violent marriage. After recounting how her mother used to tell her she was 'selfish' and would 'never keep a man', Maureen describes here how she automatically adopted a position of self-denial in an effort to 'keep' her new partner:

Maureen: I think in the early relationship I was just so frightened that he would go . . . and that I couldn't manage on my own . . . I was very anxious in the early years . . . I suppose it weighed him down, really. All I – I kept saying 'you're all I've got' erm, and I did think that he was all I had, erm, and he was the sort of one that was important. That's why I put him first, erm [*pause*]

Wendy: In what ways did you use to put him first?

Maureen: Whatever he wanted really – whether he wanted money, whether he wanted to go for a drink. Erm he'd have the best meat. He'd have the best, you know? He would just have the best. . . . He would have clothes, I'd have nothing. Only because I didn't think I was a worthy person to spend money on, not because he would say anything.

Wendy: So it wasn't coming from him?

Maureen: No it was me.

Clearly, it is necessary to problematise the fact that Bob does not appear, in the account, to challenge Maureen's self-denial; his silence and apparent lack of concern with her needs enables Bob to exploit Maureen's submissiveness. Nevertheless, Maureen's self-silencing must be seen, in itself, as deeply problematic; out of a desire to secure a relationship with someone who will care for her, she attempts, paradoxically, to render her own subjectivity invisible.

Maureen's extreme submissiveness, her obviously low self-esteem and her history of abuse make hers the kind of case which is typically the focus of explanations that root love problems in the pathology of deviant or 'dysfunctional' families (see e.g. Norwood 1986. For critical discussion see Jackson 1989; Langford 1993). However, the data in this study suggest that if Maureen's behaviour is unusual at all, it is in degree rather than in type. The same process of self-silencing can be identified throughout the women's accounts and appears as a typically feminine strategy of trying to gain affection and recognition, or of trying to *regain* the admiration which their partner had displayed towards them in the early days. In the following extract, for example, Hannah, who appeared to have relatively high self-esteem, nevertheless reflects on how her desire to be valued has overridden her sense of self in past love relationships:

Hannah: I feel very strongly that I lost part of myself, or I deliberately lose part of myself in the process of trying to work out what they want from me. And it's a situation that I've got into quite consistently . . . I mean I've got a very strong sense of myself as a person, but for some reason I lose it when I'm with people who I want to like me . . . I start to lose my sense of strong identity.

105

Again a relationship is visible between male withdrawal and female self-silencing. Hannah wants the man's affirmation but he is distant. She assumes he might be less distant if she can only work out how he might want her to be, and in the process silences her own subjective experience while putting his imagined subjectivity centre-stage.

The process of self-silencing has a clear relationship to the process of 'maternalisation'; the more women repressed or discounted their own point of view, the more 'natural' it became for them to put their partner's point of view before their own – so natural that their own perspective could easily become invisible, a fact hidden by the paradoxical feelings of power and competence which they experienced by becoming 'everybody's Mummy'. The way that 'maternal' power is underpinned by self-silencing is particularly evident, for example, in accounts where women responded to their partner's silence and emotional withdrawal by attempting to 'draw him out of his shell'. Because men often seemed genuinely to have so much trouble communicating, and because women were so motivated to try and 'sort things out', they could easily be seduced by the pleasures of becoming 'amateur therapists' whose aim was to 'help' their poor, emotionally backward partner to 'get in touch with his feelings'. Sarah, for instance, who considers herself to be the 'stronger' person in her relationship with Wayne, describes here how she 'helps' him to communicate with her:

Sarah: I try and sort of structure questions so I can make him talk about what I know he wants to talk about, but he wouldn't do it unless I question him so he had to think about what he was saying . . . I try and talk to him as if I am not in the relationship. I really do try now to do that, and er I get more out of him that way.

Wendy: So you try and put your feelings . . .?

Sarah: I just try and block them totally off.

Thus, in the process of trying to 'help' Wayne find out how he feels, Sarah actively and purposefully silences *her* feelings. In this way, while women in the study complained that men could not 'show their feelings', their accounts often revealed that they were not showing theirs either, while at the same time making considerable efforts to help partners 'get in touch with themselves'.

The more women responded to men's withdrawal in this way, the more difficult it became to uphold initial expectations that their partners would be actively concerned about them and promote their well-being. While women described the efforts they made to try and 'get through' to their partner, they also related how they more often expressed their own feelings and points of view outside the relationship. Mary, for example, claimed to know more about her husband Patrick's 'inner life' than he did himself, but this is how she responded when I asked her if she talks to him about how *she* is feeling:

Mary: No I don't, no – not any more, erm [*pause*]. No, I keep that for my women friends because I know they'll *actually listen*. They will want to engage with what I'm feeling, and they will ask me questions, and they will draw it out of me. . . . He'll engage at a superficial level, erm if you want a lift to the hospital to visit somebody, erm that kind of level. But to actually sit down and talk about how shitty you feel, and that life's bloody awful and it's not fair, and rant and rail against life, there's absolutely no engagement whatsoever.

Thus although Mary has friends who do acknowledge her subjective experience, within her relationship with Patrick she has become 'silent'. When I asked women explicitly whether they saw their own point of view as being as important as their partner's, they usually had no hesitation in responding in the affirmative: of course they did! Women were keen to assert that they were important and valuable individuals in their own right. As we have seen, however, this assertion was not supported by solid ground, and the deeper apprehension of its truth seemed largely contingent upon the vicissitudes of love. Doubts and insecurities evaporated, and a cogent and worthy selfhood was 'realised' when women underwent romantic transformation, but the hero's withdrawal all too readily stimulated the reappearance of women's self-doubt. Yet the existence of this deeper self-doubt does not in itself explain why women responded to men's withdrawal with self-objectification and self-silencing. A crucial question is therefore posed: Why, sensing the loss of that which she most desires and which she experiences herself as having found, does the heroine appear deliberately to undermine herself in the effort to regain it?

Daddy's Girl

One approach to this question is to suggest that the heroine's love betrays a habitual patterning which became established through her early attempts to 'secure herself' through object love. This process of becoming took her through a particular series of desires, fantasies, illusions and disappointments which constitute her feminine conditioning. To understand the heroine's part in counter-revolutionary love, a number of questions may then be asked: How, precisely, did her early attempts at love 'go wrong'? What fantasy of resolving the past does she harbour? How does this fantasy come to be 'realised'? What is most liable to threaten her precious illusion? How does the past determine her response to this threat? And how might her 'resolution' and her subsequent disappointment constitute the disruption and the reconsolidation of a self-denying and devalued femininity?

Because the girl does not have to renounce her attachment to her first love object, her identity has a greater continuity than the boy's and she does not develop the same fears about connection with others. Like the boy, however, the girl suffers the inevitable disappointments and disillusionments with her mother which are brought to a head at the Oedipal crisis when she finally 'realises' that her mother is 'castrated', and therefore *cannot* give her what she wants. In her continuing search for identity, which is now symbolised in the unconscious by the possession of a penis, the girl, like the boy, turns to her father for confirmation that she is like him. While the father recognises the boy, however, he thwarts the girl's attempt at masculine identification. To add insult to injury, the girl must give up her active sexual love for her mother because, being 'castrated' herself, she will never be able to satisfy her. The best hope offered by the path of feminine development is that if the girl accepts her position as the passive object of her father's desire, he will give her his penis, and eventually a baby, preferably a boy, which will make up for her own lack. Not surprisingly, the girl is not easily reconciled to her feminine identity and the Oedipal situation is much more slowly and less fully resolved than it is for the boy. While desire for, and envy of, the feminine in males is so firmly and deeply repressed that its significance is easily overlooked, most famously by Freud himself, masculine desires remain much closer to the surface in girls. Freud (1914) observed that even up until puberty, girls retain feelings of being like males and develop to some extent along masculine lines. This tendency is finally cut short when they reach feminine maturity, but even then, women 'still retain the capacity for longing for a masculine ideal that they themselves once owned' (ibid.: 24–25).

Feminine conditioning involves the 'infliction' of deep narcissistic wounds upon the girl both by the inadequate mother and by the frustrating father. As the girl represses her forbidden masculine longings, anger towards her parents for these insults is also repressed. In relation to males, this hostility takes the form of an unconscious envy and resentment, rooted in a persisting sense of injustice and a belief that they possess that which she needs to make up for her lack, but will not give it to her. The frustration of the girl's own active and aggressive tendencies leads to a turning inwards of her libidinal energies, resulting in the development of particular neurotic patterns and self-defeating tendencies. These, paradoxically, serve to defend her against the painful awareness of her wounded narcissism, her status as powerless sexual object and the 'knowledge' that she can never possess a potent and coherent identity. This possibility remains unconsciously associated with the attainment of masculinity.

Tensions and contradictions within the self may manifest in the form of desire for the 'other', commonly, although not necessarily, the heterosexual object. Through falling in love with a man, a woman aims finally to become one with the 'father' who in her mind possesses what she lacks, and thus 'achieve' the narcissistic perfection which has eluded her all her life. While this account stresses the Oedipal father–daughter dyad, it can also be suggested that the girl's fantasy of resolution, like the boy's, is many-layered. Love is the articulation of resistance to all conditioning; it aims to heal the wounds inflicted by all the 'mothers' and 'fathers', and thereby to resolve all contradictions within the self. Thus while 'the Oedipal father who relents' may be a prominent fantasy in the feminine psyche, the love object may also represent simultaneously many other manifestations of the perfect parent.

Given the contradictory nature of subjectivity, the desire to 'fall' appears readily in the presence of an object who appears as both like and, crucially, unlike the first love object. For the female, desire intensifies most predictably in response to male attention and 'affirmation'. While the romanticisation of heterosexuality endows such attractions with legitimacy and cultural meaning, desire draws its power from a deeper source. In the woman's unconscious mind, the male object may be presenting himself not only as the 'father' who through his desire for her as object bestows upon her what she lacks, but as the 'father' who is recognising her at last, who is finally confirming that she is like him. The grave risk of repeated disappointment is, of course, always there. However, to the extent that her current situation is imbued with loneliness and meaninglessness, to the extent that existential dissatisfaction and internal incoherence press themselves upon her consciousness, and even against her own better judgement, the 'girl' will feel compelled to throw herself upon the mercy of this new 'father'. Her desire for transcendence, that is, will override her deepest fear that he will, after all, turn out to be the 'frustrating father'. This father would reject her, would evade her every attempt to secure his recognition, would only want her as his sexual object, and would thus compound her deepest wounds by 'forcing' her, once again, into acceptance of her feminine conditioning. Given a mutual love, we know that to begin with everything is 'resolved'. The 'father' is besotted and the 'daughter' secures reparation for all the injustices of the past. All is forgiven, for at last she is recognised for 'who she really is'. Suddenly 'Daddy's Girl' can burst through the constraints of her existent identity and rise above all that previously held her back.

The counter-revolution part 2: her story

We already know that while feelings of transcendence are compelling, romantic transformations give rise to further transformations, producing very different manifestations of love. The question here is: What, for the heroine, triggers the onset of counter-revolutionary love, and why does it take the form that it does? The crucial factor in the 'daughter's' transcendence is her 'father's' desire and recognition. We can therefore guess that the heroine will have an acute sensitivity to the nuances of her lover's attitude towards her. Basking in his initial idealisation, which is 'proof' that she really is 'loved for herself', she will feel at her most secure. But what if her lover should become even slightly distracted? What if his devotion should become just a little less evident? What if he should begin to show interest in something other than her? To the conscious adult woman this, of course, appears perfectly reasonable; how ridiculous it would seem to desire the hero's undivided attention, to want his total, continual and absolute recognition. But at a deeper level, stirrings of self-doubt may give rise to feelings of uneasiness. The heroine may feel a little anxious if her lover's attention is elsewhere. She may feel slightly rejected if he wants to do things without her. She may, despite her newly found 'independence', tend not to be as motivated as she might be to spend time apart from him. A strange foreboding may arise within her and she may start to worry about 'the relationship'. For so crucial is the hero's attention and 'recognition' that any apparent loss of interest on his part will cause the heroine's love to be tinged with disappointment and her newly elevated self-esteem to be eroded. Just as her transformation began with her being 'valued', so her demise begins when the hero's 'aversion' first becomes apparent (*Mary*: 'What is wrong with me? Why do you not value me any more?').

None of this is to suggest that the hero does not, in fact, withdraw, but to underline the fact that neither this withdrawal, nor the 'devotion' which precedes it, have at all the same meaning for his lover as they do for him. While he withdraws because her dissatisfaction arouses his own self-doubt and invokes the spectre of feminine insatiability, she, knowing nothing of his selfish motivation, 'reads' his turning away as being due to some actual defect in herself. With her confidence thus dented, and sensing that her worst fears may be coming to pass, the heroine's resistance weakens. Anger may arise towards her frustrating lover but, being fearful of further 'provoking' his displeasure, and anxious to defend herself against further 'rejection', she is ambivalent about challenging him. It seems safer to turn her frustrated love inwards upon herself in 'acceptance' of her status as (imperfect) object. This process of 'refeminisation', manifest in women's accounts as self-silencing and self-objectification, is the strategy through which the female subject typically attempts to negotiate the growing disjuncture between her love story and the reality of the relationship in which she finds herself. It is true that this process is paradoxical and self-defeating; it is not rational to undermine yourself in the attempt to be recognised for yourself. The point is, however, that love is a manifestation of powerful unconscious forces with aims of their own. To the 'girl' who begins to 'realise' that her only hope of a potent and coherent subjectivity is to be recognised as like her 'rejecting' father, self-silencing and self-objectification may appear as the only possible way of being able to do something that will make him change his mind. We can see that these strategies are futile, but they have an important meaning for the heroine. They allow her an apparent means of exerting control in a situation where she feels powerless, and give her hope of 'saving the relationship' which, of course, represents her attempt to save herself.

Self-silencing and self-objectification do not only fail to secure the recognition the heroine desires; they compound her problem through undermining her confidence still further. The more her partner withdraws, the more she will turn her disappointment and hostility inwards upon herself with the aim of becoming that which she assumes he desires. The more the strategy fails, the more her 'inadequacy' presses itself upon her awareness, and the more her only defence against it is the means by which her loss of confidence is compounded. As the heroine comes to expect less and less recognition, the more desperately she desires that which will make up for her 'lack'. It is probably in this sense that men find women 'needy' or 'demanding', for it certainly did not seem to be the case that women in the study actually expected men to meet their needs at all (*Mary*: 'Why am I making so many demands, you know? What's wrong with me?'). The more powerful a woman's desire for recognition, the more likely she is in turn to present a threat to her partner's confidence, and the more likely he is to disappear behind the defences which to her seem more impenetrable than ever.

In theory, the heroine does have alternatives. To the extent that she is able to resist her feminine conditioning she could assert her point of view anyway, refusing the 'myth' that its existence depends upon external recognition. If her partner persists in his withdrawal, she too could 'withdraw' and pursue her quest for independent subjectivity in other directions. And indeed, these strategies of resistance were visible in the data. However, to the extent that her past conditioning has not prepared her for the self-confident pursuit of individuality, these strategies are likely to induce an anxiety in the heroine which only increases the more she declines to pursue them. And to the extent that she is in the grip of the deepest levels of her feminine conditioning, to the extent that she has projected the possibility of a 'complete' and coherent subjectivity on to the hero, so her 'instincts' will lead her to focus her energies directly upon the hopeless task of securing his recognition and 'accepting' her status as object. And the more she does this, the more the heroine becomes subject to 'paternal' governance.

As all the heroine's attempts to take refuge in the powerful 'father' fail, and as he becomes more powerful, so her disappointment grows, imbued with the painful emotion that arises from all the disappointments of the past. She could give up the relationship, but to the extent that her desire for identity and security is invested in its continuance, and to the extent that this scenario is reinforced by the many social and economic pressures and responsibilities which may have come her way, the prospect is not easily entertained. If she stays, however, how does she defend herself against the painful 'knowledge' of her powerlessness? There is one strategy which is open to her. As she becomes rehabilitated to her gender identity, an identity which for all its disappointments and disadvantages has a certain comfortableness and familiarity, she can invest her energy in the elevation of her feminine competences and the enjoyment of their compensatory gratifications. In acceptance of her adult femininity, she can bury the wounded and resentful daughter beneath the powerful and capable mother who, even in the face of the greatest adversity, can 'hold it all together'. According to this story her partner is not the powerful and rejecting father, but the hopeless little boy who cannot manage without her to prop him up and organise his life. It is really she who is in control and the reason he is unable to love her is because he is too immature. As she takes refuge in the 'pleasures' of her maternal role, however, the 'subject of love' buries her desire to 'really be herself', a desire which remains unconsciously attached to a particular fantasy of resolution. This thwarted desire now manifests as a smouldering disappointment with her frustrating love object. Periodic thoughts of abandoning him are offset by a stubborn and persisting hope that, however unlikely this now appears, things will one day 'work out'.

Summary and conclusion

I began this chapter with two particular questions in mind. Why, despite their obvious resentment and attempts at resistance, did women nevertheless appear relatively accepting of the role of 'everybody's Mummy'? And, what sense can we make of women's propensity to see men as more 'hopeless' than powerful, even though men appeared to gain and maintain structural advantages through their 'immature' behaviour? Was there, I asked, another story in the interviews, an alternative to the 'mother–son' narrative? Looking more closely at women's accounts of their partner's withdrawal, it appeared that in fact this enabled men to exert a very considerable degree of control. Men's 'silence' left women 'not knowing where they stood', their persistent evasion left women frustrated, and their assumption of a superior 'rationality' served to undermine women's self-confidence. Male behaviour may well be rooted in the defence of romantic illusion, but the defences which are constructed at once constitute a process of 'paternalisation' – the re-becoming of an identity which facilitates the exercise of a frustrating 'paternal' power.

Women's submission is not, however, a mere effect of male withdrawal. On the contrary, 'the power of the fathers' is rendered efficacious by women's own responses. Having once 'become herself' through the 'recognition' of her hero, his retreat triggers existential anxiety in the heroine, manifest as a loss of confidence and a sense of impending doom. These painful feelings, like the blissful ones which preceded them, arise upon the unconscious repetition of past dramas. They come from the long-forgotten experiences of previous 'falls from grace', other failed attempts to secure identity through object love. Of particular prevalence in the heroine's psyche is the first 'realisation' that it is a masculine identity which equates with essential selfhood and that without it she will be forever 'lacking'. Now, having at last 'attained' the potent and coherent subjectivity which has eluded her all her life, having at last become 'somebody', the 'girl' is appalled at her 'father's' distraction. Projecting her anger on to him, she blames herself for her incipient demise and tries to reverse it by attempting to 'win him back'. So begins the daughter's submission. The more she engages in the self-silencing and self-objectification which are meant to please the rejecting father, however, the more he withdraws, 'forcing' her to become reconciled to her feminine identity and rendering her subject to paternal governance.

The daughter's demise is a painful tale and not one which is often told, for

112

as the heroine loses confidence in the possibility that she can 'really be herself', so she 'forgets' what has happened and attempts to escape from the insecurity and suffering her predicament evokes by taking refuge elsewhere. Despite its limitations and dissatisfactions, a feminine identity has its 'compensatory pleasures'. Habitual self-silencing and self-objectification can become expressions of a paradoxical 'maternal power', manifest in the strength and competence of the 'woman who does everything'. In this way, the wounded daughter is hidden from consciousness by the powerful mother, and the girl's desperate desire for the recognition of the powerful and frustrating father is buried beneath a contempt for the hopeless boy who cannot satisfy her. The daughter's submission is never final, however, and hope lives on as a secret dream of revolutionary love.

6

DIALECTICS OF LOVE

Over the last four chapters we have seen how patterns of repetition in women's accounts give credence to the theory that adult love relationships are rooted in dramas of the past. We love because we want to change the outcome of past loves, and we want to do this because, in our unconscious minds, it is partly 'love gone wrong' which has brought us to an experience of existence which is unsatisfactory and full of tensions and contradictions. When dissatisfaction presses itself upon our awareness, perhaps highlighting the 'failure' of present loves to give us the satisfaction we crave, we may find ourselves drawn to new loves, compelled by a sense that perhaps this time love really could resolve everything. When we fall in love, this fantasy becomes 'reality'; at last we have found someone 'special', someone with whom we can 'find ourselves', discover 'who we really are', and realise a state of wholeness, integrity and lasting satisfaction. What we do not see is that while the superficial details of our love may well be unique, our 'salvation' is deeply and substantially a repetition of something that has gone before, perhaps many times. Having repressed this knowledge, we have also 'forgotten' that it is precisely through the subsequent failure of love that we arrived at the very situation from which we have just 'escaped'. Unaware of how the processes of love's failure helped to constitute us as we are, we inevitably 'repeat the same mistakes' and *re*constitute ourselves as before. We do this because in order to maintain the precious illusion that we really have left our old selves behind, in order to protect ourselves from the pain of disappointment, we habitually construct the same defences. We resort to the same modes of control, take refuge in the same forms of 'security' and – in so far as our partners play the appropriate part – enact the same dramas as we have before.

It is probable that the illusions of love are infinitely complex, individually unique and existent at many levels of un/consciousness. In this study, where the focus is on the particular dimensions of gender and power, I have concentrated on the elucidation of typically masculine and feminine 'love cycles', and on how the interplay between partners may be understood as the repetition of heterosexual parent–child dramas. What this analysis suggests is just how deeply the reproduction of domination and subordination inhere within love itself. Individuals may desire nothing more than to overcome the alienation and destructiveness of relationships characterised by control and manipulation. They may 'achieve' this aim when romantic transformation brings them to a blissful intimacy. But the strength of love's revolution is matched by that of a counter-revolution which destroys intimacy and brings the lovers to a state of mutual alienation, characterised by gendered dynamics of control and submission.

The strength of the reaction between revolution and counter-revolution is not the same for everyone. The desires and frustrations of love, and the exercise of power and control, have different intensities for different individuals and the character of relationships varies greatly. However, in so far as the overall picture emerging from the accounts of women in this study has any generality, two conclusions can be drawn. Firstly, to the degree that relationships are determined by falling in love, there is no evidence at all that they are, or are likely to be, characterised by lasting intimacy or equality between the partners. Secondly, to the extent that partners may succeed in developing a relationship characterised by some measure of friendliness, honesty and mutual respect, this appears as something to be achieved in spite of falling in love. In and of itself, love appears productive of relational dynamics which could hardly be more incompatible with the ideal of 'democratic love' which we examined in Chapter 1. This conclusion begs a very crucial question indeed, a question with the most far-reaching implications: In so far as couple relationships are founded through falling in love, and determined by the emotions which arise from this 'falling', is it even *possible* for these same relationships to be realised as domains characterised by lasting intimacy, 'emotional satisfaction' and equality? Or should the ideal of democratic love be renounced as a dangerous cultural myth which, once imbued with the full force of erotic ambition, leads inevitably to destruction, alienation and the reproduction of hierarchies of power?

Even given the evidence from this study, a possible defence of object love might be mounted. It might be granted that love has a cyclic manifestation and involves the compulsion to repeat. It might be granted that this repetition does indeed appear to implicate love in the reproduction of hierarchical and destructive social relations. It might be granted that love does have certain fundamentally problematic features – notably the attraction to difference, the desire to incorporate the other into the self, and the arising of hostile impulses when this aim is frustrated. The optimist might argue, however, that none of this constitutes a reason to give up on the ideal of democratic love. Rather, since neither the identities which love produces nor the processes through which these come into being are fixed or essential, it might be proposed that 'love cycles' could just as well take different, less destructive forms. It might then be suggested that the evidence from this study be used, not to damn the romantic ideal, but to find a way to save love from being corrupted by power. To this end, we could concentrate on developing a clearer understanding of how the processes of subjection are produced and reproduced. If we could isolate the 'power aspect' of love, might we not then be able to use this knowledge to 'intervene' in destructive love cycles and promote a balanced negotiation of the conflicts which arise between one selfish will and another? If we could work out how to modify love in this way, perhaps the realisation of the democratic ideal would become a real possibility?

There is one theorist whose work implies this possibility. For Jessica Benjamin (1990), domination is not an essential feature of relationships formed upon the basis of desire. Rather the problem is that in patriarchal society, the 'bonds of love' have become 'twisted' so that when we form attachments, these degenerate into expressions of control and submission. In this chapter, I will first outline Benjamin's theory before going on to use it in a further analysis of women's accounts. This will bring into focus the 'power aspect' of love and lead us to a concluding discussion of whether it is possible for falling in love to be a means through which the 'subject of love' can come to 'live happily ever after'.

Twisted bonds

Benjamin distinguishes between two possible psychoanalytic approaches to relationships: the *intrapsychic* and the *intersubjective*. The intrapsychic approach, developed by Freud, is the one which generally prevails. The focus is on uncovering the contents of the unconscious – the individual's inner world of symbol, fantasy, anxiety and defence. Looking at relationships according to this view, the individual's behaviour towards others is explained, not as a reaction to the other as a real subject, but in terms of the meaning that others and their behaviour have in relation to the self's own unconscious psychic drama. The model of love which I have developed over the last four chapters has drawn largely on this approach. Identity is reproduced through gendered 'love cycles' which repeat themselves because each partner's response to the other is determined by their own particular unconscious fantasy. Each therefore 'misinterprets' the other's behaviour, and because of this, responds to them in the way most likely to elicit this very behaviour, and so on. Within this model, the problem of love is largely defined, as Freud (1915b: 387) would define it, in terms of 'the infantile object-choice and the phantasies woven around it'.

As this understanding of love has developed, however, it has also become clear that love cycles drive, and are driven by, an actual and particular dynamic which comes into play between the partners. Men actually did 'withdraw' emotionally, women actually did 'pursue' their withdrawing partners, and the more men withdrew, the more women pursued and the more women pursued, the more men withdrew. Given this, a complementary approach to 'analysing love' is to shift the focus away from the particular nature of individual fantasy, and to look more closely at the form and momentum of this interpersonal dynamic itself. It is this kind of approach which Benjamin terms intersubjective, whereby the individual is viewed as a subject whose identity develops in and through relationships with other subjects. Individual capacities and ways of being may well be expressions of an unconscious inner world, but they are not only or simply 'internal'; they come into being in the context of particular conditions – particular kinds of interaction between self and other, and they may be *re*produced through the repetition of similar intersubjective dynamics.

Benjamin advances an intersubjective account of development in order to explain the persistence and deep-rootedness of male dominance, and to offer a vision of how it might end. Her starting point is Simone de Beauvoir's insight that woman functions as man's 'other', and that gender domination exists as a complementarity of subject and object (cf. New York Radical Feminists 1971; Firestone 1979; Frye 1983). Like de Beauvoir, Benjamin utilises a model of power developed by the philosopher Hegel (1910). In Hegel's view, the human situation is characterised by an essential and paradoxical 'doubleness of psychological reality'; in order for self-consciousness to exist, it needs at the same time both to assert itself by denying the existence of other self-consciousnesses, and to acknowledge the existence of the other in order that the other can recognise the existence of the self. For Hegel, this paradoxical tension *cannot* be maintained; it inevitably breaks down, producing a 'master–slave dialectic' in which each self-consciousness attempts to secure itself through enslaving the other. The 'master' attempts to resolve the self–other paradox by denying the self-consciousness of the other. The aim is to secure the self by forcing the other to first recognise the self, in the attempt to get the recognition needed. The 'slave' attempts to resolve the paradox by denying the self-consciousness of the self. The aim of this strategy is also to secure the self by forcing the other to first recognise the self in the attempt to get the recognition needed. 'Master' and 'slave' are not essential identities and both positions are built into the psychology of every human being. In practice, however, conditioning determines that each individual will be inclined to utilise these positions in ways which produce and reproduce particular hierarchies of power.

Benjamin differs from Hegel in one crucial respect. She disputes the inevitability of domination and believes that if we can understand the particularities of how the paradoxical tension between subjects breaks down, and thus how power relations are constructed, we can end domination. Benjamin pursues this project using object relations theories, explaining psychic development in terms of how the individual's conflicting needs for assertion and recognition are played out in the arena between self and other. The production of equal social relations is seen to depend upon the mutual maintenance of the self–other paradox throughout each phase of the child's development. In this way the self becomes increasingly strong and active within relationships which involve a continuing confrontation between subjects, and which do not encourage either denial of the self or denial of the other. In practice, however, events in both the pre-Oedipal and Oedipal worlds of the infant cause the tension between self and other to break down along the lines of gender differentiation. Girls learn to recognise the subjectivity of men while denying their own, and boys learn to assert their own point of view while denying the subjectivity of women.

The result of this one-sided differentiation is that neither males nor females grow up to be well-balanced individuals. Rather each is 'lopsided', inclining either to the 'master' or 'slave' position in Hegel's dialectic. This polarisation, moreover, produces a sense of 'deadness' and aloneness at the heart of both masculine and feminine identities; human beings find themselves locked into one of two modes of 'solitary confinement', either 'being unable to get through to the other, or be gotten through to' (Benjamin 1990: 83). This alienated situation gives rise to a desire for the other, whereby individuals seek to create the paradoxical tension between themselves and other subjects which they lack within themselves. Because of the lopsided and polarised construction of the gendered psyche, however, such attempts to find freedom and communion become twisted into relations of control and submission. Relationships between men and women are thus characterised by a cyclic re-creation and breakdown of the self–other paradox, reproducing a social structure characterised by the subordination of women to men.

Benjamin develops her own theory through a detailed analysis of sado-masochistic fantasy. She argues that this involves a re-creation and a break-down of the self–other paradox which 'replicates quite faithfully the themes of the master–slave relationship' (Benjamin 1990: 55). Perhaps more surprising is that striking parallels are visible between Benjamin's analysis and the patterns which emerged from my empirical study of 'ordinary' love relationships. Given that Benjamin's theory precisely addresses how relationships are determined by the play of power, and given the aim of attempting to rescue love from the corrupting influence of power, this correspondence demands a detailed elaboration. In what follows, then, I will explain how the counter-revolutionary manifestation of romantic love can be understood in terms of a master–slave dialectic. I will do this through returning to women's accounts and focusing on some examples of what happened when the processes of 'maternalisation' and 'paternalisation', which we looked at in Chapters 4 and 5, became intensified into particularly destructive forms.

He couldn't even see it

As we saw in Chapter 5, one central finding of this study is that women some-times appeared to put a very great deal of effort into pursuing a course which, while meant to remedy the problems in their relationships, seemed only to make things worse and to undermine their own confidence. In some accounts, women's efforts to 'make it work' had a clear downhill momentum; the less they felt valued, the more they would tend towards self-silencing and self-objectification in their efforts to overcome the growing distance between themselves and their 'absent' partners. Their partner's further distancing would only confirm their own growing self-doubt and intensify their longing to regain the appreciation they had 'lost'. Several women's accounts revealed that as they struggled to bridge the growing contradiction in their love stories, they became caught in a vicious downward spiral. One particular outcome of this was that as their anger and hurt failed to find outward expression and their desire for affirmation was repeatedly thwarted, women developed particular 'symptoms' of emotional or psychological distress. These were experienced as being directly related to the dynamics of their love relationships. Here, for example, is Ruth:

Ruth: Erm, I've had probably three long periods of depression in my life. One of these was when I was married, and certainly the relationship was the reason I was depressed, yes. Because erm, because of not feeling loved, and feeling like everything I did was wrong, and up for question and up for criticism. Erm, and just not having any validation I suppose in the relationship. Erm [*pause*] but at the time it was just that I felt he didn't love me, and I felt I couldn't bear it.

Just as Ruth saw her depression as resulting from her failure to secure Colin's 'validation', other women similarly described their suffering as specifically caused by the lack of love and attention they received from their partners. Although it is possible that this may in part be accounted for by the fact that the subject under discussion was love relationships, it was nevertheless striking how sure women felt that 'love gone wrong', as opposed to any other factor, was the cause of their ills.

A correlation between women's emotional and psychological well-being and the dynamics of love relationships has been described elsewhere (Bernard 1973; Symonds 1974; Brown and Harris 1978; Brannen and Collard 1982; Jack 1991). In a study of women suffering from clinical depression, Dana Crowley Jack (1991) concluded that a 'silencing of the self' within heterosexual relationships, associated with an identification with the partner's point of view, was the key factor. In order to preserve relationships, depressed women actively censored themselves, repressed their anger and devalued their own experience. This resulted in low self-esteem and dependency on relationships in which they sought a reciprocal intimacy which was not forthcoming. Trapped in a strategy of trying to please their partner, Jack's interviewees became so alienated from their own standpoints that they experienced the 'loss of self' and feelings of extreme worthlessness which characterise episodes of depression. The women in my study were not selected on the basis of their having suffered from severe psychological or emotional distress. Nevertheless, the parallels with Jack's findings are striking: more than half described such episodes including depression, anxiety, eating problems and phobias. Moreover, it was very clear that these experiences were embedded in an intensification of the 'normal' dynamics of counter-revolutionary love. Just as women 'rose above' their difficulties through romantic transformation, so they literally 'went into decline' in the context of a destructive intersubjective dialectic which drove, and was in turn driven by, their own 'refeminisation' and the 'remasculinisation' of their partners. The more women 'gave themselves up' in pursuit of a fulfilling relationship, the more their partners appeared to give them up in what appeared to women as an attempt to avoid 'intimacy'. Several women described how the distress they experienced became so severe that it constituted a serious emotional crisis or 'breakdown'. In each case it was conspicuous that the focus of women's angst was their partner's failure to respond to them, to recognise their unhappiness, to realise how desperate they were. In each narrative, women spoke of how, in the end, they had to be 'saved' by other people who *did* recognise their distress: women friends, a doctor, their mother. Here are three examples of such narratives from Kate, Diane and Sarah:

Kate: I just kept saying to him *'Everything* is black. I have nothing to live for, everything is black'. . . . What he couldn't see was that I was *really* depressed. I needed help. I – my female friends knew that and *really helped me through it*, bolstered me and just kept me going. But Harry, he just couldn't . . . it's out of his experience to be able to help me, so I – he never contributes to me feeling better.

Diane: If I talked to him I may as well be talking to myself . . . and I was going down and down and down and down, and other people could see it but he couldn't. Whether he didn't want to – you know? – I don't know. But I went to seven and a half stone . . . and the doctor then said to me: 'You have had a complete nervous break' – you know? – 'physical and nervous breakdown'.

Sarah: I thought I was going *mad* . . . I didn't know what I was doing. I couldn't work, I couldn't eat. I was about six stone I think. I was just smoking cigarettes all the time and not eating, and he couldn't even see it . . . I just thought I can't take any more, and I just went – and I was off work for a month . . . I just went to my Mum's and she was literally forcing food into my mouth, and making me take these anti-depressant things.

The pattern of repetition in women's accounts is striking; each describes how they went into a severe 'decline' while their partners remained indifferent and they even use the same language to describe their frustration that 'he couldn't see' their distress. The implication is always that if the man could have 'seen', and responded with the love and recognition which he had shown in the beginning, this would have 'saved' the woman. Everything had become focused on this one aim. In the interviews, women expressed anger, resentment, pity and despair at their 'hopeless', 'useless', 'pathetic', 'hard', 'callous' and 'psychopathic' partners. The analysis of love suggests, however, that within their relationships, women's frustration was largely turned inward upon themselves with seriously destructive consequences.

In attempting to account for the typically 'feminine' love cycle, we have already seen how this can be understood as a search for identity. Women experience an attraction towards embodied masculinity because, in the female subject's unconscious, this usually represents the most likely route to overcoming internal conflicts and the sense of inadequacy which imbues her experience. Romantic transformation appears to deliver the heroine from these evils and bring her to the potency and coherence which she longs to possess. But as revolution gives way to counter-revolution, it is with profound disappointment and a deep sense of injustice that she accommodates herself to the 'compensations' of a reconstituted femininity, repressing her own subjectivity while citing her partner's loss of interest as the cause of her demise. In Chapter 5 we saw that projected anger and the defences built against it help to explain this course; the 'daughter' 'submits' because she fears she has angered the 'father' and tries to 'win him back' in order to avoid the pain of further 'rejection'. However, seeing now the extent of some women's suffering, an obvious question presents itself: Why does the 'subject of love' pursue this course with such vigour? Why is she prepared not only to assume extensive 'maternal' responsibilities, but to become deeply unhappy and even give up her health and well-being? Why does she not see that her efforts to regain her partner's 'recognition' are increasingly hopeless? Why does she not think to abandon her quest and instead simply assert herself overtly?

The sheer strength and persistence of women's self-denial and its intensification through counter-revolutionary love suggests it is a classic manifestation of the 'slave' position in Hegel's dialectic. The slave's actions are irrational, paradoxical and painful, and it is important to stress that neither self-denial nor the burdens and misery it brings are 'enjoyed'. Rather suffering is *endured*, and it is endured for one reason only: the 'slave's' conditioning has led her to feel most confident in pursuing this route to subjectivity. As Benjamin stresses, then, self-denial should not be understood merely as a passive defence, but as an active and purposeful striving for self-discovery which has come about through a particular 'twisting' of the bonds of love. The more the psyche is in the grip of feminine conditioning, the more strongly and determinedly will the subject incline towards self-discovery through self-denial. It is this which helps to give the 'dialectic of love' its critical momentum; the more the 'slave' experiences herself as dependent upon the 'master's' recognition, the more anxious she is to secure and retain it, and the more anxious she is, the more willingly she denies herself in the hope of *regaining* 'recognition' which she believes herself to have lost.

In explaining how the girl's tendency towards submission becomes established, Benjamin stresses the relational conditions which give rise to it; the girl's realisation of her 'lack' may well take on a certain symbolism in her unconscious, but it comes about as a result of the particular ways in which the self–other paradox breaks down in the inter-subjective world(s) of her infancy. To the extent that the mother appears dependent on the 'other' for recognition of her own subjective existence, neither the boy nor the girl are able to establish a sense of subjectivity through identifying with her. As a result, both develop a powerful wish 'to be recognized as like the father and to share his subjectivity, will, and desire' (Benjamin 1990: 115). However, to the extent that the father rejects the girl's attempt to identify with him, she learns to see self-assertion as masculine and to experience independence as dangerous – as an exercise of power for which she has no basis in identification. Instead, the girl learns to try and realise her wish for her father's recognition by a different route; she becomes like her mother, and in the process learns that her source of power resides in self-sacrifice. Thus the developing girl's identity forms in reaction to the polarised identities of her parental figures; unable to 'find herself' in the mother and spurned by her father, she develops the particular illusion that her route to independent subjectivity lies in the provisional adoption of a submissive femininity.

Identity is always provisional, however; there is no feminine compliance without the possibility of resistance. Romantic transformation is one kind of path which resistance can take. By rebelling against the 'injustice' which has been inflicted upon her, the romantic heroine 'finds herself' at last in a father–daughter identification where her subjectivity is finally recognised and realised. The path of love leads inevitably to disappointment, however, for although the heroine's 'lopsided' feminine personality is temporarily 'transcended', her new-found 'independence' is not what it seems. We began to see this in Chapter 3, where a paradox was already visible in some women's claims that the recognition of their hero enabled them to 'really be themselves' and to know that they could 'manage without a man'. Since then we have seen what happens when the hero's 'recognition' comes into doubt: the heroine's self-assertion weakens and she lapses into old and well-worn habits of self-silencing and self-objectification. Thus she begins to play her part in the dialectic of master and slave, whereby mutual recognition gives way to mutual alienation and her desire to become 'somebody' is once again twisted into submission.

But he said he loved me

The heroine's drama is, of course, only one of two parts in the dialectic of love; women's despairing cry that 'he couldn't even see it' does not appear to be without foundation. We saw in Chapters 4 and 5 how the openness and sensitivity which men exhibited 'in the beginning' all too readily disappeared as they resorted to a 'paternal' power exemplified by the capacity to objectify women and block their attempts at communication. Here we will look at how this behaviour represents a classic manifestation of the 'master' position in Hegel's dialectic. This will help to explain why, in some accounts, men's 'passive' aggression intensifies and becomes interspersed with more overtly hostile and abusive behaviour which appears as an increasingly desperate and determined effort to silence women's 'demands'.

One area where this was particularly evident was in some women's accounts of sex. Men were commonly portayed as simply expecting that their partners would, as a matter of course, provide them with sexual pleasure – an expectation not matched by any attempt to ascertain how far women themselves desired sexual intercourse. Indeed, some men appeared determined to 'block out' evidence that was contrary to their own desire. Women described how, if they were resistant to their partner's sexual demands, he would engage in pressurising behaviours such as sulking or 'whingeing'. If she still did not agree to sex, he might be hurt and bad-tempered and the atmosphere of the relationship would become more openly difficult. This is not to suggest that women simply did not want to have a sexual relationship. Rather they said that they only wanted to have sex when they felt recognised and appreciated, and in so far as they did not feel recognised and appreciated they would experience reluctance. However, this situation was not straightforward. Given women's propensities to assume responsibility for 'making the relationship work' and given the central place of sex in ideals of a 'proper' relationship, it is not surprising that women's resistance was weak and ambivalent. Moreover, since a common complaint among women was that the only time their partners expressed affection or interest in them was when they wanted sex, neither is it surprising that women's resistance might also be undermined by their own desire to re-establish intimacy.

In practice, sex in the context of established relationships was often described as being far from intimate and the question of whether it took place at all appeared to become increasingly separate from the question of whether women themselves either desired it or found it pleasurable. As with the more general picture, women expressed anger and disappointment at their partner's selfishness and ineptitude and described their efforts at love-making as 'hopeless' and 'pathetic'. For some women, sex appeared to have become simply one aspect of their 'maternal duties', something they provided on demand which appeared no more welcome or enjoyable than doing all the housework. The following quotes from Mary and Jane are typical:

Mary: I am not really sure that it's me he is having sex with any more, not inside his head. Yes, I feel I am just a useful vehicle.

Jane: Keith has woken me in the night a few times, and you just – it is just not worth the hassle or the row or the argument or the aftermath by saying 'no, sod off'. Erm so you just go along with it, but you don't enjoy it. But they don't seem to . . . actually *realise* whether you are enjoying it or not.

In such narratives, men appeared at once as greedy and desperate for the comfort afforded by their 'mother's' body, and as assailants who expressed a violent disregard for the well-being of the woman they 'loved'. Where women continued to engage in sexual relationships on these terms, they did so – and indeed could only do so – through 'blocking out' their own experience. In the following extract, for example, Ruth reveals some of what normally remains hidden during the alienated encounters of counter-revolutionary sex:

Ruth: I've often felt quite detached when I've had sex, and I know from talking to other women that that's quite a common thing, you know? Like er you start to think like Oh God – you know? – did I iron my shirt for tomorrow or whatever – you know? – that kind of thing – Oh God, I wish this would just be over – you know? – which speaks volumes, doesn't it?

It would be hard to do justice to the question of the distress and harm inflicted upon women by their being reduced to mere instruments of their partner's gratification. I will not try, save to say that tears were shed during some interviews, and to give these two quotes from Sarah and Jean:

Sarah: It's horrible. He doesn't even like me. He doesn't look at me. . . . And I feel awful afterwards, because I just feel like I have just been used. . . . It is soul-destroying, and I think it just makes me lose all my confidence.

Jean: After it was over I would sort of just sort of lie there for a while and then come down[stairs] and break my heart, thinking *for God's sake I can't stand this*. I hated it.

Without accounts from men, it is not possible to know how they understood this violence which they exacted upon their partners. Women's accounts suggested that the aim of men's aggression was, paradoxically, to block out all knowledge of the suffering they were inflicting in their hopeless attempt to enforce the fantasy that women actually could, and wanted to, provide them with unconditional gratification. This observation would certainly correspond with the psychology of the 'master'. The master does not aim to inflict suffering for its own sake. Indeed, he might feel extremely guilty were he to allow knowledge of the slave's suffering to come fully into his awareness. The master's ability to exhibit concern or compassion for the slave is overridden, however, by his own existential drama; his aggression is aimed at reassuring himself that he has control over the independent will of the slave, whose recognition he needs to convince himself of his own existence.

However, just as the slave's submission is self-defeating, so is the master's domination. The more the master intimidates the slave, the less the slave's independent will is apparent and the more insecure the master therefore becomes. And the more insecure the master becomes, the more he feels threatened by the independent will of the slave and the more controlling he becomes in his hopeless efforts to secure her recognition. In relationships where dynamics of control and submission were intense, the whole atmosphere became infused with fear and hostility. Living with this degreee of tension meant that some women became acutely fearful of the possible consequences of expressing resistance, even where there had been no actual eruption of physical violence. In a number of relationships, physical violence had erupted or been threatened, appearing as a further stage in the man's escalating attempts to shore up his defences and 'block out' his partner's resistance. This had included acts of rape, other sexual assault and physical battering. Two women spoke of past relationships where they did not attempt to resist the man's sexual advances because there was 'no point'.

One woman's account of the ending of a past relationship described very precisely the acute sense of danger inherent in the advanced master–slave dialectic. Kate's relationship with Phil had become, and remained, extremely destructive, involving both sexual abuse and a severe physical assault upon Kate. Kate's decision to leave the relationship was not, however, simply precipitated by the actual harm that was being caused to her, but to a wider and more pervasive fear of the consequences of what had become an extremely intense and hostile relationship:

Kate: I just knew there was no way I could stay with Phil, because I felt I would be killed, and I don't mean physically, although I never quite got over that [Phil's assault on her]. I just knew I couldn't live in that environment.

Wendy: When you say you felt you would be killed, what do you mean?

Kate: I felt that I would have to give in to him, that he would break me, one of us would have to break almost, like the two of us couldn't survive together.

Kate's use of the crucial language of death and survival to describe an association which began with powerful attraction and passionate love-making seems tragic and shocking. One way of responding to this would be to suggest that Kate and Phil's relationship has gone horribly 'wrong'. Preferring to believe such explanations, and thereby avoid uncomfortable questions about love, we often construct a dichotomy so that when love is expressed as violence we no longer recognise it as 'love' at all.

Another explanation, however, is that destruction is simply a consequence of object love, in that desire for the love object necessarily implies the desire to control the other whose existence makes possible the existence of the self. In Hegel's view, the master–slave dialectic *is* a 'struggle to the death for recognition'. Through their respective attempts to enslave the subjectivity of the other, either through aggression against the other or through enduring aggression against the self, two self-consciousnesses systematically destroy the tension between self and other which makes possible the recognition of each. The process gains momentum because, as master and slave each become more insecure in their own existence, they find it increasingly difficult to recognise each other.

Being therefore even more desperate to secure the recognition they need, they become willing to inflict or endure ever greater degrees of harm in their hopeless quest to secure themselves through controlling the other. This destructiveness is perhaps most apparent in relationships where violence has a strong physical manifestation. A particularly extreme example is the case of Maureen's marriage to Jed which involved severe sexual violence and battering as well as ritualised humiliation. In a traumatic and emotional interview, Maureen described something of the ordeal she had endured in a relationship where both she and Jed were looking to be loved:

Maureen: My face was just all a bruise, it was just all bruised. And my eyes was closed. And the bruising was so severe it was on the inside as well. It was just totally bruised. Er, just a violent man. *But he said he loved me.*

Maureen lived in constant fear of Jed and endured years of escalating violence and abuse. However, it was only at the point when it became apparent to her that Jed was likely to kill her that Maureen literally fled from the marriage:

Maureen: I was frightened for my life – erm, you know? It would have just built up and built up . . . it had come to the stage where to survive I had to go. I *had* to go. So I went.

Such was the force of Jed's love for Maureen, and so utterly inseparable was it from his willingness to destroy her, that she was forced to spend many months 'on the run' in fear for her life, taking refuge with different friends. Eventually Maureen tried to settle in a new part of the country, but Jed managed to find her and committed a serious assault upon her. On this occasion Jed was convicted and imprisoned and Maureen spent a number of weeks in hospital recovering from her injuries. Even this did not end the matter, however. For many years after Jed's release from prison, Maureen lived in fear of the man who continued to contact her and tell her that he still loved her.

Individuals are all different. Relationships are all different. The persistence and severity of the violence which Jed inflicted upon Maureen is unusual and extreme. Certainly no other woman in this study had endured so many horrific experiences in the name of love. While pronounced differences are visible between women's accounts, however, equally visible is the similarity of the underlying processes of counter-revolutionary love. The struggle of love may, in exceptional cases, lead literally to physical death, but infinitely more common is the slow and unremitting crushing of the spirit that, from the 'slave's' perspective, comes from being persistently ignored and undermined by the person whose affirmation is most desired. We have already looked at how and why the 'slave' might learn to endure such suffering. We must now ask how and why the 'master' learns to inflict it; how does the propensity to aggress against the other come to be 'written into' the masculine psyche?

For Benjamin (1990), the male's tendency towards domination does not simply result from the boy's differentiation from his mother, nor even from a need to defend himself against the powerful pre-Oedipal mother, as Chodorow (1978, 1989) and Dinnerstein (1976) suggest. Rather, as for the girl, it is the *submissiveness* of the mother that is the problem, since the infant's relationship with her offers no basis for identification which does not at once require a repression of autonomy and independent subjectivity. Drawing on Margaret Mahler's (1975) theory of separation–individuation, Benjamin argues that maternal submissiveness creates the ideal conditions for the development of masculine 'lopsidedness'. She concentrates on the boy's *rapprochement* crisis', a phase where the infant must come to terms with its growing sense of separateness and independence. In order to negotiate this in such a way as to maintain the tension between self and other, the infant needs to be able to assert himself *and* to come up against an other who cannot and will not give him everything he desires. The mother who makes this most possible is one who experiences herself as independent and entitled to a separate existence. She recognises the infant's desires, but is also prepared to frustrate these and has confidence that he will survive the conflicts which result. However, if the mother attempts to fulfil her own narcissism through engaging in 'self-obliteration' and does not put sufficient boundaries on the child's will, she pushes him back into an 'illusory oneness' where others appear merely as extensions of himself. The frightened child will react to this by attempting to become even more dominant in order to break out of the emptiness and loneliness of his isolation. Submissive femininity, then, makes the growing boy feel insecure and to the extent that his mother does not appear as a subject in her own right, he will learn to pursue his quest for subjectivity aggressively, not merely by repressing femininity as different, but by *repudiating* femininity as inferior.

While Benjamin does not particularly discuss the father–son relationship, it is important to stress that although the boy, unlike the girl, is 'recognised' by the father, his successful masculine identification merely consolidates his lopsidedness. To the extent that the father is masculine, the 'subjectivity' and 'autonomy' which he embodies will also have been attained and maintained through denying the subjectivity of the other. Therefore while the boy may appear, especially to the 'envious' girl, to have gained independent subjectivity, this is not what it seems. It is true that, unlike her, he may come to feel relatively comfortable in asserting himself. However, while the girl grows up to be relatively comfortable in close relationships, the boy does not; he has learned to equate others' desire for his recognition with a threat to his independence, and therefore experiences anxiety should others make such 'demands' upon him. In his attempt to assuage this fear, he may exhibit an apparent indifference to others and resort to the kinds of 'paternal' control which we examined in Chapter 5. However, this self-defeating strategy only undermines his self-confidence and increases his anxiety, for in cutting himself off from others, he at once cuts himself off from the recognition *he* needs in order to 'be himself'.

The isolation and alienation which the male habitually brings upon himself give rise to desire. It can be suggested that this typically finds expression in the form of a particular fantasy of resolution: if only he could find a 'mother' whose desire for him originated entirely from within herself, whose subjectivity was independent of his recognition, then he could recognise her without fear of losing himself and be freed from the compulsion to withdraw and become controlling. When the man falls mutually in love this very resolution 'comes to pass', an appearance which can be readily understood by reference to women's own accounts of what they were like 'in the beginning': self-confident, 'independent', and apparently able to 'do anything' without the need for a man. At last the hero can 'be himself', free from the fear and anxiety which normally inhibits his expression of sensitivity and relationality, free to enjoy the affirmation which appears to flow independently and unambivalently from the heroine. However, the oneness of illusion and reality is soon in doubt. No sooner is the true nature of the heroine's 'independence' glimpsed than anxiety will begin to arise, triggering the commencement of the withdrawal through which the hero attempts to cling to his resolution. As we have seen, this process may come to be expressed through silence, through evasion, through derogation of the other, and even through physical and sexual violence. All have one aim: through attempting to force his partner to give him the unconditional recognition which he once took, quite mistakenly, to be his, the hero tries to regain what he thought he had found and in so doing plays the 'master's' part in the drama of love's destruction.

The security paradox

Once the power aspect of love is understood in terms of the dialectic of master and slave, this in turn helps to explain a phenomenon which was particularly apparent in many women's accounts: their entrapment within a 'security paradox'. Sarah, for example, was very unhappy in her current relationship with Wayne. Yet the worse things had become, the *more* difficult she found it to contemplate ending it. Instead, Sarah found herself putting an increasing effort into trying to please Wayne and regain his recognition:

Sarah: I spend a lot of my time trying to get affection from him, so much so that it makes me tired sometimes because I try so hard, and I don't usually get anywhere . . . I just try and do what he wants . . . I just do things to keep him happy, and he just does what he wants. . . . Last Sunday, I went to watch him play football, and I *hate* it. I hate standing there in the freezing cold, but I went because he wanted me to go . . . I just did it because it would put him in a good mood, and I thought if I did that he would be nice to me for the rest of the day, which he was. But I *hate* someone having that sort of power over me. I hate it.

By this point in the relationship, Sarah has become painfully aware of her submissiveness, but this merely compounds feelings of low self-worth which manifest as a fear that she is unlovable. Thus she has come to fear that Wayne is her 'only hope', a fear that compels her to continue trying to please him so that he will not abandon her. Wayne, meanwhile, does nothing to reassure Sarah and adopts the indifferent stance typical of the 'master' position:

Sarah: I've got no commitment from him, whereas I used to have. I don't know from one day to the next what his mood is going to be like. . . . He can't decide if he wants to stay with me or not. When I ask him, he just says 'Oh I don't know. I'm not sure. I'll think about it.' He will never give me a 'yes' or 'no' answer, *ever* . . . he's never had to decide before. In previous relationships his girlfriends have always left him, *always*, and he says it is because . . . he doesn't know if – if he'd change his mind or not if he decided to go. So he doesn't decide.

It is clear that these dynamics allow Wayne to exploit Sarah; while he 'can't decide' whether or not he wants to stay with her, Sarah described how she put great efforts into her appearance so that she 'looks good' all the time, does all the domestic work and maintains their 'relationship' single-handedly, all in the hope that Wayne might eventually 'commit himself'. However, although Sarah 'loves' Wayne, her 'commitment' to the relationship does not appear due either to any particular appreciation of him as an individual, nor even to any positive benefit which the liaison currently affords her. On the contrary, Sarah readily admitted that the reason she stayed with Wayne was because she felt 'too insecure' to leave without first finding someone else to take his place.

In one sense, Sarah's miserable predicament may seem a very long way from her original feelings that she could 'do anything' because she was in love with Wayne (see Chapter 3). However, the one is a direct consequence of the other. To the extent that desire for existential security and potent selfhood is once 'realised' in relation to a particular person, the more liable the individual is to continue looking to that relationship for affirmation and security, even when this *undermines* their self-confidence, and reinforces painful contradictions in their lives. This 'security paradox' is visible elsewhere. For example, one thing that struck me when looking at some women's accounts was their similarity to what has been termed 'the battered woman syndrome' (Walker 1988; Barnett and LaViolette 1993). A crucial feature of the battered woman syndrome is that the one thing women perceive they can do to save themselves, that is, leave the man, becomes increasingly frightening because, as their sense of self collapses, they experience themselves as increasingly dependent upon the recognition of their abuser. Particularly destructive relationships are often pathologised and set apart from 'normal' or 'healthy' love, but this similarity suggests that the underlying relational processes may be no different. Depending on the individuality of the partners, the 'chemistry' of their inter-action and the extent of their existential investment in love, the counter-revolution will have more or less destructive outcomes and the 'security paradox' will be more or less crucial.

Certainly in this study, the 'security paradox' was not only visible in the sto-ries of women who, like Sarah, were particularly unhappy; it could also be identified where women believed themselves to have been relatively 'lucky in love'. Here too, the 'emotional security' which women experienced in their relationships appeared to have a strikingly contradictory quality. To illustrate this, I will look at the case of Jenny, who at the time of the interviews was experiencing considerable ambivalence concerning her eighteen-year marriage to Peter. On the one hand, Jenny felt dissatisfied and unhappy and said that she had contemplated ending the marriage; on the other, she felt the relation-ship had been relatively successful, saw herself as fortunate, and feared that leaving Peter would turn out to be a dreadful mistake. Central to Jenny's dilemma was the 'security' the relationship gave her:

Jenny: It certainly gave me a lot of emotional stability . . . in a sense it's nur-tured me, and made me a lot more stable, stable enough to be able to cope with the outside world. . . . It's given me a lot of confidence to go out there and try things . . . Peter is such a secure base. . . . It seems *ridiculous* to give it up – erm – when – you know – that's what every-body wants really, isn't it – you know? Maybe I'm just being stupid by – you know – almost trying to throw it all away . . . I mean I'm very, very lucky. . . . He gives me all the freedom I ever need – you know? Why do I want to leave it? Why do I want to throw that away?

While Jenny sees herself as 'very, very lucky', however, her account of her relationship with Peter reveals familiar patterns. Peter, she says, is a 'closed book' emotionally and there is no intimacy in the relationship. Relations are polite and harmonious and there is no open conflict, but Jenny complains that Peter does not see her 'as a person' and feels threatened by her having a point of view. How can this contradiction be explained? How can Jenny believe that her marriage has 'nurtured' her and given her confidence, when she does not even feel able to express her own point of view within it?

Further analysis of Jenny's account finds this contradiction paralleled by a second. Jenny says that she has always believed that she could not manage on her own and expresses a great lack of confidence in her abilities. Yet these feel-ings contrast with the fact that she has actually achieved much during her marriage to Peter, including bringing up children, doing a university degree, undertaking a professional training and holding down several responsible paid jobs. Indeed Jenny appears as a successful and talented woman. However, she does not represent herself as an autonomous individual and plays down her own agency, while attributing her achievements to her relationship and assuming that she would not have been successful were she not married to Peter. So, while Jenny feels constrained in her marriage and expresses a powerful desire to see if she can cope without it, she is at once fearful of taking the step because it feels to her that this would mean giving up the 'security' which has enabled her to get this far in life:

Jenny: In a sense it's proving to *me* that I could survive on my own . . . I'm very conscious that – you know – I'm throwing, or trying to throw away, erm, a very, very solid rock really, and it's very scary. But somehow I've got this drive in me that wants to do that . . . I have this awful feeling in me that if, erm – you know – I was on my own, as hard as it would be, this sounds awful, but I almost feel that I would *fly*, that I would *thrive*, that I would do, really – you know? I have this feeling in me. I don't want to recognise that, at the same time.

Wendy: Why not?

Jenny: Because it's even more damaging to the relationship, isn't it? . . . I would fly, *soar* in a way, and that's – and I struggle with that because I feel I shouldn't feel that, erm – you know? Erm, Peter, I think would find it very difficult.

It appears here, then, that the security which Jenny values so much has been bought at the price of her denying her independent subjectivity. Indeed this denial seems to be the very reason *why* Jenny feels so 'secure' in her relationship. Exhibiting a typically 'feminine' fear of her own individual potential, Jenny bases her life on the illusion that she would simply collapse without the 'solid rock' of the marriage to support her and struggles to repress her 'awful' feeling that she would '*fly*' and '*soar*' and '*thrive*' if she left Peter.

The illusion that a sense of emotional security can be preserved through giving up autonomy and subjectivity thus seemed to produce a kind of psychological imprisonment in women. Through 'giving themselves up' for love, women came to feel too insecure to leave relationships which were incompatible with their desire to 'be themselves'. In the following quote, another woman, Jane, looks back on the many years she spent in this position:

Jane: I *really don't know why* I stuck it so long . . . I have spoken to a few other people who have been in the same position, and it is just this – this feeling of the unknown. It is as if you are standing next to a big, high wall and you are dying to have a look on the other side, and you are thinking well, there has got to be better than this. But just that fear of actually making the plunge and doing something about it, or realising that . . . you *can* do something about – you *can* change the events – you know? You can change your life to suit you, and live it the way *you* want.

Women's entrapment within the security paradox thus manifests as the antithesis of 'true love'. While romantic transformation lifts the heroine 'above' her struggles with autonomy and self-confidence, the counter-revolution consigns her to a circumscribed life determined by the fear of displeasing others. Love was supposed to set her free but now her only hope is to break out of the confines of love itself and see what lies 'on the other side'. Immobilised by her fear of freedom, Jane herself remains 'eternally grateful' to an older woman at her workplace who, recognising that Jane was in dire straits, insisted on taking her home one lunchtime to collect her personal belongings and having her to stay at her house. Jane never returned to her marriage.

Breaking the spell

There can be no better illustration of the paradoxical nature of the 'security' of love than some women's accounts of what actually did happen when relationships ended. Sharon, for example, spent many years in a marriage where the master–slave dialectic had long since brought her and her husband to a miserable life of mutual alienation. She reflects here on what it was like:

Sharon: I was just so ill and depressed because of everything that happened that your perspective goes completely. . . . I think now looking back – you read about these people that get kidnapped and fall in love with the people that have kidnapped them – you know? And it's sick isn't it? Well it's like that, marriage, in a bad marriage, like that. It's *sick*, and it's a form of sickness, and there's no hope for anybody in that situation. There's only one hope and that's to get out of it. And you know, sometimes you don't have the strength of character.

Sharon did not leave John because she believed that she would be unable to cope without him. However, when John finally left her, Sharon's terror of being abandoned proved completely unfounded. Instead of causing her to 'fall apart' as she had feared, John's exit produced the opposite effect:

Sharon: I started to recover from the minute he went. What actually happened was he left me . . . and more or less from the day he went, I was *forced* to take responsibility for myself completely, naturally, and I became – I began to recover and become healthy and normal and happy and have a laugh. . . . So it was like an overnight sensation, you know?

Through being 'forced' to take responsibility for herself, Sharon was thus freed from her compulsion to continually surrender her sense of self in order to 'save' the relationship which she believed she could not do without. Even though Sharon's 'destruction' through the master–slave dynamic had left her without the 'strength of character' to make this choice for herself, her release from 'security' nevertheless allowed her to experience her denied autonomy and gave her at least the *possibility* of gaining a sense of control over her own life.

Some women did find the strength to 'break the spell' of the security paradox themselves. Their accounts are particularly interesting because they reveal that, just as Sharon's capacity for autonomy suddenly returned when her husband left her, so the act of a woman threatening to leave her partner appeared to have a corresponding effect upon him. This took the form of a sudden and dramatic return of his capacity for emotional openness and recognition of her feelings. This occurred, for example, when Ruth decided to end her marriage to Colin. In this extract, Ruth describes Colin's response when, after several years of feeling uncared for, she finally told him that she had 'had enough' of his coldness and indifference towards her:

Ruth: He was totally, totally unsupportive, until the day when I said 'I'm leaving you', and then he just switched overnight. Overnight he was entirely different . . .

Wendy: . . . how did he change?

Ruth: Well he seemed to go into *shock*. And then he was saying 'Oh no look really I *don't* want this' and 'I'm so sorry'. . . . Erm and 'Oh I couldn't bear it if you left me. I love you. I do *really* love you. I've just been so stupid.'

Ruth's threat to end the relationship, and the sudden reversal of Colin's emotional withdrawal, dramatically restored the intimacy of their early relationship and Ruth agreed to give the relationship another chance. The change, however, was very temporary and soon they were back in the same old dynamic. Just before Ruth finally left Colin, she remembers a second occasion on which he 'reappeared' from behind his defences:

Ruth: I came back from work this evening and he was *crying his heart out*. . . . And what had happened was, he'd been going through my things . . . I'd written this poem about how I felt about him, about his *hardness* – you know – and my inability to get through to him. And he'd read this and he was saying 'I had no idea you felt like this. . . . Won't you give me another chance? Isn't there another chance?'. . . I can remember sitting on the edge of the bed thinking what the fuck are you talking about, you had no idea I felt like this. I've been *telling* you this for *two years* – you know? And I *had*, you know? . . . I can remember saying to my counsellor – you know – 'What the hell's he *talking* about' – you know? 'He had no idea. How could he not have any idea?'

Two particular features of Ruth's story are echoed in other accounts of 'scenes' where women had threatened to leave their partners. Not only was it then, and only then, that the man would let down his otherwise impenetrable facade, but he would sometimes appear quite genuinely to believe that his partner had been happy and even that the relationship had been relatively successful. Like Ruth, women themselves expressed complete astonishment at this. However, it is perhaps not so surprising once it is seen that the whole point of men's withdrawal is to 'block out' women's dissatisfaction, avoid their 'demands', and thus maintain their own romantic illusions.

Women's threats to leave 'emotionally absent' partners did not only result in the sudden revelation of men's hidden and denied vulnerabilities; they also highlighted women's own hidden and denied autonomy. In the following extract, for example, Mary recounts how she told Patrick that she had 'had enough' and was going to leave him. Mary's account is striking in its revelation of the mixture of excitement and fear experienced by a woman confronting the myth of her own 'lack':

Mary: He was almost pleading not – for me not to leave him, and he would do anything to keep me. It was the most – it was frightening because I had so much power there in my hands, and I knew that I could do anything. At that moment I could have done *anything* I wanted. . . . It was like *anything I wanted I could have*, anything I want you to do I can have. I can destroy you at this moment if I want to. I can crush you and humiliate you, and – you know – well, destroy you as a person if I want to at this moment. That was – that was quite frightening. It was very – it was *very heady* because suddenly you think . . . this is – you know – *this is the sort of power I have always wanted* . . . I could describe it as a palpable presence, and we both knew it, we both *knew* it.

Sarah, too, has found that her own feelings of powerlessness, as well as Wayne's indifferent attitude towards her, have all suddenly evaporated when she has threatened to leave him:

Sarah: I feel the only way I will ever get him to give me any kind of respect is to dump him, because when I have done it . . . then he's been a different person, and he'll do anything for me . . . he panics when he thinks he is going to lose me, and then I know I am in control. It's like I can feel myself taking over.

Feelings like '*this is the sort of power I have always wanted*' and '*It's like I can feel myself taking over*' are highly significant; they represent the 'slave's' realisation that her subjectivity is not, after all, entirely dependent upon the recognition of the 'master'. This revelation in turn makes possible, and is made possible by, the revelation of the 'master's' vulnerability and his 'admission' that he is not indifferent to the 'slave' at all, but every bit as dependent upon her recognition as she is upon his.

Facing up to the possible ending of a love relationship and thereby redefining it as *in*secure could thus release the 'master' and the 'slave' from the deadening grip of the security paradox. The relative fixity of their polarised masculine and feminine identities might be disrupted once again, reintroducing the tension between self and other which intimacy demands. The man might reassert his love for, and admiration of, the woman and she might regain some of her lost confidence. Both might experience renewed hope that the relationship is 'worth it' after all. Cruelly, however, under the weight of all that the counter-revolution had brought to pass, this intimacy was but a brief echo of 'true love'. Further attempts to 'make it last' led quickly to the reassertion of old and familiar patterns and returned the couple to the 'security' of their mutual alienation. Given this contradiction between intimacy and stability, it is not surprising that a repeated playing out of the drama of 'ending the relationship' was a feature of some relationships. Sarah, for example, had 'ended' her relationship with Wayne several times. However, the fact that the relationship still continued meant that Sarah's threats were losing their efficacy. Thus she was facing the ultimate paradox of love: the only way in which her relationship with Wayne could 'work out' was to end it altogether.

The security paradox represents the failure of love to heal the contradictions within individual identity. While these contradictions may be unique to the individual, the analysis of prevailing gendered 'love cycles' has highlighted two aspects of this failure: the failure of love to reconcile masculinity with recognition of the other, and to reconcile femininity with assertion of the self. We began the story with the heroine's attempt to 'find herself' through romantic transformation, and we have followed the subsequent process of her 'losing herself' to the point where, in order to 'find herself' again, she must separate from the 'cause' of her liberation. Indeed, quite paradoxically, the heroine may come to find that she was more herself before she tried to find herself. Hannah, for example, has had four attempts at 'lasting love', and gives this ambivalent reflection on her experience as a whole:

Hannah: It's losing sight of who I actually am. . . . All my relationships have had *some* positive aspects where I've kind of gleaned other ideas and other ways of being, but only in the sense that I've almost scrubbed out the old me and immersed myself in this new person, and then had to find the old me again and integrate it with this new stuff. It's quite painful really. It's not an easy process, which is why it's probably always a relief to finish a relationship, because it means that I can then get back to me.

135

However, while it is a relief for Hannah to get back to the sense of self which she tends to 'scrub out' in relationships, her problems are not simply resolved by ending a love relationship. How, then, are they to be resolved? One possibility consistently presents itself; we saw in Chapter 2 how Hannah, now single, found it 'very problematic being on your own as a woman'. We saw her experiencing a 'gap' in her life which to her represented the relationship she did not have. And we saw how Hannah was 'yearning' for exclusive intimacy with someone who would see her as special. What should Hannah do? Should she risk another fall and another bumpy ride on the 'big wheel of love'?

Love and love's untwisting

Jessica Benjamin is an optimist. She does not underestimate the extent of domination and argues that the twisting of the bonds of love to produce a polarised opposition between a paternal subject and a maternal object is replicated throughout social and intellectual life, everywhere undermining any conscious commitment to equality and freedom. Nevertheless, the logic of paradox means that 'if breakdown is "built into" the psychic system, so is the possibility of renewing tension. If the denial of recognition does not become frozen into unmovable relationships, the play of power need not be hardened into domination' (Benjamin 1990: 223). Personal and social transformation can arise from the understanding that 'breakdown and renewal are constant possibilities: the crucial issue is finding the point at which breakdown occurs and the point at which it is possible to recreate tension and restore the condition of recognition' (ibid.). Benjamin's conclusion begs a very crucial question indeed: What conditions are most favourable to 'renewal', 'restoration' and to the realisation of 'untwisted' human relationships? A full and systematic answer to this question is well beyond the scope of this study, but an important contribution can be made by posing a more specific question: To what extent might it be possible for the master–slave dialectic to be arrested and reversed within relationships which come into being through falling in love, and which retain the resulting emotional bond as their foundation and *raison d'être*? Can love itself, that is, make any positive contribution to the conditions required for its own 'untwisting'? Benjamin herself suggests that strong emotional attachments are no necessary impediment to equality; we should aim, she argues, 'not to undo our ties to others but rather to disentangle them; to make of them not shackles but circuits of recognition' (ibid.: 221). However, having seen how readily and how generally dynamics of power and control became established in women's relationships, and having seen the destructive intensification of some dialectics of love, the possibility of acting directly to 'disentangle' very powerful emotional attachments appears ambitious. What would it require?

The construction and maintenance of 'circuits of recognition' would require that we gain an ever greater awareness of the subtleties of relationships, so that we could increasingly act out of appreciation of the other as a subject, inde-

136

pendent of any fantasy we may have about them. We would need to become more aware of how we do violence to others by greeting their openness with indifference or by asserting our ego in ways which serve to undermine and discredit their point of view. We would need to become sensitive to how we do violence to ourselves by failing to be responsible for our own point of view while projecting the possibility of our self-determination on to others. We would need to become conscious of how we employ either or both of these strategies out of a desire to control the independent existence of those upon whom our own existence is felt to depend. This would in turn require us to struggle against our 'natural' inclinations. To the extent that we habitually employ 'feminine' or submissive tendencies, we would need to overcome anxieties concerning autonomy and agency and learn that to become and remain 'alive' we must 'take up space', instead of seeking control through 'shrinking away'. To the extent that we habitually employ 'masculine' or domineering tendencies, we would need to overcome anxieties concerning the relational 'demands' of others and learn that we can only become and remain 'alive' through 'coming up against' the other, something that becomes impossible when the other is repeatedly 'destroyed'. And all of this in turn requires that we become aware of deeply ingrained proclivities of which we may yet be hardly conscious.

Even on the basis of this brief consideration, it would be hard to imagine worse conditions for the realisation of love's untwisting than those brought into being by falling in love, for love at once blinds us to all that needs to change. No longer need we grapple with the contradictions in our experience; love 'heals' them all, replacing discord with harmony, deadness with vitality, self-doubt with confidence and dissatisfaction with joy. No more need we struggle with gendered fears and insecurities; love 'transforms' us into 'women who can do anything' – no longer limited by the fear of our own potential, and 'men who are not men' – tender, compassionate and no longer trapped by an alienating fear of recognising the other. No more need we envision a compassionate society; love 'overthrows' a social order characterised by hierarchies of power and replaces them with mutuality and collectivity. No longer need we strive to realise our deepest yearnings for a meaningful life; through love we are transported into a 'transcendent' dimension. In short, since love appears supremely and uniquely beneficial, there may be no state in which the creation of humane and equal relationships appears a less pressing concern; for those in love, this great task is always already achieved.

Once all desire for existential security, all craving for emotional satisfaction and all aspiration for a better world has been 'realised', love has but one aim: the maintenance of, and the returning to, a state of being which is not and never was. Lovers strive to maintain and recapture the blissful intimacy that came into being when romantic transformation 'created' a paradox of self and other. In fact, neither lover came to terms with the threat posed by the 'other' at all. On the contrary, each merely engaged in the fantastical overcoming of this threat through the illusion that the other already was that which they most desired them to be: a source of unconditional recognition of the self. Lovers long to retain and recapture the confidence, coherence and well-being they experienced when romantic transformation lifted them out of the confines of a limited, discordant and gendered selfhood. In fact, they never really gained that splendid state at all; repressed and undeveloped aspects never were developed and integrated, but split off, projected on to the other, and 'actualised' through the illusory integration that is the 'bond' of love. Lovers yearn for the world of kindness, trust and mutual appreciation which romantic transformation once revealed. In fact they never developed those capacities any further than they could exercise them already, but simply experienced the idealisation and self-satisfaction that results from the belief that what is most desired has come into one's possession.

It might be argued that love's illusoriness is not, in itself, the problem so much as the particular forms these illusions take. Benjamin herself appears to take this view; while the drama of master and slave begins when individuals seek reparation in adult attachments, this latter compulsion is portrayed as a problem only in so far as individuals have a 'lopsided' predisposition. The implication is that if individuals were subject to the 'right kind of illusions', illusions which predisposed them equally to assert themselves and recognise the other, they would still make emotional attachments, but these would not become mutilated by the will to domination. However, is it not precisely the desire for attachment in itself, realised *par excellence* through falling in love, that inclines even the more 'well-balanced' individual towards tactics of control and manipulation? After all, through love, everything is magically transformed; by attaching ourselves to an object in the world we 'transcend' our existential predicament, whatever we believe, consciously or unconsciously, that predicament to be. And regardless of its particularities, one thing is true of each and every love: whatever wound that love has 'healed' we do not want exposed, and whatever we 'gain' from falling in love we do not want to 'lose'. It is the desire to prevent this pain and loss which impels us to act upon the object which the ego has taken for its own 'completion'. It is true that this controlling action may be direct or indirect, depending upon which 'habit' the subject manifests. The point is, however, that neither the habit of master nor the habit of slave would develop, or be enacted or reinforced, were there no illusion and no 'intention' to persist in this state of mind.

The self-conscious maintenance of self–other paradox may be a logical possibility, but the whole point is that power is largely exercised as a result of our *unconscious* motivations. The 'point of breakdown' in love is *theoretically* recognisable; it is the point at which, at some level of (un)consciousness, the subject recognises a disjuncture between their fantasy of resolution and the behaviour of the love object. However, how can this crucial moment be recognised in experience when our most powerful desires are at play? There may be evidence if we are receptive to it – subtle stirrings of doubt and anxiety may be telling us that our new 'refuge' is not what it appears. But who, believing themselves to be in the most splendid, fortunate and intensely pleasurable state known to humankind, is able to 'wake up' at this point, consider the possibility that they are merely dreaming the same old dream, and act against their own desire? More likely by far is that, having once allowed ourselves to 'fall', we will simply act upon our emotions as habit dictates, producing a counter-revolution which will be well advanced before we admit to ourselves that there is anything 'wrong', if indeed we do at all. Moreover, in so far as we resist disillusionment, and therefore 'still feel the same way', any problem appears to lie only with the object of our desire, whose behaviour is increasingly at odds with what it 'ought' to be. We have seen in this study, for example, how women experienced the cause of love's demise as their partner's emotional withdrawal and could not understand why he was behaving like this when he *said* that he loved them. Meanwhile, male partners appeared equally mystified; if women really did love them, why were they being so 'needy' and 'demanding'? Without answers to these questions the lovers' frustrations merely grow and, by their own most determined efforts, they destroy that which they are trying to save.

Summary and conclusion

Having seen that for the women in this study, falling in love provided no basis for the practice of equal or 'democratic' love, and having further concluded that such an outcome appears an unlikely one, the crucial question under consideration in this chapter has been the very *possibility* of realising the new, egalitarian, romantic ideal. Could love's counter-revolution be modified so that we could still fall blissfully in love, but not become trapped by destructive and alienating emotional dynamics? Could we instead live happily, intimately and equally ever after?

The hope of lasting love hinges upon the possibility of identifying and eliminating the power aspect of love, so that lovers no longer destroy their own love through control and manipulation. Jessica Benjamin's analysis implies this possibility; domination inheres in adult attachments, she argues, but is not essential to them. It results from the twisting of the child's early bonds with its parent figures, whereby it fails to develop the ability to maintain the paradox of self and other which is necessary for equal and intimate relations. There are two forms of twisting: feminine conditioning produces anxiety concerning assertion and a tendency to seek control through self-denial, while masculine conditioning produces anxiety concerning recognition of the other and a tendency to seek control through over-asserting the self. 'Lopsided' individuals are alienated and lacking in vitality, and attraction to their 'opposite' arises from their desire to create the paradoxical tension which those individuals lack within themselves. The attempt fails however, for their habitual tendencies mean they simply reproduce polarisation and domination.

139

Having seen how romantic transformation facilitates the 'transcendence' of gendered identities, and how the counter-revolution involves their re-becoming, the consideration of love as a dialectic has helped us to further understand why this re-becoming can take such destructive forms. We have seen how women's self-silencing and self-objectification exemplify the position of the 'slave' who 'gives herself up' in the pursuit of her 'master's' recognition. We have seen how, as their mounting frustration was channelled into this strategy, some women suffered severe and debilitating psychic distress. Of the greatest significance was the fact that, in spite of all their suffering, their part-ner 'didn't even notice'. We have seen how men's silent control and 'blocking out' of their partner's subjectivity typify the position of the 'master' who increasingly 'locks himself away' in his attempt to control his 'slave's' decreas-ing capacity to recognise him. Some men resorted to physical and sexual as well as emotional violence. We have further seen how the dynamic between master and slave can lead to entrapment within a 'security paradox'; as women lost their confidence they further repressed the desire for freedom for fear that they could not 'cope', and looked for their 'security' to the very relationship that was undermining them.

Having seen the suffering that 'breakdown' can bring, there can be few more worthy aims than to slow down, to mitigate, and eventually stop the dialectic of love. Success is a logical possibility; if we can identify the point at which breakdown occurs and work against our 'natural' tendencies, we may learn to create and maintain 'circuits of recognition'. This task is immense, however; it requires a well-developed ability to recognise and promote the independent subjectivity of the other and an acute awareness of tendencies within the self to draw back from that recognition and promotion. Falling in love could not be less conducive to this aim; it involves entering into a particularly deluded state of mind, wherein the other appears as the object of a most grandiose self-seeking fantasy. The attempt to remain in love involves the further attempt to remain deluded; evidence in contradiction to the individual's preferred fantasy is denied, while a systematic effort is made to manipulate the other into con-formance. The love object's 'non-compliance' leads to the arising of hostile impulses which, once channelled through even the most slightly 'lopsided' tendencies, reproduce polarisation and fuel the dialectic of love. Domination in romantic love relationships is not an aberrant tendency; love of this kind is not something essentially innocent that can be rescued, otherwise intact, from the corrupting influence of the patriarchal society which it helps to reproduce and maintain. Rather, the attempt to control the other inheres in the bond of love itself and the attempt to base their lives upon it impels some individuals to lit-erally 'love each other to destruction'.

7

MISGUIDED REVOLUTIONS

Prevailing theories about love, like the contemporary romantic ideal itself, are deeply contradictory. Love is held to be powerful, anarchic and essentially mysterious, yet at once tameable and readily amenable to the principles of social democracy. Modern 'individuals' have supposedly won the freedom to act upon passions beyond their ken, while at once being dispassionate enough to make their love a contract and negotiate the intimacy and emotional satisfaction they crave. Evidence from previous studies suggests that in practice, this contradiction is hard to contain; researchers find distant men, dissatisfied women and couples who have stayed together anyway, despite their inability to get beyond a state of mutual bafflement. Meanwhile, the contradictions of love seem only to be intensifying. Entry into intimate coupledom is advocated as a route to happiness and security, yet a growing army of therapists and lawyers live off the misery and insecurity that often follow. Love is portrayed as the one thing that can really satisfy us, yet love is everywhere characterised by dissatisfaction. Love may even seem to represent the promise of ultimate salvation, yet its 'realisation' merely returns us to the mundane. Perhaps what is most remarkable is that while love appears as both supremely important *and* as remarkably difficult and unsatisfactory, we remain strangely reluctant to penetrate love's mystery, to subject love itself to systematic enquiry, to ask ourselves what *is* love, anyway?

One striking exception to this persisting romanticism is the radical feminist analysis. Focusing particularly on the power aspect of love, feminists highlighted the cruelty and violence which flourish unseen within the 'private sphere', often denied by women themselves who – once having fallen in love – live their lives in the grip of a particularly deluded state of mind. The initial critique was cutting and insightful; it aimed at the roots of domination and cited love as the emotional underpinning of an exploitative patriarchal society. However, the critique has been poorly sustained and the analysis has remained largely undeveloped. *Revolutions of the Heart* has aimed to advance and deepen understanding of the relationship between love and power, a task given further import by contemporary claims that love is in the process of shaking off the last vestiges of tyranny. The new romantic ideal is a 'democratic' ideal, but what does this really represent and how far can it be realised? Democratisation may well mean that attachment love is no longer subject to the mores of a formal and overtly hierarchical society, but does the freedom to love really mean that we are more free, more compassionate, more humane and more equal? Or is this a myth which we choose to believe while we fail to notice how the forces of domination have us by the heart? Does the new romantic ideal represent our liberation, or hide the very means by which we subject ourselves and each other to a most insidious form of governance? *Revolutions of the Heart* has sought to answer these crucial questions through the construction of a provisional 'anatomy of love' which embraces, contains and begins to account for some of its confusions and contradictions. While the account is theoretical, it has sought to avoid abstraction through grounding analysis in the accounts of a group of ordinary women as they tell of how they fell in love and tried to live happily, intimately and equally ever after.

After setting the scene in Chapter 1, the story began with a consideration of how love represents a desire for transformation which arises upon prior conditions: the subject's experience of existence as unsatisfactory and contradictory. Within women's accounts this had a particular visibility in the form of 'single dissatisfactions'; women had a deep conviction that the experience of life as lonely and meaningless, as well as particular fears concerning autonomy, self-value and personal adequacy, might be transcended through intimacy with someone to whom they would be 'special'. This conviction contradicted and undermined a more 'rational' belief that they 'did not need a man to be happy' and fuelled a propensity to fall in love. Having located a suitable 'hero', women attempted to realise their salvation by 'writing themselves into love', a process through which they gave order and coherence to events and emotional experiences by incorporating them into a particular 'script'. This narrativisation allows the prospective heroine a sense of control and helps to assuage the 'risk anxiety' invoked by her making herself vulnerable to the hero's potentially transforming gaze. Ultimately, however, the project of love requires that control be relinquished; the individual must, at some level of experience, 'let go'. We saw that if the risk pays off, the subject is 'lifted out of herself' and transformed. She becomes the heroine in her own romance and looks to a future of happy companionship.

Leaving the heroine poised on the threshold of her new life, we considered some important questions concerning women's 'romantic transformations'. If they were illusory, why was their reality so cogent? If they simply represented the articulation of cultural narratives, what made them so deeply 'moving' at the emotional level? And if love was actually something mundane and unremarkable, what accounts for its compelling 'spiritual' dimension? With help from another researcher who, a century ago, also 'analysed' women's falling in love, we constructed and elaborated a theory which embraces love's contradictions. Romantic transformations may appear as narratives of quite exact cultural specificity, but their articulation is underpinned by other, older transformations, knowledge of which has been lost from consciousness. To the subject, the characters, the setting and the events of love are immediate and original, but at the emotional level love is something more: the reinvocation of an old drama which the subject projects on to the world in an attempt to achieve the happy ending that past (re)productions failed to deliver. Love may be traced back through many repetitions, but its intense and crucial emotions of fear, of anxiety, of excitement, of bliss are ultimately those of the tiny infant who, apprehending its own separate and imperfect existence in a constantly changing and frustrating world, attempts to escape from itself through identification with powerful – and in the child's fantasy, perfect – parent figures. Again and again, the developing child suffers the inevitable hurts and indignities of a kind of love which can never give it the satisfaction it desires, but, knowing no other way to defend itself from the painful knowledge it habitually represses, it attempts to love again, and again. . . .

Reflecting on romantic transformations as repetitions, we began to make sense of some of the 'symptoms' of love that women described. We saw, for example, how their attempts to 'find themselves' involved their 'losing themselves'. This loss of identity was not superficial but involved deep emotions and compelling perceptions of 'merging' with the hero, of 'spinning in time', of losing defences and inhibitions. The 'finding' was similarly underpinned by extreme emotions; the heroine did not only feel better – she felt like 'the most wonderful person on earth'. At the same time, the ugly frog was transformed into a handsome prince as though something had been 'released into [her] bloodstream'. All of this may be understood as representing the regression of the ego, the projection of the ideal self on to the object who represents the perfect parent, the idealisation of the perfect self/parent, and the bliss of thus 'realising' narcissistic perfection.

While these general processes may have a more or less universal manifestation, the repetitions of love are at the same time unique. Freud himself worked at the very particular level, seeking to identify specific early traumas which lay at the root of neurotic illnesses. Between the universal and the specific lies the possibility of identifying how particular patterns of conditioning might give rise to particular patterns of repetition, involving particular psychological processes and emotional experiences, especially in respect of gender difference. In women's accounts, love certainly appeared to have a strongly gendered manifestation. Women did not only feel wonderful when in love, but 'transcended' particular fears and insecurities concerning autonomy and self-efficacy. They found these qualities in themselves and felt they could now 'do anything' without the need for a man. Women's accounts also described men in love who were 'not men', who displayed an unusual capacity for tenderness and emotional openness. Part of love's realisation, it seems, is a 'breaking out' of the particular limits of gender identity and the expression of potentials contained within the ideal self, but repressed or undeveloped through masculine or feminine conditioning. As 'merging' reunites the individual with the possibility of their own completeness, feelings of intense well-being arise which draw their force from previous occasions when ego, object and ego ideal 'became' one.

The 'healing power' of love has made it a cause for celebration and even those writers who admit it to be a narcissistic illusion have nevertheless praised the apparent benefits which it brings. However, our undertaking was never merely concerned with the illusions of love, but rather with what happens when we act upon those illusions – when, having found 'true love', we attempt to 'live happily ever after'. Once it becomes the *raison d'être* of an actual relationship, the bond of love is deeply problematic. It is of a fragile, contradictory and unstable constitution, while invested with fantasies which are experienced as crucial and yet which are at once largely unconscious. Success requires each lover, having only just grasped a nascent identity and having given up their usual defences, to take on – unbeknown to themselves – the task of being their partner's perfect parent, of embodying the projection of their ideal self. Lasting love is an ambition indeed! In the bliss of mutual 'refinding' no problem is apparent, for mutual idealisation causes positive emotion to flow between the lovers. Little hurts and 'misunderstandings' will be laughed at – dismissed as 'lover's tiffs', for neither wants to see that the worm is already in the bud, nibbling away at love's heart.

Suspecting already, then, that love's tragedy was about to unfold, we stepped over the threshold with the heroine and watched as revolution gave way to counter-revolution, fuelled by the frustration and the disappointment which are the counterparts of love's blissful emotions. We witnessed three dramas which evolved as love's repetition caused defences to be re-erected, gender identity to be re-consolidated, power to be exercised and suffering to be inflicted. Firstly, we followed the story of 'everybody's Mummy'. We saw how, for women, the bliss of true love gave way to feelings of hurt and rejection as male partners appeared to lose interest and withdrew emotionally. 'Abandoned', women began to lose the feeling that they were special – loved for themselves. Attempting to talk to their partners about this loss did not usually help, since men appeared baffled and complained that women were 'demanding'. If challenged, the man might state that he still loved his partner, but this appeared to be in contradiction to his 'unloving' behaviour. As women lost the initial sense that the relationship was a shared project, they assumed responsibility for 'holding it all together' – a task which could become quite extensive. Some women experienced their situation as grossly unfair and men were frequently described as lazy, irresponsible, selfish and immature. Overall however, women had an ambivalent response to the development of the 'mother–son' dynamic in their relationships. On one level they were deeply hurt, disappointed and frustrated. On another, being 'everybody's Mummy' provided certain 'compensatory gratifications'; women could feel pride in their 'strength' and competence in comparison to their 'hopeless' and easily manipulable partners. And, even though in strictly limited and paradoxical ways, it afforded an exercise of control which appeared to be experienced as such by male partners whose distant and frustrating stance was combined with an apparent desire to be a 'good boy', to please 'Mummy', and to hide things which might get him into trouble.

To explain how true love might give rise to this particular drama, we (re)constructed the typically male heterosexual counter-revolution, the story of 'Mummy's Boy'. We saw how the relationship dynamic which women described may reflect deep male fears stemming from the boy's early relationship with his mother; distancing and domineering behaviour aims to defend the ego against a threat of engulfment. However, male behaviour in love does not simply reflect the outcome of gender development, but rather the process of its re-becoming. This process crucially begins through the attempt to cling on to love's illusion, an attempt which is motivated by the desire to keep repressed the disappointment, the suffering, the fear, the hostility and the self-doubt which disillusionment would reveal. In the male psyche, this desire manifests as the attempt to split off and control 'Bad Mummy' in all of her many-layered manifestations. In the beginning no problem is apparent, for the male's 'romantic transformation' occurs when he finds and falls in love with 'Good Mummy', a compound illusion representing many or even all of his previous experiences of 'salvation'. 'Good Mummy' is bounded and self-contained. She is 'complete' unto herself, not dependent upon him for her existence, and is delighted with him and satisfied by him. In short, she is a source of unconditional love and, through her appearance, all the hurts that 'Bad Mummy' ever caused are healed. The hero's outworn defences are cast aside, and he is restored to narcissistic perfection. We know that the heroine of the story has an agenda of her own, an agenda that causes her to display disappointment and dissatisfaction. For the hero, however, this does not indicate the appearance of another human being with desires of her own, but the appearance of 'Bad Mummy', a woman of the most evil intent. Huge and engulfing, unpredictable and uncontrollable, 'Bad Mummy' tricks him and teases him, chastises him and belittles him, and makes demands which he cannot satisfy. Then, to add insult to injury, it turns out that she is inadequate and never could have satisfied him anyway! No wonder, when 'Bad Mummy' starts to appear, the hero attempts to keep her at bay. No wonder he hides his fears and vulnerabilities, feigns disinterest and independence, and wants to show he can dominate her. Little does he realise, however, that all his efforts merely cause 'Bad Mummy' to 'materialise' before his very eyes, *as though he had conjured her up himself!*

Being subject to this male hysteria was no joke for women. We saw how, as the sensitive boy became hidden by the process of 'paternalisation', men came to exercise forms of control which had actual and demoralising effects upon their female partners. As men lapsed into silence and hid their vulnerabilities, women became increasingly anxious and uncertain. They felt alienated and tried to close the gap by developing an exaggerated sensitivity to their partner's emotional state in the effort to 'work him out', and by trying to persuade him to 'have a talk' about what was wrong. Their efforts were rebuffed, however, for silence was only the first line of defence. It was backed up by a strategy of evasion whereby men blocked women's attempts to 'get through' by finding jobs to do, falling asleep or pretending not to hear what their partners had said. They appeared outwardly unruffled while women grew more frustrated. If women insisted on forcing their way through their partner's 'stonewalling', a third line of defence was manifest; men would insist on communication being calm and 'rational' and if their partners showed emotional upset or expressed a point of view they did not understand, they might not only appear mystified but accuse her of being 'irrational', apparently unable to recognise a perspective that was different from their own. As communication became more difficult and undermining, women would often give up trying for much of the time, enabling the couple to live a 'harmonious' life belied by a 'festering atmosphere'. Some men became bad-tempered and unfriendly for much of the time, and some women became fearful of resisting, aware that if they 'pushed too far', a fourth line of defence was a possibility – the use of physical violence, something to which some women had indeed been subjected.

Since the exercise of 'paternal' power was so frustrating, dispiriting and often frightening for women, it was unclear why their resistance was not stronger, at least in the beginning. And when things did become extreme, why did they not simply end the relationship altogether? What actually emerged was that while women could see the destructiveness of love in other people's relationships and in their own past relationships, a certain 'blindness' prevailed in respect of current relationships. Partners were portrayed as 'hopeless' rather than powerful, while women were more aware of their own 'maternal' power. The 'compensations' afforded by 'maternalisation' were not, however, a sufficient explanation for the re-becoming of feminine conditioning. To develop our understanding, we needed to 'unearth' women's own love story, to look beneath the more conscious drama of 'everybody's Mummy' and identify women's own investments in love. What was the illusion that women did not want to relinquish? This illusion kept women trying to 'make it work' and allowed them to conceal from themselves that which they did not want to see.

This second, more 'repressed' story emerged as the drama of the 'daughter's submission'. Just as the 'son' has two mothers, the 'daughter' has two fathers. The father who is the 'cause' of her romantic transformation, and who represents the compound illusion of many or all of her previous experiences of 'salvation', is the father who affirms his daughter, recognises her true worth, welcomes her identification with him, and shows a sensitivity and vulnerability which demonstrates that he is like her. With this father, women felt confident and special: they were loved 'for themselves'. We may know that this 'father' has an agenda of his own and that his 'recogniton' and his openness are contingent. For the 'daughter', however, whose love is aimed only at herself, the merest sign of his wavering is enough to trigger anxiety that another 'father' is about to appear. This father is indifferent to his daughter and does not recognise her worth. He rejects her attempts to identify with him and denies the sensitivity and vulnerability which show that he is like her. With the 'appearance' of this father, the daughter begins to lose her confidence and the sense that she is loved 'for herself'. Projecting her disappointment on to her partner, and acting upon the apprehension that she is somehow 'unacceptable' to him, she tries to 'win back' the affirming father by silencing and objectifying herself, putting up with his silent aggression and gradually assuming her 'maternal' responsibilities. The tragedy of the daughter's submission is that, as she buries the pain of her 'rejection' and turns her hostility inwards upon herself, she is unaware that her actions merely create the ideal conditions for the rejecting father to materialise, *as though she had conjured him up herself!*

Through the dramas of 'everybody's Mummy' and the 'daughter's submission', we thus came to see how each lover's illusion of having found 'true love', combined with their most determined efforts to 'make it work', helps to create the very conditions in which love's failures are most readily reproduced. Acting habitually upon the basis of unconscious fantasies, the lovers reconstruct their ego defences, reconstitute their gender identities and reproduce dynamics of domination and submission. Meanwhile, evidence of the supposed arrival of 'democratic' love was strikingly absent from women's accounts which rather suggested that few conditions would be less favourable to its birth than those brought into being by romantic transformations. This gave rise to a crucial question indeed: is it *possible* for romantic love, in and of itself, to become a 'democratic' phenomenon? Given that this kind of love is driven by a compulsion to repeat, could love's repetitions be modified? Could we become more aware of love's dangerous deceptions, identify and eradicate the 'power aspect' of love, and in so doing render the 'love cycle' innocuous?

We explored this possibility with the help of Jessica Benjamin, whose psychoanalytic work on 'the problem of domination' implies a way forward. The exercise of power is seen to arise from an essential situation in which human self-consciousness, of being unable to embrace the paradox of self and other, attempts to resolve it through enslaving the subjectivity of the other upon whose recognition its own subjective existence is felt to depend. There are two possible methods for attempting to secure the self: domination and submission. Both are available to each individual but the nature of conditioning inclines us to manifest one or the other, depending upon the particular circumstances we are in. 'Master' and 'slave' inclinations have a correspondence to gender, and in a sense the heterosexual relationship provides conditions for the archetypal power struggle. Women's accounts of love showed a striking correspondence to the drama of master and slave, allowing us to reflect upon the counter-revolution in a third way, as a 'dialectic of love'. The starting point for the master–slave dialectic is the point at which the paradox of self and other has been re-established, something we find ways of doing in order to escape from the alienation and loss of vitality which 'breakdown' brings. Romantic transformation is a most dramatic instance of re-creation, allowing lovers to 'transcend' the loneliness and meaninglessness of an alienated existence. In so doing, however, they enter upon a crucial existential situation whereby, fatefully, their very 'existence' is felt to depend upon the recognition of the other. Unable to bear the sense of jeopardy this implies, the lovers soon lapse into habitual attempts to control the other, and the dialectic of love commences. The more recognition is sought through recourse to power, the less it can be experienced as 'recognition' at all and the less the subject feels recognised, the more desperately they seek to impose control upon the other. Each advance merely fuels love's destructive repetitions.

Women's self-silencing and self-objectification exemplify the position of the 'slave' who attempts to secure recognition through self-denial, forcing the other to first recognise her subjectivity before she is 'able' to return it. As the 'master' becomes more reluctant or less able to recognise the slave, the slave's self-denial intensifies, fuelled by a more desperate effort to regain the recognition she has lost. We saw how, as women's frustration was turned inwards upon themselves, many experienced symptoms of psychological or emotional distress, even 'breakdowns', which they attributed to their relationships. The most distressing aspect of this was the fact that their partner 'couldn't even see it'. They wanted him to recognise their suffering, and thus to restore them to a state of well-being. The strategies of 'paternal' control which men appeared to utilise exemplify the domination of the 'master' position. The master tries to 'block out' the slave's subjectivity, forcing her to first recognise him before he is willing to recognise her. We saw how, as the counter-revolution advanced, men appeared more and more indifferent to the suffering of their partners and even attempted to get the recognition and gratification they desired through coercive means. We saw how in one case, the degree of physical violence which the man was prepared to use was so extreme as to threaten his partner's life, a graphic example of how the master–slave dialectic can literally become a 'struggle to the death for recognition'.

Once lovers are in the grip of an advanced and intensifying master–slave dialectic, their love for one another can become a most evil curse. Their craving for recognition and their clinging to illusion may manifest as a more or less thinly disguised hatred and a willingness to inflict or endure the most terrible suffering. This situation, in a more or less extreme form, can become a way of life. In women's accounts, the underside of love was visible in the form of a 'security paradox' – a kind of psychological imprisonment whereby, having once attributed their sense of security to a particular relationship, women felt extremely fearful of leaving it, however much it caused them suffering, limited their lives and undermined their sense of confidence in themselves. The illusion of security was often dramatically dispelled when relationships did end, or an end was contemplated. 'Breaking the spell' might produce a sudden and unexpected 'empowerment' of women characterised by the realisation that they could take responsibility for their own existence after all. It might also produce a sudden disruption of the 'master's' defences and the revelation that he was not indifferent after all. However, while ending a particular relationship allowed new possibilities, the disenchanted state was fertile ground for a new romantic transformation. . . .

By the end of our third drama, then, we had gained both an understanding of how love's repetitions are based upon particular illusions and of how the play of power is rooted in the existential situation which accompanies their 'realisation'. The crucial question is: Is power separable from love? Could the breakdown of love's paradox be prevented? Benjamin's theory suggests that paradox might be maintained through developing and applying knowledge of how girls learn to seek selfhood through the provisional adoption of a submissive femininity, and how boys learn to seek selfhood through aggression and dominance. We concluded, however, that while such theories have proved useful in understanding love, this understanding merely confirms that falling in love creates the most unlikely conditions for an end to domination. The ability to maintan paradox would require the development of a very great awareness of one's own tendencies to control and their origins. The whole point of love is that our actions are motivated by what we are *un*aware of. The ability to maintain paradox would require a great capacity to recognise and respect the independence of the other. Falling in love is aimed entirely at the self, at *overcoming* the threat posed by the other. The maintenance of paradox would require that we channel our energies into finding real resolutions for the contradictions and dissatisfactions of our lives. When we fall in love, everything is already resolved and our efforts are wasted in propping up this illusion through the attempt to control the love object. The maintenance of paradox requires that we respond to the difficulties and imperfections of the other with kind recognition. The illusion of love, based on the craving for satisfaction, predisposes us to hostility towards the other who cannot but frustrate us.

This conclusion has profound implications because it suggests that beliefs and assumptions about love which currently prevail in Western society are wrong. Firstly, love is widely assumed to be a path of individual freedom and self-development. It is not that we think love is easy; women in this study were probably no exception in their apprehension that the path of love was a difficult and painful one. However, our deep emotional investment in love compels us to try and 'make it work', to believe that 'it will be worth it in the end', and to see our strivings as a kind of heroic struggle. We are comforted by the wisdom that 'the path of true love never runs smoothly' and urged on by the belief that to tread this path is 'perhaps the most important of our cultivated freedoms . . . perhaps in our time the primary vehicle for self-realization, transformation and transcendence' (Person 1990: 353–354). Wanting to 'believe in love', we separate the fall from its consequences and fail to see how the blissful self-expansion of romantic transformation heralds the frustrated self-contraction of the ever after. Once we recognise the counter-revolution, we can see that love's path is a circuitous one. We may feel that love takes us 'somewhere we've never been', an observation reflected in many popular songs, but all it really affords is a tantalising glimpse of something 'transcendent' which impels us thenceforth to channel our desire into the backward-looking never achieving of it. Love in itself does not so much take us higher, as round in circles; it takes us nowhere that we have not been before and does not allow us to develop into anyone substantially different from who we were in the first place.

While love's path is circular, however, its overall effects are not neutral. Love does not merely fail to give us what we desire but in so doing compounds painful feelings of dissatisfaction and low self-esteem. After all, it was to solve the problem of our unsatisfactory existence that we fell in love in the first place, and underneath feelings of hostility and frustration with the love object lurks a lack of faith in our own potential. Love's painful failure and the problems it reveals have become the subject of a proliferation of professional advice, counselling and self-help literature. We could hardly fail to be aware that love does not bring lasting happiness. Strangely, however, we look to almost any explanation for this but the fact that we fell in love in the first place. Indeed, quite often the cure prescribed for love is more love – 'don't worry, you'll meet someone else'. While we blame ourselves, our partners, our parents, 'men', 'women' and society, we fail to see that love fails because love is bound to fail. Love may, temporarily, bring pleasure, excitement and feelings of great joy. Love will challenge us and provide us with many opportunities to learn. But *love in itself* cannot develop our potential, heal our wounds or set us free. It can, however, hold us hostage to oppressive forces, lock us ever more securely within the confines of a stunted selfhood, and twist our desire for freedom into a neurotic and destructive craving.

Our mistaken view of love finds expression in a second prevalent assumption: relationships which have attachment love as their *raison d'être* are necessarily the most important and valuable kind of human connection. We look to the love bond for the satisfaction of a wide range of needs and desires and, believing it to be the context in which we can be most 'ourselves', this relationship has become the primary focus for our expression of sociality. A trend towards an increasingly 'privatised' social life has long been observed by sociologists. At the centre of this trend is the prioritisation of attachment love, reflected in a proliferation of discourse concerning sexual love which at once assumes other kinds of adult relationship to be of subsidiary importance. Indeed the very term 'relationship' has itself come to be synonymous with sexual coupledom. The more we look to love, however, the more we may fail to notice that, paradoxically, love in itself may actually limit self-expression and inhibit the positive demonstration of sociality. This study has shown that while we may look to love because we want to be 'ourselves', love can cause both men and women to 'silence themselves', to hide from themselves and from each other what they feel and experience. We may look to love for someone who will care for us, but the hostility aroused by the counter-revolution may leave us feeling unloved or even harmed by the person who was 'supposed to' care for us. We may look to love for a sense of 'security' but the dynamics of love may make us feel insecure. And we may look to love as the mainstay of our social life, only to find that we feel lonely – distanced from the person to whom we are 'meant' to be closest.

All this is not simply an inevitable result of attachment love. It is rather that, failing to see the limitations of this kind of love, we endow it with a meaning and significance which is misguided and idealistic. Mistaking love as a source of everything we most desire, we attempt to build upon it an exclusive world where we will be safe and happy. This creates love as a crucial existential situation and – to the extent that the couple relationship is founded only upon the illusions of love – one which is most inclined towards 'breakdown', since there exists no basis for mutual recognition. In these 'hothouse conditions', love is bound to produce its worst effects and – to the extent that the couple is prioritised over the development of wider social ties – these effects will not be mitigated by recognition from elsewhere which might reassure each of their existence. With ever more hungry hearts, the couple feed off the poisonous fruits which their love produces in abundance and descend into the hell of mutual alienation. Once isolated from wider humanity, even if these individuals manage to 'break out' of the prison they have helped to build around themselves, they emerge into an apparent social wasteland where 'everyone else' is assumed to be happily coupled up. Salvation appears then to lie only in finding someone 'special' and retreating once again into the dangerous dependency of exclusive coupledom, along with any offspring they may have produced along the way. Appearing as the last refuge of those who long for kindness, companionship and meaningful human connection, love has become the most revered of relationships. In such circumstances, however, it will surely prove to be one of the most destructive.

Our failure to appreciate fully the dangers and limitations of love is reflected in a third erroneous assumption: a society founded upon an 'ethic of intimacy' is a just and humane society. According to this supposition, the practice of forming and dissolving relationships upon the basis of a self-referential quest for 'satisfaction' is not only compatible with the cause of egalitarianism, but actually advances it. This is not so. It is true that the tendency to form relationships through attraction and emotional attachment is a universal one, and that attachment love needs to have a positive place within any human society. But this does not mean that it is a good thing for such relationships, entered into for their own sake, to determine the course of our lives or be the foundation of our social being. This does not result in a society determined by equity and humanity at all, but one in which the individual is either subject to the insidious regulation of 'government by love' or cast aside like a piece of flotsam upon the whim of love's unruly passions. It is also clear, however, that no remedy is to be found in a reactive return to the regulation of love along traditional lines. Justice and humanity cannot thrive through the imposition of a repressive moral order and the institutionalisation of oppressive practices.

It might seem that the ideal of 'democratic love' represents a way forward – a middle way between the repression of the past and the chaos and cruelty of 'free love'. Love is contained, but by contractual negotiation between individuals rather than by rules imposed from without. Yet by what is love's regulation to be determined? The ideal depends, of course, on the abstracted 'individual'. This individual is self-aware and operates on the basis of reason. Knowing what they want, and what is good for them, they are able to negotiate fairly – representing their own interests but without resorting to tactics of control and manipulation. This individual is the individual that most of us would probably like to be. It is not, however, the individual who most of us are. It is certainly not the individual who loves. Individuals who love may have partial self-awareness, but their motivations and volitions are based upon fantasies of which they are almost entirely unaware. Finding themselves fearful, hurt and confused, individuals who love are gripped by compulsions which they do not understand. Individuals who love act largely out of unconsciousness and irrationality. They control, manipulate and hurt themselves and each other, often while suffering from the delusion that their behaviour is based upon reason. While the ideal of democratic love stands apart from the realities of the human heart, however, its effects are not neutral. It facilitates the practice of a blind amorality, whereby the exercise of domination and submission can flourish unseen. It enables us to invest our efforts in 'making it work', while hiding from ourselves the inhumanity we inflict upon ourselves and each other. In this way our energies are channelled into the reproduction of a social order characterised by gendered polarisation, alienation and hierarchies of power, while we at once articulate the discourse of egalitarian coupledom.

Belief in the democratic ideal is not disingenuous; it merely reflects a deep attachment to romantic love – love's blindness finds expression in both personal and theoretical forms. Our desire for a humane and equitable society may be genuine and heartfelt, but we may still be reluctant to engage in a deeper exploration of the nature of our own investments. Given this, it is all too easy to assume that power and the will to domination reside elsewhere: in outdated and unjust laws, in a repressive Christian morality, in a patriarchal society where power is possessed by men, or in a heterosexist society which pathologises homosexual love. Through such constructions, we aim to retain love while defeating power. We may even adopt love as the cause of a heroic struggle against forces which corrupt it and deprive the individual of the possibility of loving happily every after. Power *is* of course exercised through the repression of love, but we have seen how love's resistance itself is an expression of power which can wreak as much destruction upon the individual as any repressive law or social more. Love itself is not essentially innocent. Love itself is not essentially anything. Love is an expression of psychic energy in search of satisfaction. When we invest another human being with the projection of our own idealistic fantasies, love's energy all too easily turns to hostility. This, finding expression in habitual forms of control, twists our longing for satisfaction into the reproduction of everything we hoped to overcome. The more we invest in attachment love, the more intense these processes become.

What is it that prevents us from seeing that love's revolution is so misguided? Why do we remain so loyal to the romantic ideal? Ultimately, the strength of our deluded attachments depends upon the *spiritual* significance that love has in our lives. Love – an energy process bringing transitory pleasures and inevitable suffering – has become elevated into a particular kind of attempt to resolve the human situation. Despite everything we believe in love. We have faith in love. We have a blind faith in love. Because of this we see love as a means of salvation without noticing how it is a form of re-becoming. If we loosen our attachments and begin to see love for what it is, we cannot but face a crisis of faith for if not love, what then would we place our hearts upon?

APPENDIX

The women interviewed for the study[1]

Jenny (37) is a white, English woman from a working-class birth family. She considers herself to have become middle class through marriage and subsequently through education and occupation. Jenny has worked in a 'caring profession' for much of her married life, and currently does so part-time. She has vocational qualifications and a university degree, and is currently undertaking a higher degree through part-time study. Jenny married Peter eighteen years ago, at the age of 19. He was her first boyfriend, and she has had no other love relationships. Peter (45) is a white middle manager from a middle-class background. He was educated to GCE O level. They live in a jointly owned suburban semi with their teenaged child.

Rose (37) is a black, working-class, English woman from a working-class, Afro-Caribbean birth family. She has no academic or professional qualifications. Rose has always worked full-time in factory or clerical work, and currently has an administrative job. She has had six significant relationships, mostly of around one to two years' duration. The exception is her current partner Ken, who she has been seeing 'off and on' for thirteen years. Ken (44) is a black, working-class, English man. He has no formal qualifications and works in a clerical job. Ken lives with his female partner of twenty-two years' standing and their children. Rose lives in a council house with her two children from previous relationships.

Jean (45) is a white, Scottish woman from a working-class birth family. She considers herself to have moved into the lower middle class through marriage to Ron twenty-three years ago, after an eighteen-month courtship. Jean and Ron have one teenaged child. Jean has combined childcare and domestic responsibilities with a series of part-time paid jobs including bar work, shop work and clerical work. She is currently a part-time charity worker. Jean is educated to O level standard, and is currently undertaking a vocational course at her local adult college. Ron (45) is a white, lower middle-class, English man who is educated to O level standard, and works as a travelling salesman. Jean, Ron and their child live in a jointly owned semi in suburbia. Jean had one significant love relationship prior to their marriage and has had two affairs since, although neither is current. To Jean's knowledge, Ron has had at least one significant extra-marital affair.

Maureen (43) is a white, working-class, English woman. She has always worked full-time in factory work or clerical work apart from a period of involuntary unemployment. Maureen currently works in an administrative job. Maureen has no academic qualifications but has City and Guilds vocational qualifications. She is currently studying part-time for a further vocational qualification at an adult college. Maureen has had four significant sexual relationships, including a seven-year marriage, and her current fourteen-year relationship with Bob with whom she cohabits in their jointly owned urban semi. Bob (35) is a white, working-class, English man. He has no formal qualifications and has always worked in unskilled and semi-skilled manual work. Neither Maureen nor Bob have any children.

Jackie (36) is a white, working-class, English woman. She has City and Guilds vocational qualifications, works part-time in catering, and has previously worked as a care assistant. Jackie has been married to Dave for eleven years after a one-year courtship. She has had one other significant love relationship prior to her marriage. Dave (32) is a white, English man from a lower middle-class background. He has CSE qualifications, has worked previously in catering, and is currently a residential care worker. Jackie and Dave have one child and live in a council house.

Diane (45) is a white, English woman from a working-class birth family who considers herself to have become middle class through marriage. Diane has a City and Guilds vocational qualification in care work and works full-time as a care assistant. She has had two significant love relationships: a five-year marriage which ended in divorce, followed by her current seventeen-year marriage to John. John (44) is a white, English man from a middle-class birth family. He has a higher degree and works in a professional job. They have two children and live in a privately owned detached house.

Lucy (53) is a white, middle-class, English woman from a middle-class birth family. She has a professional qualification and worked full-time as a young woman. Since leaving her job to have children, Lucy has been a full-time 'housewife'. She has had two significant love relationships: a previous four-year marriage which ended in divorce, and her current marriage of twenty-seven years' standing. Lucy's husband Thomas (51) is a white, middle-class, English man who has a higher degree and works in higher education. They live in a privately owned semi and have two grown-up children.

Hannah (29) is a white, English woman from an Irish immigrant working-class birth family. She now considers herself middle class through her education to higher degree level, and her professional employment. She has had four significant love relationships of between six months' and four years' duration but has never married or cohabited. Hannah has recently ended her last relationship. She has no children and lives with her female lodger in her own terraced house.

Mary (44) is a white, English woman from a working-class birth family who considers herself to have become middle class through marriage. She has a university degree, vocational qualifications in childcare, and works part-time as well as studying for a further academic qualification. Mary has been married to Patrick for twenty-four years. They started 'going out' as teenagers and, until Mary recently embarked on an extra-marital affair, this had been her only love relationship. Patrick (44) is a white, Irish man from a working-class birth family who has moved into a middle-class occupation through promotion in his work. Mary's current lover Barry (48) is a middle-class Welsh man. He is also married. Mary and Patrick live in a jointly owned detached house and have two grown-up children.

Helen (33) is a white woman from a Scottish working-class birth family who moved to England as a child, and who now considers herself to have moved into the lower middle classes. Helen has secretarial qualifications but has not been in paid work for about ten years. During most of this time she has been a full-time 'housewife and mother', but is now combining this with doing a full-time university degree. Helen has had two significant love relationships: a two-year 'engagement' as a teenager, and her current fourteen-year relationship with Jonathan (35) to whom she has been married for nine years. Jonathan is a white, English man from a working-class background. He has a trade apprenticeship but currently works in a lower managerial position in industry. To Helen's knowledge Jonathan has had one extra-marital affair. This involved a temporary separation. They live in a privately owned urban semi and have two children.

Jane (26) is a white, working-class, English woman from a working-class birth family. She has secretarial qualifications and works as a full-time secretary. Jane has had two significant love relationships: a previous marriage involving a five-year relationship, and a current relationship of nine months' standing to her fiancé Paul (32). Paul is a white, working-class, English man from a working-class background. He is a semi-skilled manual worker and has no educational qualifications. Jane and Paul have bought a house together, but Paul will continue to live with his parents until their forthcoming wedding. Neither has any children.

Sarah (28) is a white, middle-class, English woman from a middle-class background. She has a university degree and is studying part-time for a higher degree. Sarah works part-time in a skilled technical job. Sarah has had two previous significant love relationships and one 'marriage of convenience'. She currently lives with Wayne (26), a white, working-class, English man. Wayne is an unskilled factory worker with no educational qualifications. He has regular 'flings' with other women of which Sarah is aware. Sarah and Wayne have been 'together' for three years. Neither has any children.

Kate (30) is a white, middle-class, English woman from a middle-class, English/European birth family. She has a university degree, works in education, and is studying for a higher degree. Kate has had five significant love relationships, including one marriage and her current relationship of three years' standing with Harry (36). Harry is a white, middle-class, English man. He is a skilled tradesman with professional qualifications and his own business. Kate and Harry live together in a privately owned terraced town house with their baby, and Kate's three children from her marriage.

Sharon (38) is a white, working-class, English woman. She has secretarial qualifications and has had various jobs in waitressing, bar work and factory work, as well as periods of voluntary and involuntary unemployment. Sharon currently works full-time as a telephone operator. She has had six significant love relationships of between one and eight years' duration, including two marriages. Her current partner Ravi (46) is a black, working-class, Asian immigrant with no educational qualifications. Ravi is a single parent and lives with his children from a previous marriage. He works as a driver. Sharon is also a single parent and lives in her own urban terraced house. Ravi also has an ongoing relationship with another woman.

Ruth (36) is a white, middle-class, English woman from a working-class birth family. She has a university degree and is studying for a higher degree as well as working part-time. Ruth has had five significant love relationships, including a seven-year marriage, and her current five-year relationship with Nick (33). Nick is a white, middle-class, English man from a working-class birth family. He is a full-time student on a professional training course. Ruth and Nick live together with Ruth's two children from her marriage in their jointly owned terraced house.

NOTE

[1] These descriptions were prepared at the time of each woman's first interview. References to ethnicity and class location are as defined by the women themselves. All names have been changed, as have some biographical details where these might be recognised.

BIBLIOGRAPHY

Alberoni, F. (1983) *Falling in Love*, trans. L. Venciti, New York: Random House.

Allen, H. (1982) 'Political Lesbianism and Feminism – A Space for Sexual Politics?', *m/f* 7: 15–34.

Altman, L. L. (1977) 'Some Vicissitudes of Love', *American Psychoanalytic Association Journal* 25: 35–52.

Aron, E. N. and Aron, A. (1986) *Love as the Expansion of Self: Understanding Attraction and Satisfaction*, New York: Hemisphere.

—— (1996) 'Love and Expansion of the Self: The State of the Model', *Personal Relationships* 3: 45–58.

Aron, E. N., Paris, M. and Aron, A. (1995) 'Falling in Love: Prospective Studies of Self-concept Change', *Journal of Personality and Social Psychology* 69: 1102–1112.

Atkinson, T. (1974) *Amazon Odyssey*, New York: Links Books.

Averill, J. (1985) 'The Social Construction of Emotion: With Special Reference to Love', in K. Gergen and K. Davis (eds) *The Social Construction of the Person*, New York: Springer.

Bak, R. (1973) 'Being in Love and Object Loss', *International Journal of Psychoanalysis* 54: 1–8.

Barnett, O. W. and La Violette, A. (1993) *It Could Happen to Anyone: Why Battered Women Stay*, London: Sage.

Bartky, S. L. (1990) *Femininity and Domination: Studies in the Phenomenology of Oppression*, London: Routledge.

Beck, U. and Beck-Gernsheim, E. (1995) *The Normal Chaos of Love*, trans. M. Ritter and J. Wiebel, Cambridge: Polity Press.

Bell, C. and Newby, H. (1976) 'Husbands and Wives: The Dynamics of the Deferential Dialectic', in D. Leonard Barker and S. Allen (eds) *Dependence and Exploitation in Work and Marriage*, New York: Longman.

Belsey, C. (1992) 'True Love: The Metaphysics of Romance', *Women: A Cultural Review* 3(2): 181–192.

Benjamin, J. (1990) *The Bonds of Love*, London: Virago.

Berger, P. L. and Kellner, H. (1974) 'Marriage and the Construction of Reality', in R. L. Coser (ed.) *The Family: Its Structures and Functions*, London: Macmillan.

Bergmann, M. S. (1971) 'Psychoanalytic Observations on the Capacity to Love', in J. McDevitt and C. Settlage (eds) *Separation–Individuation: Essays in Honour of Margaret S. Mahler*, New York: International Universities Press.

—— (1987) *The Anatomy of Loving: The Story of Man's Quest to Know What Love Is*, New York: Columbia University Press.

158

—— (1988) 'Freud's Three Theories of Love in the Light of Later Developments', *Journal of the American Psychoanalytic Association* 20(3): 347–373.

Bernard, J. (1973) *The Future of Marriage*, London: Souvenir Press.

Blood, R. and Wolfe, D. M. (1960) *Husbands and Wives: The Dynamics of Married Living*, New York: Free Press.

Bologh, R. W. (1987) 'Max Weber on Erotic Love: A Feminist Inquiry', in S. Whimster and S. Lash (eds) *Max Weber, Rationality and Modernity*, London: Allen & Unwin.

Brannen, J. and Collard, J. (1982) *Marriages in Trouble: The Process of Seeking Help*, London: Tavistock.

Brown, G. W. and Harris, T. (1978) *Social Origins of Depression*, London: Tavistock.

Brunt, R. (1988) 'Love is in the Air', *Marxism Today* (February): 18–21.

Burgess, E. W. and Locke, H. J. (1945) *The Family*, New York: American Books.

Campbell, B. (1987) 'A Feminist Sexual Politics: Now You See It, Now You Don't', in *Feminist Review* (eds) *Sexuality: A Reader*, London: Virago.

Cancian, F. (1985) 'Gender Politics: Love and Power in the Private and Public Spheres', in A. S. Rossi (ed.) *Gender and the Life Course*, New York: Aldine.

Chessick, R. D. (1988) 'On Falling in Love II: The Two-Woman Phenomenon Revisited', *Journal of the American Academy of Psychoanalysis* 17(2): 293–304.

—— (1992) 'On Falling in Love and Creativity', *Journal of the American Academy of Psychoanalysis* 20(3): 347–373.

Chodorow, N. J. (1978) *The Reproduction of Mothering*, Berkeley: University of California Press.

—— (1989) *Feminism and Psychoanalytic Theory*, Cambridge: Polity Press.

Christian-Smith, L. (1990) *Becoming a Woman Through Romance*, London: Routledge.

Comer, L. (1974) *Wedlocked Women*, Leeds: Feminist Books.

de Beauvoir, S. (1988) *The Second Sex*, London: Pan Books.

Dinnerstein, D. (1976) *The Mermaid and the Minotaur*, New York: Harper.

Dion, K. K. and Dion, K. L. (1996) 'Cultural Perspectives on Romantic Love', *Personal Relationships* 3: 5–17.

Douglas, C. A. (1990) *Love and Politics: Radical Feminist and Lesbian Theories*, San Francisco: ism press.

Duncombe, J. and Marsden, D. (1993) 'Love and Intimacy: The Gender Division of Emotion and "Emotion Work" ', *Sociology* 27(2): 221–241.

Dworkin, A. (1976) *Our Blood: Prophecies and Discourses on Sexual Politics*, London: Harper & Row.

Edgell, S. (1980) *Middle-Class Couples: A Study of Segregation, Domination and Inequality in Marriage*, London: Allen & Unwin.

Eichler, M. (1981) 'Power, Dependency, Love and the Sexual Division of Labour', *Women's Studies International Quarterly* 4(2): 201–219.

The Feminists (1973 [1969]) 'The Feminists: A Political Organization to Annihilate Sex Roles', in A. Koedt, E. Levine and A. Rapone (eds) *Radical Feminism*, New York: Quadrangle Books.

Firestone, S. (1979) *The Dialectic of Sex: The Case For Feminist Revolution*, London: Women's Press.

Fogarty, T. F. (1976) 'Marital Crisis', in P. J. Guerin (ed.) *Family Therapy: Theory and Practice*, New York: Gardner Press.

Freud, S. (1905) 'Three Essays on the Theory of Sexuality', in S. Freud (1977) *On Sexuality: Three Essays on the Theory of Sexuality and Other Works*, Harmondsworth: Penguin.

159

—— (1912a) 'Contributions to the Psychology of Love: The Most Prevalent Form of Degradation in Erotic Life', in S. Freud (1956) *Collected Papers* Vol. 4, trans. J. Riviere, London: Hogarth Press.

—— (1912b) 'The Dynamics of the Transference', in S. Freud (1957) *Collected Papers* Vol. 2, trans. J. Riviere, London: Hogarth Press.

—— (1914) 'On Narcissism: An Introduction', in S. Freud (1956) *Collected Papers* Vol. 4, trans. J. Riviere, London: Hogarth Press.

—— (1915a) 'Instincts and their Vicissitudes', in S. Freud (1956) *Collected Papers* Vol. 4, trans. J. Riviere, London: Hogarth Press.

—— (1915b) 'Further Recommendations in the Technique of Psycho-Analysis: Observations on Transference-Love', in S. Freud (1957) *Collected Papers* Vol. 2, trans. J. Riviere, London: Hogarth Press.

—— (1917) 'The Libido Theory and Narcissism', in J. Strachey (ed.) (1963) *The Standard Edition of the Complete Psychological Works of Sigmund Freud* Vol. 16, London: Hogarth Press.

—— (1922) *Group Psychology and the Analysis of the Ego*, London: International Psychoanalytical Press.

—— (1930) 'Civilization and its Discontents', in J. Strachey (ed.) (1961) *The Standard Edition of the Complete Psychological Works of Sigmund Freud* Vol. 21, London: Hogarth Press.

Frye, M. (1984) 'In and Out of Harms Way: Arrogance and Love', in M. Frye (ed.) *The Politics of Reality*, Trumansburg, NY: The Crossing Press.

Gaylin, W. (1988) 'Love and the Limits of Individualism', in W. Gaylin and E. Person (eds) *Passionate Attachments: Thinking About Love*, New York: The Free Press.

Gaylin, W. and Person, E. (eds) (1988) *Passionate Attachments: Thinking About Love*, New York: The Free Press.

Giddens, A. (1992) *The Transformation of Intimacy: Sexuality, Love, and Eroticism in Modern Societies*, Cambridge: Polity Press.

Goode, W. J. (1974) 'The Theoretical Importance of Love', in R. L. Coser (ed.) *The Family: Its Structures and Functions*, London: Macmillan.

Goodison, L. (1983) 'Really Being in Love Means Wanting to Live in a Different World' in S. Cartledge and J. Ryan (eds) *Sex and Love: New Thoughts on Old Contradictions*, London: The Women's Press.

Greer, G. (1970) *The Female Eunuch*, London: Granada.

Hegel, G. W. F. (1910) *The Phenomenology of Mind*, trans. J. B. Baillie, London: George Allen and Unwin.

Hite, S. (1988) *Women and Love: A Cultural Revolution in Progress*, London: Viking.

Hitschmann, E. (1952) 'Freud's Conception of Love', *International Journal of Psychoanalysis* 33: 421–428.

Hochschild, A. R. (1983) *The Managed Heart: Commercialization of Human Feeling*, London: University of California Press.

Jack, D. C. (1991) *Silencing the Self: Women and Depression*, London: Harvard University Press.

Jackson, C. (1989) '12 Steps to Heaven', *Trouble and Strife* 17: 10–17.

Jackson, S. (1993a) 'Even Sociologists Fall in Love: An Exploration in the Sociology of Emotions', *Sociology* 27(2): 201–220.

—— (1993b) 'Love and Romance as Objects of Feminist Knowledge', in M. Kennedy, C. Lubelska and V. Walsh (eds) *Making Connections: Women's Studies, Women's Movements, Women's Lives*, London: Taylor & Francis.

160

Jeffreys, S. (1990) *Anticlimax*, London: The Women's Press.

Jung, C. G. (1931) 'Marriage as a Psychological Relationship', in H. Read (ed.) (1954) *C. G. Jung The Collected Works* Vol. 17: *The Development of Personality*, trans. R. F. C. Hull, London and Henley: Routledge & Kegan Paul.

Kayser, K. (1993) *When Love Dies: The Process of Marital Disaffection*, New York: Guilford Press.

Kernberg, O. (1974) 'Barriers to Falling and Remaining in Love', *Journal of the American Psychoanalytic Association* 22: 486–511.

Komarovsky, M. (1988) 'The New Feminist Scholarship: Some Precursors and Polemics', *Journal of Marriage and The Family* 50: 585–593.

Komter, A. (1989) 'Hidden Power in Marriage', *Gender and Society* 3(2): 187–216.

—— (1991) 'Gender, Power, and Feminist Theory', in K. Davis, M. Leijenaar and J. Oldersma (eds) *The Gender of Power*, London: Sage.

Langford, W. (1993) 'The Sexual Politics of Loving Too Much: Discourses of Popular Advice on Heterosexual Relationships', Lancaster University: Centre for Women's Studies (Occasional Paper).

Leach, W. (1981) *True Love and Perfect Union*, London: Routledge & Kegan Paul.

Leeds Revolutionary Feminist Group (1981) *Love Your Enemy: The Debate Between Heterosexual Feminism and Political Lesbianism*, London: Onlywoman Press.

Lester, E. (1985) 'The Female Analyst and the Eroticized Transference', *International Journal of Psychoanalysis* 66: 283–293.

Luhmann, N. (1986) *Love as Passion*, Cambridge: Polity Press.

McRobbie, A. (1981) 'Just like a *Jackie* Story', in A. McRobbie and T. McCabe (eds) *Feminism for Girls: An Adventure Story*, London: Routledge & Kegan Paul.

Mahler, M., Pine, F. and Bergmann, A. (1975) *The Psychological Birth of the Human Infant*, New York: Basic Books.

Mainardi, P. (1975) 'The Marriage Question', in Redstockings (eds) *Feminist Revolution*, New York: Redstockings.

Mansfield, P. and Collard, J. (1988) *The Beginning of the Rest of your Life: A Portrait of Newly-wed Marriage*, London: Macmillan.

Meyer, J. (1991) 'Power and Love: Conflicting Conceptual Schemata', in K. Davis, M. Leijenaar and J. Oldersma (eds) *The Gender of Power*, London: Sage.

Millett, K. (1971) *Sexual Politics*, London: Granada.

Modleski, T. (1984) *Loving With a Vengeance*, London: Methuen.

Morgan, K. P. (1986) 'Romantic Love, Altruism, and Self-Respect: An Analysis of Simone de Beauvoir', *Hypatia* 1(1): 117–148.

Napier, A. Y. (1978) 'The Rejection–Intrusion Pattern: A Central Family Dynamic', *Journal of Marriage and Family Counseling* 4: 5–12.

New York Radical Feminists (1971) '1969 – Politics of the Ego: A Manifesto for New York Radical Feminists', in J. Hole and E. Levine (eds) *Rebirth of Feminism*, New York: Quadrangle/The New York Times Book Co.

Norwood, R. (1986) *Women Who Love Too Much: When You Keep Wishing And Hoping He'll Change*, London: Arrow Books.

O'Connor, P. (1991) 'Women's Experience of Power within Marriage: An Inexplicable Phenomenon?', *Sociological Review* 39(4): 823–842.

Parsons, T. and Bales, R. F. (1956) *Family: Socialization and Interaction Process*, London: Routledge & Kegan Paul.

Pateman, C. (1988) *The Sexual Contract*, Cambridge: Polity Press.

Pearce, L. and Stacey, J. (eds) (1995) *Romance Revisited*, London: Lawrence & Wishart.

Person, E. S. (1980) 'Sexuality as the Mainstay of Identity: Psychoanalytic Perspectives', *Signs* 5(4): 605–630.

—— (1985) 'The Erotic Transference in Women and Men: Differences and Consequences', *Journal of The American Academy of Psychoanalysis* 13: 159–180.

—— (1990) *Love and Fateful Encounters: The Power of Romantic Passion*, London: Bloomsbury.

Radway, J. (1984) *Reading the Romance: Women, Patriarchy, and Popular Literature*, Chapel Hill, NC, and London: The University of North Carolina Press.

Reich, A. (1953) 'Narcissistic Object Choice in Women', *Journal of the American Psychoanalytic Association* 1: 22–44.

Reik, T. (1974) *Of Love and Lust*, New York: Jason Aronson.

Rich, A. (1980) 'Compulsory Heterosexuality and Lesbian Existence', *Signs* 5(4): 631–660.

Rose, J. (1987) 'Femininity and Its Discontents', in *Feminist Review* (eds) *Sexuality: A Reader*, London: Virago.

Rubin, L. (1983) *Intimate Strangers*, New York: Harper & Row.

Safilios-Rothschild, C. (1976) 'A Macro- and Micro-Examination of Family Power and Love: An Exchange Model', *Journal of Marriage and The Family* 38: 355–362.

Śāntideva (1995) [seventh century]) *The Bodhicaryāvatāra*, trans. K. Crosby and A. Skilton, Oxford and New York: Oxford University Press.

Scanzoni, J. (1972) *Sexual Bargaining: Power Politics in the American Marriage*, Englewood Cliffs, NJ: Prentice-Hall.

Seidler, V. (1989) *Rediscovering Masculinity: Reason, Language and Sexuality*, London: Routledge.

—— (1991) *Recreating Sexual Politics: Men, Feminism and Politics*, London: Routledge.

—— (1994) *Unreasonable Men: Masculinity and Social Theory*, London: Routledge.

Seidman, S. (1991) *Romantic Longings: Love in America, 1830–1980*, London: Routledge.

Shorter, E. (1976) *The Making of the Modern Family*, London: Collins.

Snitow, A. B. (1984) 'Mass Market Romance: Pornography for Women Is Different', in A. Snitow, C. Stansell and S. Thompson (eds) *Desire: The Politics of Sexuality*, London: Virago.

Sternberg, R. J. (1994) 'Love is a Story', *The General Psychologist* 30: 1–11.

—— (1996) 'Love Stories', *Personal Relationships* 3: 59–79.

Stone, L. (1979) *The Family, Sex and Marriage in England 1500–1800*. London: Penguin.

Symonds, A. (1974) 'Phobias after Marriage: Women's Declaration of Dependence', in J. B. Miller (ed.) *Psychoanalysis and Women*, Harmondsworth: Penguin.

Tannen, D. (1986) *That's Not What I Meant!: How Conversational Style Makes or Breaks Your Relations with Others*, New York: William Morrow.

—— (1992) *You Just Don't Understand: Women and Men in Conversation*, London: Virago.

Tennov, D. (1979) *Love and Limerance: The Experience of Being in Love*, New York: Stein & Day.

Thompson, S. (1989) 'Search for Tomorrow: On Feminism and the Reconstruction of Teen Romance', in C. Vance (ed.) *Pleasure and Danger: Exploring Female Sexuality*, London: Pandora Press.

Van den Haag, E. (1974) 'Love or Marriage', in R. L. Coser (ed.) *The Family: Its Structures and Functions*, London: Macmillan.

Verhulst, J. (1984) 'Limerance: Notes on the Nature and Function of Passionate Love' *Psychoanalysis and Contemporary Thoughts* 7: 115–138.

Viederman, M. (1988) 'The Nature of Passionate Love', in W. Gaylin and E. Person (eds) *Passionate Attachments: Thinking About Love*, New York: The Free Press.

Voaden, R. (1995) 'The Language of Love: Medieval Erotic Vision and Modern Romance Fiction', in L. Pearce and J. Stacey (eds) *Romance Revisited*, London: Lawrence & Wishart.

Walker, L. (1988) 'The Battered Woman Syndrome', in G. T. Hotaling, D. Finkelhor, J. Kirkpatrick and M. Strauss (eds) *Family Abuse and its Consequences*, London: Sage.

Weber, M. (1948) 'Religious Rejections of the World and Their Directions', in H. Gerth and C. Wright Mills (eds) *From Max Weber: Essays in Sociology*, London: Routledge & Kegan Paul.

Weeks, J. (1995) *Invented Moralities: Sexual Values in an Age of Uncertainty*, Cambridge: Polity Press.

Wile, D. B. (1981) *Couples Therapy: A Non-traditional Approach*, New York: Wiley.

Wilkinson, S. and Kitzinger, C. (1993) *Heterosexuality: A Feminism and Psychology Reader*, London: Sage.

Wilson, A. (1981) 'Statements from Individual Members of the Collective', in Onlywoman Press (eds) *Love Your Enemy: The Debate Between Heterosexual Feminism and Political Lesbianism*, London: Onlywoman Press.

Young, M. and Willmott, P. (1973) *The Symmetrical Family*, London: Routledge & Kegan Paul.

INDEX

Van Den Haag, E. 16–17, 24, 51
Verhulst, J. 46, 47
Viederman, M. 25, 58
violence 77, 91, 123–8, 146
Voaden, R. 38

Walker, L. 129
Weber, M. 2–3, 17–18, 19, 24, 41, 51, 64
Weeks, J. 9–10
Wilkinson, S. 7, 54
Willmott, P. 8
Wilson, 7
withdrawal, male 65–7, 72, 81, 90–100, 116, 128
Wolfe, D. M. 3, 11
women: feeling abandoned 65–7, 99, 144; able to 'do anything' when in love 50–2, 132; as 'amateur therapists' 106; and anger/hostility 68, 72, 93–5, 120, 123, 147; on being single 26–9, 50–1, 142; blind to male power 74, 99; and confidence/self-esteem 26–9, 35, 50–2, 57–60, 78–9, 100–2, 105, 119, 129; decline of health and well-being 118–22; as 'demanding' 67–9,

83, 86, 104, 144; desire to feel 'special' 13, 67, 142, 144; enjoying sex 39–40; evaluating love in terms of 'absence of negatives' 68–9; experiencing devaluation 100–2; seen as 'irrational' 95–7, 146; exercise of 'maternal' power 74–84, 89–90, 144–5; fear of autonomy 26–9, 50–2, 129–35, 139, 142, 143, 148; fear of partners 78, 125–6, 146; feeling over-burdened 71–3; feeling strong and capable 79–81, 144; as partners' 'mothers' 72–3; pressurised into sex 123–4; response to partner's withdrawal 70–3, 99, 100–7, 109–11, 118–22; seeing relationships as 'absence of negatives' 68–9; and self-objectification 102–4; and self-silencing 104–7; as 'slaves' 118–32, 132, 149; as subject to 'paternal' power 100–13, 146–7; trapped by desire for security 128–32; trying to 'make the relationship work' 70–3, 92–3, 99, 118, 123, 128

Young, M. 8